At the Boundaries of Homeownership

In the United States, homeownership is synonymous with economic security and middle-class status. It has played this role in American life for almost a century, and as a result, homeownership's centrality to Americans' economic lives has come to seem natural and inevitable. But this state of affairs did not develop spontaneously or inexorably. On the contrary, it was the result of federal government policies established during the 1930s and developed over the course of the twentieth century. *At the Boundaries of Homeownership* traces how the government's role in the housing market became hidden from public view and how groups of citizens who found themselves excluded from otherwise submerged homeownership programs came to recognize and reveal the hidden hand of the state. Through organizing and activism, these boundary groups transformed laws and private practices governing who gets access to mortgage credit, and on what terms. This book describes the important policy consequences of their achievements and how it should shape our understanding of American political development.

CHLOE N. THURSTON is Assistant Professor of Political Science at Northwestern University.

At the Boundaries of Homeownership

Credit, Discrimination, and the American State

CHLOE N. THURSTON
Northwestern University

CAMBRIDGE
UNIVERSITY PRESS

CAMBRIDGE
UNIVERSITY PRESS

University Printing House, Cambridge CB2 8BS, United Kingdom

One Liberty Plaza, 20th Floor, New York, NY 10006, USA

477 Williamstown Road, Port Melbourne, VIC 3207, Australia

314–321, 3rd Floor, Plot 3, Splendor Forum, Jasola District Centre,
New Delhi – 110025, India

79 Anson Road, #06–04/06, Singapore 079906

Cambridge University Press is part of the University of Cambridge.

It furthers the University's mission by disseminating knowledge in the pursuit of
education, learning, and research at the highest international levels of excellence.

www.cambridge.org
Information on this title: www.cambridge.org/9781108434522
DOI: 10.1017/9781108380058

© Chloe N. Thurston 2018

First published 2018

Printed in the United States of America by Sheridan Books, Inc.

A catalogue record for this publication is available from the British Library.

Library of Congress Cataloging-in-Publication Data
NAMES: Thurston, Chloe N., author.
TITLE: At the boundaries of homeownership : credit, discrimination,
and the American state / Chloe N. Thurston.
DESCRIPTION: 1 Edition. | New York : Cambridge University Press, 2018.
IDENTIFIERS: LCCN 2017051565 | ISBN 9781108422055 (Hardback) |
ISBN 9781108434522 (Paperback)
SUBJECTS: LCSH: Home ownership–United States. | Home ownership–Government
policy–United States. | Mortgage loans–United States. | Housing–United States–Finance.
CLASSIFICATION: LCC HD7287.82.U6 T48 2018 | DDC 333.33/80973–dc23
LC record available at https://lccn.loc.gov/2017051565

ISBN 978-1-108-42205-5 Hardback
ISBN 978-1-108-43452-2 Paperback

For JJ and EDM

Contents

Figures

Tables

Acknowledgments

This book is about the ubiquity of boundaries in social, economic, and political life, yet my first order of business is to acknowledge the many people whose kindness, generosity, and, most of all, patience through the process of writing and revising it seem to know no boundaries. I am glad to finally be able to thank them properly.

This project began as my dissertation at the University of California at Berkeley, and my first debt of gratitude goes to my committee members. Paul Pierson, Margaret Weir, Nick Ziegler, and Neil Fligstein's support and feedback have improved and sharpened this project in countless ways. I am grateful for their guidance and for their willingness to read and comment on many, many drafts.

At Berkeley, I found a vibrant intellectual community that helped shape how I think about political science more broadly, and how I approached this project more specifically. I would like to thank Jack Citrin, Steve Vogel, Jonah Levy (who generously chaired the prospectus committee), and Vinnie Aggarwal for their support, as well as my class-mates Akasemi Newsome, Dann Naseemullah, Chris Chambers-Ju, Devin Caughey, John Henderson, Rebecca Hamlin, Peter Hanson, Amanda Hollis-Brusky, Adrienne Hosek, Nina Hagel, Erin Hartman, John Hanley, Ruth Bloch Rubin, Aris Grigoriadis, Alex Theodoridis, Travis Johnston, Abby Wood, and Phil Rocco. In addition, the Berkeley Institute for International Studies provided funding for the dissertation research.

The UC Washington Center provided a home away from Berkeley and a respite from the National Archives and Library of Congress. Melanie DePuis, Amy Bridges, Bruce Cain, Genevieve Lester, and Peter Ryan all weighed in on earlier formulations of this project, as did a broader network of people in and around DC, including Matthias Matthijs, Neil Shenai, Alex Reisenbichler, Lee Drutman, Jim Greer, Jonathan Rose, and David Karol. At Johns Hopkins, where I spent a year as a postdoctoral fellow, Danny Schlozman, Adam Sheingate, Steve Teles, Mimi Keck, David Dagan, Lester Spence, and Emily Zackin all offered helpful advice.

Northwestern has been an ideal place to finish this project, both for the large community of scholars interested in public policy and historical-institutional scholarship, and for the library's unusually extensive collection of obscure real estate literature from the 1920s and 1930s. I am grateful for the support I have received both from the political science department, which generously funded a book manuscript workshop in Fall 2015, and from my colleagues here, including Al Tillery, Traci Burch, Reuel Rogers, Julie Merseth, Tom Ogorzalek, Quinn Mulroy, Edward Gibson, Sara Monoson, Tony Chen, Laurel Harbridge, Jamie Druckman, Deb Thompson, Ann Orloff, and Dan Galvin. Thanks also to John Mocek, Bonnie Gordon, and Pamela Straw for their logistical support. Finally, the political science department's Farrell Fellowship program and Weinberg College's Undergraduate Research Assistant Program generously funded three of the research assistants working on this project.

Many people read and commented on earlier versions of the manuscript and chapters, including Mark Blyth, Amy Bridges, Bruce Cain, Tony Chen, Jim Greer, David Karol, Jonah Levy, Matthias Matthijs, Mike McCarthy, Quinn Mulroy, Akasemi Newsome, Alex Reisenbichler, Jonathan Rose, Danny Schlozman, and Neil Shenai, as well as workshop participants at UC Berkeley, the UC Washington Center, Johns Hopkins, Northwestern, Uppsala University, and the American Bar Foundation. Conversations with Gunnar Trumbull and Greta Krippner were very helpful in refining my argument and bringing my attention to other possible data sources. Finally, I offer a special thanks to Emily Zackin, Phil Rocco, Margaret Weir, and Dan Galvin, who have read and commented on more drafts than can reasonably be expected of anybody, as well as to the participants in my Fall 2015 book manuscript workshop, in particular Ann Orloff, Des King, Kimberly Morgan, and Adam Sheingate, who served as discussants.

If the long list of names above has not served as enough of a hint that academic books are collective endeavors, then hopefully the one to follow will. Amelia Strauss, Kimberly Chow, Gus Berrizbeitia, and Libby Berry provided valuable research assistance. The prose was much improved by Pamela Haag's keen eye for historical narrative. I am grateful to the archivists across the country who helped me navigate their collections, in particular Kenneth Chandler at the National Archives for Black Women's History, Jill Waycie at Northwestern University's Special Collections, and Allen Fisher at the Lyndon B. Johnson Library (the LBJ Foundation also provided a travel grant to fund my visit there). Portions of Chapters 1 and 4 are drawn from my article "Policy Feedback in the Public-Private Welfare State: Advocacy Groups and Access to Government Homeownership Programs, 1934–1954," which was published in *Studies in American Political Development* 29, no. 2 (2015): 250–67, and is reprinted with permission from Cambridge University Press. Finally, I would like to thank my editor at Cambridge University Press, Sara Doskow, for her unwavering support of this project and expertise in guiding me through the publication process, and to as well as the four reviewers, for their valuable suggestions on how to improve the manuscript.

For years, my friends, family, and extended family have offered their support and encouragement as I completed first the dissertation and now the book. My sincere thanks go to Tanya and Ernie Goldsmith, Debby Applegate and Bruce Tulgan, Cliff Egel and Nancy Harris, Mary Lassila and Brian Israel, George Jakubowski, Robin and Arthur Jameson, Jerome Fox, Jonathan Rose and Jane Dokko, Marc and Kimberly Goldwein, Leila Lackey and Danny Gossett, Melissa Hidrobo and Fernando Sedano, Leslie and Terry Malley, Kathy Murray, Mike Thurston, Patricia Thurston, Liz Gilbert, Andrew and Paul Egel, Linda Manganiello, and my parents, Tom and Debra Thurston. Finally, I thank Daniel and Julia for helping keep things in perspective.

Abbreviations

ACLU	American Civil Liberties Union
AFL	American Federation of Labor
CHOMC	Consolidated Home Owners Mortgage Committee
CNPR	Center for National Policy Review
CPC	Community Participation Committee
CWPS	Center for Women's Policy Studies
ECOA	Equal Credit Opportunity Act
FaHA	Farmers Home Administration
Fannie Mae	Federal National Mortgage Association
FDIC	Federal Deposit Insurance Corporation
FHA	Federal Housing Administration
FHLBB	Federal Home Loan Bank Board
FHLBS	Federal Home Loan Bank System
Freddie Mac	Federal Home Loan Mortgage Corporation
GAO	US Government Accountability Office
HHFA	Housing and Home Finance Agency
HOLC	Home Owners' Loan Corporation
HUD	Department of Housing and Urban Development
LHA	Local Housing Authority
MBAA	Mortgage Bankers Association of America
MHB	Mississippi Home Builders
NAACP	National Association for the Advancement of Colored People
NAHB	National Association of Home Builders
NAREB	National Association of Real Estate Boards/National Association of Realtors

NCCF	National Commission on Consumer Finance
NCCRC	National Consumer Credit Reporting Corporation
NCNW	National Council of Negro Women
NHA	National Housing Act
NOW	National Organization for Women
NPHC	National Public Housing Conference
OEO	Office of Economic Opportunity
PWA	Public Works Administration
RFC	Reconstruction Finance Corporation
SNCC	Student Nonviolent Coordinating Committee
USBLL	United States Building and Loan League
VA	Veterans Affairs (Home Mortgage Guaranty Program)
VHMCP	Voluntary Home Mortgage Credit Program
WEAL	Women's Equity Action League
WIMs	Workshops in Mississippi

I

Politics, Markets, and Boundaries

A belief in spontaneous progress must make us blind to the role of
government in economic life.

$\qquad$ – Karl Polanyi, 1944[1]

Sharyn Campbell married her law school classmate when she was twenty-
five. Shortly after, the couple picked up from New York and moved to
Washington, DC. The year was 1970. When it came time to buy a car,
Campbell filled out a loan application. The loan was approved, but she
was taken aback when she noticed that the lender had issued the credit in
her husband's name and not her own. Not only had Campbell applied for
the loan independently, her husband had no credit history to speak of and
a less compelling work history than she had. This happened again when
she applied for a bank card, finding that, too, issued in her husband's
name only.

Already frustrated by these two experiences, the couple's biggest shock
came when they decided to buy a house. Both lawyers with relatively high
incomes and stable jobs in the federal government, they found a place
within their price range and applied for a loan from the local VA office.
The loan officer told the couple that there was only a fifty-fifty chance that
Campbell's income would be counted toward the loan, because of the risk
that she might become pregnant and quit her job.[2] In order to get a loan,

[1] Karl Polanyi, *The Great Transformation: The Political and Economic Origins of Our Time* (Boston: Beacon Press, 1944), 39.
[2] Sharyn Campbell, in "October 1972 Meeting of Citizens' Advisory Committee on the Status of Women," Records of the Citizens' Advisory Committee on the Status of Women, Library of Congress Manuscripts Collection (hereafter CACSW), Reel 6, 149; "Loans to

Campbell needed to submit "an affidavit to the VA promising not to become pregnant and assuring them that I would continue to work under any circumstances."[3] She did get the loan, but learned later that she was much more fortunate than many others.

Initially, Campbell had assumed the problem had something to do with her recent move to DC – perhaps Washington lenders had not caught up with the times. Reflecting two years later, she said, "It didn't occur to me that this would have happened to me in New York if I would have stayed in New York after I had gotten married also."[4]

By the time she was twenty-seven, Campbell was at the forefront of a movement to transform women's access to credit. She had become active with the Women's Legal Defense Fund, which had been inundated with credit-related requests during its first few months of existence. Campbell became the coordinator of the fund's Credit Counseling Project, and eventually went on to run the National Organization for Women's Task Force on Credit. She was also active with the Citizen's Advisory Council on the Status of Women. All of these activities she did on her own time, when she was not working as an attorney for the Securities and Exchange Commission.

Women's groups such as the ones Campbell was involved with targeted likely culprits, including financial institutions and retailers, that they had suspected of discrimination. However, they also targeted the federal government, which they argued had enabled and encouraged discrimination by designing earlier underwriting standards that restricted women's access to credit, and by condoning discriminatory behavior on the part of private lenders that they regulated or otherwise conferred benefits upon.

Campbell could have viewed her exclusion – and initially did view it – as driven by idiosyncrasies of the local market in which she sought a loan. Instead, Campbell, along with members of groups that she worked with, identified a vast public–private structure in the United States, in which the federal government helped some categories of citizens gain access to social benefits while excluding others. By 1974, the movement had succeeded in getting Congress to pass legislation to outlaw sex discrimination in

---

Women: A Case for Questioning Lending Criteria," *Savings and Loan News* (January 1974), in National Council of Negro Women, National Archives for Black Women's History (hereafter NCNW), Series 34, Box 2, Folder: Women and Housing Mortgage Credit Discrimination, 1973–1974.

[3] Campbell, "October 1972 Meeting," 148–9.   [4] Ibid., 168–9.

mortgage and consumer credit lending. Hers was one of many social movements that acted similarly to get the government to intervene not only in issues of lending, but also in a whole host of policy areas often considered too mundane to attract public attention and consequently considered primarily in the purview of private interests.

* * *

At the root of Campbell's experience is a story about the American welfare state. Beyond that, it is a story about the struggle to expand the American state's authority over areas traditionally viewed as dominated by private market actors. On the one hand, it should surprise few social scientists that citizens, such as Campbell, who were excluded from accessing a publicly provided benefit would mobilize to be included on equal footing. On the other hand, it *is* surprising when we consider that conventional scholarship holds that citizens should be unlikely to recognize access to homeownership or credit as a publicly provided benefit. In this area of the "public-private welfare state," a government largely out of sight issues regulations and designs incentives to encourage the private provision of social benefits, but does not engage in any direct provision itself.

Scholarship typically holds that such a melding of public and private power obscures the role of the government from citizens' view and instead empowers private providers, for example, Campbell's lender. This was not how Campbell's case unfolded, however, nor the other cases examined in this book.

This book challenges this conventional view of the public–private welfare state as part of the government out of sight. It examines the development of a policy area that exemplifies the United States' out-of-sight government: its promotion of homeownership by indirect support of the mortgage market through loan guarantees and insurance, secondary markets, and a host of other regulatory mechanisms.[5] It depicts cases in

---

[5] The public–private infrastructure includes private loan insurance, loan guarantees, and interest rate subsidies through the Federal Housing Administration (developed in 1934) and the Veterans Administration (as part of the GI Bill of 1944). It also includes the government's creation and support of the Federal Home Loan Bank Board in 1932 to support thrifts, as well as its creation of and support for the secondary mortgage market, establishing Fannie Mae in 1938 and Freddie Mac and Ginnie Mae in the 1960s and 1970s. Another means of promoting homeownership has been through the tax code, via a combination of tax deductions and tax credits that have increased the appeal of homeownership versus renting.

which the primary drivers of policy, regulatory, and even private-sector change were not business actors engaging with this area of the state most directly. Instead, the drivers of policy change were citizens' groups whose constituents had found themselves excluded from access.

This book's argument, in brief, is that citizens' groups that have found their constituents *excluded* from the public–private welfare state have, against expectations, recognized that exclusion as being generated by government policies and practices. Like the organizations to which Campbell belonged, these groups have engaged in activities to reveal precisely how complex and opaque government policies and regulations to extend homeownership to millions of Americans also operated to exclude millions more on the basis of race, sex, marital status, and income. By highlighting that exclusion was not solely the result of the workings of an impartial market mechanism, but also shaped by the activist hand of the federal government, marginalized groups built a case that the federal government not only had the authority to intervene in order to ensure more equitable terms of access to homeownership, but also had an obligation to ensure that the private providers it partnered with for provision did the same.

A WELFARE STATE OUT OF SIGHT

Conventional wisdom long characterized the United States as a developmental laggard that has lacked strong centralized state power for much of its history and whose government has taken a hands-off approach to economic and social welfare that extends to the present day.[6] Recent

---

[6] See, for example, Alexis de Tocqueville *Democracy in America* (New York: McGraw-Hill, 1981 [1835]), vol. I, chap. XII; Seymour Martin Lipset and Gary Marks, *It Didn't Happen Here: Why Socialism Failed in the United States* (New York: W. W. Norton, 2013); Seymour Martin Lipset, *American Exceptionalism: A Double-Edged Sword* (New York: W. W. Norton, 1997); Arthur Schlesinger, *Paths to the Present* (New York: Macmillan, 1949); Louis Hartz, *The Liberal Tradition in America: An Interpretation of American Political Thought* (San Diego: Harcourt Brace & Company, 1955); Stephen Skowronek, *Building a New American State: The Expansion of National Administrative Capacities, 1877–1920* (Cambridge: Cambridge University Press, 1982). On the mischaracterization of the American state as weak, see also Gerald Berk, *Louis D. Brandeis and the Making of Regulated Competition, 1900–1932* (Cambridge: Cambridge University Press, 2009). The irony of American liberalism in the presence of a highly regulated state has not gone undetected. As William Novak points out, it was recognized as early as 1887 by Albert Shaw, writing, "Never for a moment relinquishing their theory [of laissez-faire], the people of the United States have assiduously pursued and cherished a practical policy utterly inconsistent with that theory, and have not perceived the discrepancy." William Novak,

scholarship has challenged this characterization of the American state as minimalist on several fronts.[7] Brian Balogh and others have cast doubt on the assumption of a laissez-faire economy in the US prior to the Progressive Era and the New Deal, pointing out that, if anything, the laissez-faire stance constituted a blip in a much longer history of robust state action across many realms of the economy and polity.[8] Looking across the Atlantic, Monica Prasad has noted that in several areas of the economy, the United States was far more interventionist than its Western European counterparts. Elsewhere, scholars have begun to note that what makes the American welfare state exceptional is not so much its size, but its form, with benefits channeled to citizens indirectly through employers, the tax code, the regulatory system, credit support, and even tort law.[9] Bolstering the claim of an activist American state throughout its history is a vast

"The Myth of the 'Weak' American State," *American Historical Review* 113, no. 3 (2008), 752–72; 753.

[7] Novak, "The Myth of the 'Weak' American State"; Desmond King and Robert C. Lieberman, "Ironies of State Building: A Comparative Perspective on the Weak American State," *World Politics* 61, no. 3 (2009), 547–88; Peter Baldwin, "Beyond Weak and Strong: Rethinking the State in Comparative Policy History," *Journal of Policy History* 17, no. 1 (2005), 12–33; Elisabeth Clemens, "Lineages of the Rube Goldberg State: Building and Blurring Public Programs, 1900–1940," in Ian Shapiro, Stephen Skowronek, and Daniel Galvin (eds.), *Rethinking Political Institutions: The Art of the State* (New York: New York University Press, 2006), chap. 8.

[8] Brian Balogh, *A Government Out of Sight: The Mystery of National Authority in Nineteenth-Century America* (New York: Cambridge University Press, 2009); Richard John, *Spreading the News: The American Postal System from Franklin to Morse* (Cambridge, MA: Harvard University Press, 1995); Richard John, "Governmental Institutions as Agents of Change: Rethinking American Political Development in the Early Republic, 1787–1835," *Studies in American Political Development* 11, no. 2 (1997), 347–80; John Lauritz Larson, *Internal Improvement: National Public Works and the Promise of Popular Government in the Early United States* (Chapel Hill: University of North Carolina Press, 2000); Richard Bensel, *The Political Economy of American Industrialization, 1877–1900* (Cambridge: Cambridge University Press, 2000); James Sparrow, William Novak, and Stephen Sawyer (eds.), *Boundaries of the State in US History* (Chicago: University of Chicago Press, 2015).

[9] Jennifer Klein, *For All These Rights: Business, Labor and the Shaping of America's Public-Private Welfare State* (Princeton, NJ: Princeton University Press, 2003); Marie Gottschalk, *The Shadow Welfare State: Labor, Business, and the Politics of Health Care in the United States* (Ithaca, NY: Cornell University Press, 2000); Jacob Hacker, *The Divided Welfare State: The Battle over Public and Private Social Benefits in the United States* (New York: Cambridge University Press, 2002); Christopher Howard, *The Hidden Welfare State* (Princeton, NJ: Princeton University Press, 1997); Suzanne Mettler, *The Submerged State: How Invisible Government Policies Undermine American Democracy* (Chicago: University of Chicago Press, 2011); Kimberly Morgan and Andrea Campbell, *The Delegated Welfare State* (Oxford: Oxford University Press, 2011); James Morone, "American Ways of Welfare," *Perspectives on Politics* 1 (2003), 137–46.

literature that examines specific industries, agencies, and institutions shaped by a combination of market and government power.[10]

In short, far from being weak or nonexistent, the American state has simply manifested itself differently from the Weberian-style states that scholars had used earlier for comparison.[11]

If this expansive American state has been with us in some form or another for centuries, then why has it taken so long for scholars to acknowledge its role in social, political, and market affairs? Part of the answer has to do with its complexity, which tends in various ways to conceal the exercise of state authority. Power is dispersed across different layers of government, as is the range of activities and outcomes that it affects. This dispersion is thought to conceal and obfuscate.[12] The exercise of state power is also concealed by private actors that state officials empower as partners in the allocation of resources. The state grants power and authority to private actors not only through subsidies or regulatory incentives, but also more fundamentally by defining the private sphere itself; for example, by sanctioning the establishment of associations and corporations.[13] The legal system – especially the state's role in defining what constitutes a legitimate legal grievance – offers yet another channel for governing private outcomes while disguising public authority.[14] The masking of state activity through its sheer complexity can be seen in the labels that scholars have used to describe various parts of the American state: Balogh's nineteenth-century activist government was largely "out of sight"; Christopher Howard and Suzanne Mettler's

---

[10] Susan Hoffman, *Politics and Banking: Ideas, Public Policy, and the Creation of Financial Institutions* (Baltimore: Johns Hopkins University Press, 2001); Kathryn Lavelle, *Money and Banks in the American Political System* (Cambridge: Cambridge University Press, 2013); Karen Orren, *Corporate Power and Social Change: The Politics of the Life Insurance Industry* (Baltimore: Johns Hopkins University Press, 1974).

[11] Novak, "Myth of the 'Weak' American State"; Clemens, "Lineages of the Rube Goldberg State"; Julie Novkov and Carol Nackenoff (eds.), *Statebuilding from the Margins: Between Reconstruction and the New Deal* (Philadelphia: University of Pennsylvania Press, 2014); Kimberly Morgan and Ann-Shola Orloff, eds., *The Many Hands of the State: Theorizing Political Authority and Social Control* (New York: Cambridge University Press, 2017); Sparrow, Novak, and Sawyer, *Boundaries of the US State*.

[12] Novak, "Myth of the 'Weak' American State," 765; Adam Sheingate, "Why Can't Americans See the State?" *The Forum* 7, no. 4 (2009), art. 1; Clemens, "Lineages of the Rube Goldberg State."

[13] Novak, "Myth of the 'Weak' American State," 769.

[14] Charles Epp, *Making Rights Real: Activists, Bureaucrats, and the Creation of the Legalistic State* (Chicago: University of Chicago Press, 2010); Sean Farhang, *The Litigation State: Public Regulation and Private Lawsuits in the U.S.* (Princeton, NJ: Princeton University Press, 2010).

welfare states were "hidden" from public view, "submerged" even from those who used their benefits on a regular basis.

WHO MOBILIZES WHEN THE STATE IS HIDDEN FROM VIEW?

Just as the complexity of the American state has deflected scholarly attention, it has also placed the state's operations out of many citizens' view. State complexity is thought to generate a distinctive kind of politics. For instance, a government social program channeled to citizens indirectly through private providers may be less prone to policy feedback effects among its beneficiaries, partly because citizens are less able or inclined to trace back to the government the particular benefit they enjoy (be it higher education, health insurance, or a house).[15] Recent survey research corroborates that there is a possibility that a program's design can shape people's perception of the government's role in their lives; even citizens who benefit from indirectly provided programs often fail to recognize that the government helped to provide those benefits. Suzanne Mettler sums up this lack of recognition as the "quintessential experience of the submerged state: it benefitted them [citizens], providing opportunities and relieving financial burdens, *without them even knowing it.*"[16]

The particular distributional mechanisms of a policy are said to affect who mobilizes in support or opposition, once it is enacted.[17] When lines from the government to a beneficiary are clear and unambiguous, policies can mobilize beneficiaries (for example, senior citizens in favor of preserving or expanding Social Security benefits) or backlash groups (for example, conservative groups against Aid to Families with Dependent Children, more colloquially known as "welfare"). As the link between the government and beneficiaries becomes more intricate and elaborate, the nature of conflict can change. Actors in more direct proximity to the state are still likely to mobilize politically in support of or opposition to

---

[15] Chloe Thurston, "Policy Feedback in the Public-Private Welfare State: Advocacy Groups and Access to Government Homeownership Programs," *Studies in American Political Development* 29, no. 2 (2015), 250–67. On visibility and traceability, see also R. Douglas Arnold, *The Logic of Congressional Action* (New Haven: Yale University Press, 1990).

[16] Mettler, *Submerged State*, 11.

[17] Andrea Campbell, "Policy Makes Mass Politics," *Annual Review of Political Science* 15 (2012), 333–51; Joe Soss and Sanford Schramm, "A Public Transformed? Welfare Reform as Policy Feedback," *American Political Science Review* 101, no. 1 (2007), 111–27.

policy or regulatory changes that could affect their position.[18] For instance, Mettler notes that, with a few exceptions, members of the student loan industry were more likely to mobilize to preserve and expand the federal student loan program than were college students who actually received the loans. Moreover, where private litigation has replaced federal enforcement, we might expect public interest lawyers to mobilize to protect or expand the "market" for private litigation.[19]

Citizens further removed from the process may be more prone to attributing benefits they receive to the proximate provider, rather than notice the government institutions and incentives that enabled their provision in the first place. When taking out a home mortgage or student loan, saving for college or retirement, or filling out paperwork for employer-provided health care, it is easy to associate each of these benefits with one's ability to save, hold good credit standing, or get a good job. To the extent that citizens are likely to mobilize around these benefits, they do so most often in their capacity as consumers in a market; for example, when they bargain with the provider for better terms or threaten to walk away. But because those same citizen beneficiaries tend not to see the role of the state in shaping their ability to access goods, they are theoretically less likely than providers to mobilize *politically*. For example, Jack Buckley and Mark Schneider's study of DC charter schools found that charter schools (publicly funded but privately managed) had a positive impact on parental trust and involvement in schools (in short, mobilizing at the level of the provider), but no measurable impact on trust in government or parents' personal sense of political efficacy. The authors concluded that this is likely due to the fact that they do not identify charter schools as government-provided.[20]

---

[18] E. E. Schattschneider predicted this development in the 1930s, suggesting that trade policies that ultimately would lower prices for consumers were more likely to be pushed through by producers. See E. E. Schattschneider, *Politics, Pressure, and the Tariff: A Study of Free Private Enterprise in Pressure Politics, as Shown in the 1929–1930 Revision of the Tariff* (New York: Prentice Hall, 1935). I thank David Karol for this insight.

[19] Farhang, *The Litigation State.*

[20] Jack Buckley and Mark Schneider, "Are Charter School Parents More Satisfied with Schools? Evidence from Washington, D.C.," *Peabody Journal of Education* 81, no. 1 (2006), 57–78. Not every study has recovered evidence that citizen beneficiaries were unaware of the role of the state. More recently, David Fleming, et al., found that school voucher programs increased parental involvement by introducing competitive pressure to school choice, and that vouchers actually made the role of the government in schooling more visible rather than less. David Fleming, William Mitchell, and Michael McNally,

The expectations of a sidelined citizenry and mobilized private (usually business) actors align with many accounts of the development of the hidden state in the US and abroad, including the "quiet politics" associated with low-salience and highly technical areas such as the regulation of managerial pay and corporate takeovers. In such cases, as work by Pepper Culpepper shows, businesses have exceptional power to martial their claims of technical expertise in ways that shape policies in their preferred direction, with little awareness by, let alone input from, the public. But extant scholarship also reveals many counterpoints to the quiet politics account, even in areas considered too mundane to attract much citizen attention.[21] Sometimes, as work by Daniel Carpenter shows, bureaucrats may be the driving force that expands the authority of the state over private activities.[22] In other cases, focusing events, accompanied perhaps by the efforts of a policy entrepreneur, can bring short-term public attention to a complex problem. This occurred when policy-makers considered removing the home mortgage interest deduction as part of the 1986 tax reforms, to great public outcry.[23] In other instances, the demands of private, concentrated interests may still lose out to other voices, including a diffuse public interest, or competition from other private concentrated interests.[24] Even if institutional conflicts of this sort are largely fought outside the realm of popular politics, scholars have yet to exhaust the list of potential drivers of policy change.

"Can Markets Make Citizens: School Vouchers, Political Tolerance, and Civic Engagement," *Journal of School Choice* 8, no. 2 (2014), 213–36.

[21] Pepper Culpepper, *Quiet Politics and Business Power: Corporate Control in Europe and Japan* (Cambridge, MA: Cambridge University Press, 2010). Though Culpepper's term "quiet politics" specifically refers to the politics of corporate control across France, Germany, Japan, and the Netherlands, I adopt the term occasionally throughout this book to describe the politics also thought to attend low-salience and highly technical areas of public policy more broadly.

[22] Daniel Carpenter, *The Forging of Bureaucratic Autonomy: Reputations, Networks, and Policy Innovation in Executive Agencies, 1862–1928* (Princeton, NJ: Princeton University Press, 2001); Daniel Carpenter, *Reputation and Power: Organizational Image and Pharmaceutical Regulation at the FDA* (Princeton, NJ: Princeton University Press, 2010).

[23] See, for example, Dennis Ventry, "The Accidental Deduction: A History and Critique of the Tax Subsidy for Mortgage Interest," *Law and Contemporary Problems* 73, no. 1 (2009), 233–84.

[24] Gunnar Trumbull, *Strength in Numbers: The Political Power of Weak Interests* (Cambridge, MA: Harvard University Press, 2012).

BOUNDARY GROUPS AND THE VISIBILITY OF THE DELEGATED STATE

While recent work tends to stress the obscurity of the delegated state from ordinary citizens, this book argues instead that scholars have simply been looking in the wrong place for evidence that such policies generate any recognition by and mobilization from citizens. It argues that the contours of the delegated welfare state are often visible to those who lie at its boundaries. That is, citizens' organizations whose constituents are located on the margins of inclusion in and exclusion from delegated state programs can and have come to attribute their constituents' exclusion not to some impersonal market logic, but instead to activities (or inactivity) of the federal government. Further, these organizations have waged new conflicts around the terms on which citizens may access the delegated state's benefits, challenging the state's role (whether through active involvement or inactive complicity) in the constituents' exclusion. I call these organizations "boundary groups."

Boundary groups are typically preexisting groups that may temporarily take on new missions (whether alone or in consort with others), rather than new groups that form in response to general patterns of exclusion from a delegated state benefit. This is precisely because the contours of the delegated state often impede collective mobilization, since people's experiences with their benefits are highly individualized. Likewise, individuals may attribute their exclusion to impersonal and individual market forces and fail to see their individual grievances against market actors as grounds for collective political contestation generated by a common cause. These factors make it difficult for organizations to emerge spontaneously. Existing civil society groups already possess resources – material, symbolic, organizational – that enable them to collect individual experiences into common problems. (That boundary groups are typically drawn from existing organizations also means that the known inequalities of representation and voice are likely replicated, and in some sense amplified, in the public–private welfare state issues such groups take on.)

Boundary groups engage in particular forms of collective action when they come to find their constituents excluded from delegated programs. They may decide to challenge specific public policies and regulations that directly, or indirectly, sanction their constituents' exclusion. Or, they may target private actors who partner with the state in the provision of services. They can do this by calling on the state to withdraw support from providers who deny their constituents access to goods indirectly provided by the state. They may also appeal to providers for better terms of access by trying to persuade them that they have missed profitable markets by refusing to see their members.

Some of the political activity and mobilization characteristic of boundary groups are generated by the very structure of the delegated state. First, when the state collaborates with third-party providers to help distribute social benefits, it can fundamentally change the interests of those providers. It invests them as stakeholders in upholding government policies and programs. The delegated state also recasts the relationship between the government and private providers. Arguably, it gives private providers increased sway in policy negotiations. But it also subjects them to increased risk in the form of government sanctions or programmatic retrenchment. Second, public–private programs operate by creating incentives to encourage private-sector providers to expand their provision of goods *beyond what they would otherwise provide*. But they cannot provide to everybody without incurring too much risk. This means that part of the federal government's role is to define the terms on which citizens and providers will be eligible or ineligible for indirect government support. Ultimately, this means that even when the purpose of delegation is to remove the government from thorny distributional issues, the government unleashes the power of market providers by defining and then defending market boundaries.[25]

This has implications for how citizens react to being excluded from the delegated state, because it means that they may be able to challenge the legitimacy of the state's role in supporting their exclusion from its benefits, as well as argue that the state actually has the authority to ensure their inclusion. Businesses and other third-party providers may also see their future fortunes at stake, depending on how the state governs these areas. In short, not only can the delegated state empower some groups of citizens even while it remains out of view by those who benefit, its own structures can provide some of the raw materials that outsider groups use to contest their exclusion.[26]

---

[25] See also Theodore Lowi and Norman K. Nicholson, *Arenas of Power: Reflections on Politics and Policy* (New York: Routledge, 2009).

[26] For a similar discussion on how the structure of policies can provide the "raw material" outsider groups can use to contest them, see Sandra Levitsky, *Caring for Our Own: Why There Is No Political Demand for New American Social Welfare Rights* (New York: Oxford University Press, 2014).

This argument, that the public–private collaboration in and of itself generates the tools and raw materials for citizen mobilization, cuts against the assumption that the private sector, laden with technical expertise and other advantages, enjoys a profound upper hand in the politics of the delegated state. To understand why, it is necessary to delve further into the form and features of delegation. It is also necessary to think about how these relate to the overarching goal of delegation, namely, to create incentives to entice private third-party providers to extend benefits that they would not otherwise provide.

Reconsidering the Political Power of Private Providers

Policy-makers often justify their decision to delegate service provision to private actors on the grounds that the private sector has invaluable preexisting knowledge and capacities, and can encourage gains in efficiency or effectiveness through further specialization. For example, recognizing a professional association's authority over occupational licensing may be preferable to locating this power in a federal or state government bureaucracy. Similarly, devolution of responsibility for a program's provision to local and state governments can improve efficiency by harnessing the local knowledge of lower-level political actors.

If a benefit is especially complex to provide, then delegation to private providers reduces the state's burden by drawing on providers' existing administrative capacity and expertise.[27] For instance, as urban mayors and federal policy-makers began to worry about the decline of American cities in the 1960s, they started to look toward the "genius of private industry" to become partners in the resolution of urban problems. As they were already successful at providing housing to the middle class, policy-makers hoped that businesses would be able to lend their expertise to help manage the complexities of housing America's urban poor.[28]

The fact that third-party providers already possess expertise underlies much of the rationale for business influence in the public–private welfare state. It is argued that businesses have both a greater interest in the political decisions made in these "quiet" arenas because they are clearly

---

[27] See, for example, Morgan and Campbell, *The Delegated Welfare State*, 7.
[28] Alexander von Hoffman, "Calling Upon the Genius of Private Enterprise: The Housing and Urban Development Act of 1968 and the Liberal Turn to Public-Private Partnerships," *Studies in American Political Development* 27, no. 2 (2013), 165–94.

affected by them, and greater resources to expend in these arenas. In some cases, this is precisely because they have profited from these programs.[29]

What is sometimes neglected by these views, however, is that the expectations and activities of private actors can change in important ways once they partner with the state. In some cases, the introduction of new state programs requires that private actors invest in new capacities.[30] Providers may be called upon to offer entirely new products (for example, mortgages with longer repayment terms and lower down payments than traditionally offered). They might also need to scale up their operations to accommodate new demands. This could include having to create new staff positions or entire offices in order to accommodate new paperwork, compliance, and accounting demands. It also could require them to move into markets and activities that they felt justified in avoiding in the past.[31] This increases the cost of doing business (even if those costs are offset by greater profits) and the risk of losing their newly expanded market.

Politically, these factors – the expertise and capacity that private actors bring to the table, the investments they are asked to make, and the expectations they form in response to new institutional powers and incentives – challenge (if subtly) the assertion that these kinds of policy areas are dominated by business interests, while being largely invisible to citizens. To be sure, as the submerged state view might predict, the technical expertise, development of capacities, and knowledge of local conditions can give private actors an upper hand in negotiations with state officials. But by the same token, businesses take on new risks when they invest in new capacities and undertake new activities (especially ones that, for whatever reason, they were previously reluctant to take on). For example, the UK government's project to build a market for pensions during the Thatcher era required an expanded fleet of sales agents. As Alan Jacobs and Steven Teles highlight, these sudden new requirements stretched financial firms as they discovered the risks of expanding their

---

[29] Culpepper, *Quiet Politics*; Mettler, *Submerged State*.

[30] Paul Pierson, "The New Politics of the Welfare State," *World Politics* 48, no. 2 (1996), 143–79; Jacob Hacker and Paul Pierson, "After the 'Master Theory': Downs, Schattschneider, and the Rebirth of Policy-Focused Analysis," *Perspectives on Politics* 12, no. 3 (2014), 634–62.

[31] See, for example, Mettler's discussion of banks' discomfort with getting involved in student lending, an area of the market they deemed too risky, given the characteristics of the borrowers. Suzanne Mettler, *Degrees of Inequality: How the Politics of Higher Education Sabotaged the American Dream* (New York: Basic Books, 2013), 61.

ranks of sales agents beyond their ability to effectively train and monitor
these new employees.[32]

To the extent that state complexity empowers private actors by providing regulatory benefits and incentives or other powers, it can also leave
private actors vulnerable to outside threats to remove those incentives,
benefits, or powers, or to threats from potential business competitors.
And if private providers gain some political currency through their ability
to claim that they have technical expertise, then just as surely others can
cast doubt on whether those firms are the experts they claim to be. With
new benefits to providers signing on to the public–private welfare state
come new vulnerabilities. As we will see, boundary groups have at times
seized on these vulnerabilities to raise challenges about the appropriate
role of the government and market actors in areas defined by public and
private power.

One implication of this dynamic is that scholars of the public–private
welfare state should not misread the government's use of private actors to
channel social benefits to the public as the conferral of unchecked power.
By becoming incorporated into the public–private welfare state, businesses and other third-party providers may also become more vulnerable
to threats of programmatic retrenchment, or to individual sanctions by
policy-makers or bureaucratic agencies. This suggests that potentially
there are more constraints on their power than the submerged state school
ascribes to these obscure and highly technical policy areas. It is true that,
much of the time, these policy areas do indeed remain obscured from
public view. However, when they are made visible, and when they are
seen as the results of political choices, then these previously "quiet"
interests may find themselves vulnerable to the threat of rollbacks unless
they make new concessions. Given the investments that such policies may
have caused them to make, these rollbacks can be costly.

Boundaries and the Scope of State Authority

Another reason for some skepticism of the quiet politics view of delegated
state arrangements is that in encouraging private actors to take on new
activities, to produce new goods, and to expand their distribution into
areas they may have otherwise viewed as unprofitable, government actors

---

[32] Alan Jacobs and Steven Teles, "The Perils of Market Making," in Marc Landy, Martin
Levin, and Martin Shapiro (eds.), *Creating Competitive Markets: The Politics of Regulatory Reform* (Washington, DC: Brookings Institution Press, 2007), 170.

typically must draw *boundaries* to determine who will be included and excluded, and on what terms. These include formal laws and regulations that stipulate important aspects of provision, including who may be the providers. It also includes specification of the terms on which citizens may have access to the benefits of the delegated state.

Markets also draw their own boundaries. Abstractly, competition, preferences, and tastes become reconciled through the price system, which then allocates access. Some people may simply be priced out as the prices of goods rise, or they may have no interest in procuring the goods at the prevailing price, or perhaps any price. Others may be excluded by discrimination from providers (be they employers, lenders, or others) based on personal taste, perceived group characteristics, or perceived effects on other customers or employees.[33] It is the interplay of these three sources of boundaries – laws, implementation, and markets – that characterizes who gets what and on what terms in the delegated state. This also helps to shape how people recognize the role of the state and how they interact with (or decline to interact with) the state.

The history of homeownership policy illustrates this well, as it is replete with instances of the federal government helping to define for private actors the boundaries around safe and risky lending. In 1934, Congress created the Federal Housing Administration (FHA) to insure private mortgage lenders against default risk. As policy-makers discussed the FHA's creation, they explicitly recognized their responsibility for drawing the border around safe and unsafe lending by private actors. Speaking in front of the House Banking and Currency Committee, one of the designers of the FHA asked:

[H]ow much of a shoe string do you want a man to have before he is entitled to home ownership? On that, of course, we are dealing again with a social problem. I think everyone grants that the stability of a system such as ours is dependent, to a large extent, upon the desirability of home ownership, and that it is advisable for the Government to encourage home ownership. We then try to set a figure at a point that people will not get in without any capital of their own, entirely on a shoe string. We try to find out at what point that shoe string should be set.[34]

---

[33] See Gary Becker, *The Economics of Discrimination* (Chicago: University of Chicago Press, 1957); Edmund Phelps, "The Statistical Theory of Racism and Sexism," *American Economic Review* 62, no. 4 (1972), 659–61.

[34] Frank Watson, testimony in US Congress, House, Committee on Banking and Currency, *National Housing Act: Hearings before the Committee on Banking and Currency*, 73rd Cong., 2nd sess., 1934, 151.

Even after policy-makers set that "shoe string" to delineate safe, FHA-insurable lending from risky, non–government-insured lending, FHA officials came up against the limits of many of the market boundaries that they themselves had helped to define. In the years since the FHA's creation, officials have revisited a number of earlier constraints within the original (and then revised) program, provoked either by agency initiative or outside agitation. In 1945, the FHA commissioner appointed a "No-Man's Land Committee" to help figure out how the FHA could expand housing opportunities to groups who were too poor to qualify for mortgage insurance, but not poor enough to live in means-tested public housing.[35] In the intervening years, new laws have raised statutory limits on the maximum insurable loan limits, decreased the amount of money an applicant is required to set aside as a down payment, and expanded the types of lenders that can offer FHA-insured loans and the types of properties that can qualify for FHA insurance. The program has also been revised to allow for insuring mortgages in geographic areas that previously were beyond the FHA's reach (including urban, remote rural, and natural disaster areas).

At the level of implementation, the FHA's *Underwriting Manual* has been revised numerous times as well, including the removal of explicit criteria that held racial minorities and women to separate standards. Over the years, the manual's underwriting criteria for an applicant's credit-worthiness have shifted from the evaluator's own judgment on a number of criteria (one question in a 1935 FHA model credit report asked, "Does his wife lend encouragement to him?"; another inquired about "his personal reputation as to honesty"), toward a standardized and auto-mated system of individual credit scoring.[36] Discussions over the boundaries of access persist to this day, recently over whether government housing agencies have made sufficient efforts to ensure that same-sex couples have access to privately originated loans backed by the FHA and other Department of Housing and Urban Development (HUD)–associated benefits on the same terms as heterosexual couples.

---

[35] See, for example, a series of letters between FHA Commissioner Abner Ferguson and the chairman of the No Man's Land Committee, B. C. Bovard, from 1945 and 1946, in National Archives at College Park, Record Group 31, Federal Housing Administration, Commissioner's Correspondence and Subject Files, (hereafter RG31 CCSF), Box 4A, Folder: Middle Income Housing.

[36] Guy Stuart, *Discriminating Risk: The U.S. Mortgage Lending Industry in the Twentieth Century* (Ithaca, NY: Cornell University Press, 2003), 93.

Finally, at the level of on-the-ground practices, the housing market has been bounded not only by laws and regulations and their implementation on the ground, but also by the practices of buyers, sellers, and myriad other members of the housing industry. These types of barriers have featured persistently in the history of African Americans' exclusion from federal homeownership programs, even after the formal policy boundaries to their exclusion (including racial criteria contained within the *Underwriting Manual*) had been erased. The community reinvestment movement in the late 1970s, for example, was driven by community leaders' desire to demonstrate the systematic exclusion of African American neighborhoods by private lenders, despite new laws, court decisions, and administrative decisions over the previous two decades that were intended to eliminate discrimination in housing and lending.[37]

Why Boundaries Matter in the Delegated State

To some extent, boundaries are an inherent feature of the standards setting (or standards enforcement) that characterizes state activity across a wide variety of realms, from weights and measures to citizenship to the American character itself.[38] More narrowly, boundaries are an important feature of public policy-making. Social Security initially excluded farm and domestic workers from eligibility for the program, de facto writing most Southern blacks out of the program without resorting to any explicit racial language in the policy itself. But, as Robert Lieberman shows, the structure of the Social Security program's benefits and finances endowed it with an expansionary logic. As a result, bureaucrats looking to maintain the program's long-term financial and political health gradually

---

[37] Boundary setting is not limited to overt designations of who is and is not eligible for inclusion. Even policies providing for seemingly universalistic access can contain implicit boundaries. For example, until 1986, the home mortgage interest deduction allowed every household with a mortgage to reduce their federally taxable income. Despite its seeming universality, the deduction implicitly excluded citizens who did not or could not own their homes and has been viewed by many as an implicit tax on renters.

[38] See Desmond King and Mark Stears, "How the U.S. State Works: A Theory of Standardization," *Perspectives on Politics* 9, no. 3 (2011), 505–18, esp. 512–13. The theoretical concept of boundaries in political and social life has received a great deal of attention as well. See Andrew Abbott, "Things of Boundaries," *Social Research* 62, no. 4 (1995), 857–82; Michele Lamont and Virag Molnar, "The Study of Boundaries in the Social Sciences," *Annual Review of Sociology* 28 (2002), 167–95; Damon Mayrl and Sarah Quinn, "Defining the State from Within: Boundaries, Schemas, and Associational Policymaking," *Sociological Theory* 34, no. 1 (2016), 1–26.

shifted the SSA's "color line," essentially redrawing the boundaries of access to the program.[39] Similarly, John Skrentny documents how the minority rights revolution of the 1960s and 1970s was not just a conflict over whether minorities should have equal constitutional protections, but also, more fundamentally, over *who* ought to be considered a minority in the first place. This meant that some minority groups were not officially included within the purview of the Equal Employment Opportunity Commission, which excluded white ethnics and included, but neglected, Asian Americans and American Indians. It also meant the extension of minority status to women – a disadvantaged group, to be sure, but not numerically a minority group.[40]

What differentiates boundary creation in the delegated state from boundary creation and enforcement that is endemic to state activity is that citizens may be more likely to attribute the former to impersonal market practices than to an activist government. Individuals can find themselves unable to qualify for a home loan, or unable to obtain a job that provides health insurance, without ever linking their inability to gain these goods to actions of the federal government. However, when they do manage to recognize the role of the state in their exclusion from such benefits, the role of government-generated boundaries takes on particular political importance.

Most importantly, if identified, the state's role in defining and defending boundaries to access can open up an angle of attack for groups unable to access benefits on equal terms. These boundaries have been useful in several ways to challengers. They have provided focal points around which to mobilize members, tangible targets for political change, weapons to contest the legitimacy of the state's sponsorship of benefits, and tools to help redefine the authority and obligation of the state toward citizens in areas of ambiguous public and private power.

Yet collective political mobilization is not an automatic response to policy-generated boundaries. Informational barriers can deter or prevent collective mobilization, particularly in the delegated state. Markets tend to atomize individuals, making it difficult for them to recognize their problems as collectively shared. Boundaries to access also need to be linked to the "mighty" hand of the state rather than solely attributable

---

[39] Robert Lieberman, *Shifting the Color Line: Race and the American Welfare State* (Cambridge, MA: Harvard University Press, 1998), chap. 3.

[40] John D. Skrentny, *The Minority Rights Revolution* (Cambridge, MA: Harvard University Press, 2004).

to the invisible hand of the market.[41] Markets tend to encourage individuals to interpret their difficulties accessing goods as the byproduct of impersonal market forces, not state actions. Moreover, it can be difficult to convince private providers to expand the scope of provision, because of their concerns about profitability as well as their confidence that their day-to-day practices reflect their superior understanding of the market.

FOUR ROLES OF BOUNDARY GROUPS: DETECTION, INFORMATION, CONTESTATION, EXPANSION

This is where boundary groups come in. By aggregating individual experiences into collective problems, by conducting and disseminating their own research, and by mobilizing across multiple venues, boundary groups work to dislodge earlier ideas and practices that previously barred large numbers of their constituents from accessing benefits shaped by the state. Boundary groups can also challenge the market position of third-party providers. They can threaten providers with the loss of benefits and position if the providers fail to expand provision, or they can point to new market opportunities. Finally, they can call on the state to overturn policies that promote exclusion or force providers to operate more inclusively.

It is important to emphasize the "group" aspect of boundary groups. Groups do things that individuals cannot do, and this is especially the case in policy realms that tend to be obscured from public view.[42] In such cases, groups have helped to expand the scope of conflict around issues that otherwise might be regarded as individual, idiosyncratic, or private problems. They have done so by reinterpreting independent problems as collective grievances, defined by the state, defended by the

---

[41] See Louis Hyman, *Debtor's Nation: The History of America in Red Ink* (Princeton, NJ: Princeton University Press, 2011); Freund, *Colored Property*; Richard Rothstein, *The Color of Law: A Forgotten History of How Our Government Segregated America* (New York: Liverlight, 2017).

[42] See, for example, Hacker and Pierson, "After the 'Master Theory,'" 648. While the focus in this book is on challenger groups that find themselves outside of these arrangements, organized groups have also been brought into the delegated state in order to act as coalitional partners, helping to forge links between previously unconnected groups; to institutionalize coalitional engagement through changes in the rules, allowing for more participation and transparency; and to participate in regulatory decision-making from a variety of angles. See Charlie Eaton and Margaret Weir, "The Power of Coalitions: Advancing the Public in California's Public-Private Welfare State," *Politics & Society* 43, no. 1 (2015), 3–42.

state, and contestable through collective action. Examining three different forms of exclusion and mobilization, this book details four main activities of boundary groups: boundary detection, information gathering, contestation, and expansion.

Boundary Detection

First, boundary groups can play an important role in *boundary detection*. They serve as repositories for their members' individual grievances and can aggregate them into broader patterns. For example, few users of so-called submerged social programs view themselves as beneficiaries of government social programs, in part because the benefits of the public-private welfare state are typically experienced as individual market transactions or rewards for individual accomplishments rather than as collective social goods. A person unable to obtain financing for a house, or deemed ineligible for a student loan, or unable to afford individual health insurance may not necessarily link these difficulties to public policies. He or she may also be unaware that others share these difficulties.

Organizations can help to transform individual problems into collective grievances. To return to Sharyn Campbell's experience highlighted in the beginning of this book, it took decades of differential treatment by lenders of male and female credit applicants before women began to view their individual credit difficulties as a collective problem. After hearing anecdotal evidence of women's credit exclusion from its members, the National Organization for Women formed a national task force to study the scope and causes of the problem. Reaching beyond its own membership, NOW placed articles in women's interest magazines, including *Glamour, Ladies' Home Journal*, and *Ms.*, encouraging women to write to the organization if they had encountered similar difficulties trying to get a mortgage or charge card. In response, NOW received thousands of letters from women, many detailing similar experiences of credit denial.[43] By aggregating these individual experiences, an organized group was able to redefine the problem from an issue of individual credit denial to articulate a much broader – and suspect – pattern (Chapter 5).

---

[43] Letters to the NOW Task Force on Credit, 1972–1975, in Schlesinger Library, Records of the National Organization for Women, MC 496 (hereafter NOW), Box 44, Folder 31, through Box 45, Folder 16.

Information Gathering

Second, boundary groups have filled an important role in *information and linkage*. They gather information about the nature and scope of their members' exclusion and then trace it back to specific public policies, regulations, and business practices on the ground. Once the issue is defined as a collective problem, organized groups may have the resources to study and in some cases debunk the preeminent explanations provided by bureaucratic agencies and private providers for the inequality in access.

For example, civil rights groups from the 1930s through the 1950s identified many of the formal boundaries that excluded African Americans from participation in the housing market on equal terms as whites, pointing to racial underwriting criteria in the FHA's *Underwriting Manual* and model restrictive covenants. Restrictive covenants were prevalent across the country, yet as Marian Wynn Perry recognized in a letter to Thurgood Marshall (both in the National Association for the Advancement of Colored People's legal department), the NAACP was ideally situated to serve as a national repository for information on restrictive covenants. After returning from a conference on the topic in 1946, Perry reported:

I was struck with the fact that we in the NAACP appear to have the greatest amount of material on restrictive covenants and certainly have the greatest knowledge of what is happening in every State. As a method of impressing people with the value of coordinated effort so that they will cooperate with us in our restrictive covenant campaign, as well as for its intrinsic value, I would recommend that I spend some time collecting a manual on race restrictive covenant cases. I envision this as including a preliminary statement on the need for coordinated activity, the effect which one decision has on work all over the country, and so forth.[44]

The NAACP eventually coordinated activities with other advocacy groups, the private housing industry, and government housing agencies. It also worked with other organizations to disseminate research that cast doubt on the FHA's and private providers' insistence that the differential opportunities for credit for whites and blacks was wholly attributable to differences in creditworthiness and profitability between the two groups.

---

[44] Memo to Thurgood Marshall from Marian Wynn Perry, October 22, 1946. In Library of Congress Manuscript Division, Papers of the National Association for the Advancement of Colored People (hereafter NAACP), Group II, Box A 315, Folder: Housing Pamphlets 1945–54.

Instead, advocates' research found that private lenders, builders, and the real estate industry were ignoring profitable opportunities by focusing mainly on housing white Americans (Chapter 4).

Boundary Contestation

Civil rights groups then brought these discoveries to the attention of government actors across multiple venues and reached out directly to representatives of the housing industry, which points to a third role of boundary groups: they engage in multiple forms of *boundary contestation*. Boundary groups can do this by challenging the legitimacy of a policy or regulatory structure that provides benefits to some citizens while seemingly arbitrarily foreclosing those same opportunities for others. Outside groups have accomplished this by, among other methods, directly appealing to bureaucrats and elected officials and insisting that they identify and rectify boundaries to access. They can also do this by arguing that the benefits the state confers on private providers come with an obligation that providers do not arbitrarily deny access to benefits.[45] For example, in 1972, a coalition of thirty citizens' groups representing African Americans, women, senior citizens, and others filed a petition with the Federal Home Loan Bank Board and other banking regulators. They were drawing attention to a proposed regulation that they felt would encourage lenders to discriminate against them. In making the case for a change in policy, the petition argued that the federal regulators who had conferred benefits on banks had an obligation themselves to ensure that banks under their authority did not discriminate against borrowers on the basis of race, sex, marital status, or age.[46]

---

[45] To the extent that these arguments could be considered rights claims, they are distinct from the types of claims contained in the protest letters investigated by Lovell that also invoked rights-based arguments in 1939. The writers of those letters were private citizens expressing grievances to the government, which included a legal rhetoric of rights even if they lacked an understanding of whether and how those rights could be enforced by the government. In contrast, the claims I examine in this book come from organizations with legal expertise, aimed at specific policy and regulatory targets. Where individual letter writers have made rights claims, they tended to occur in the context of organized groups attempting to collect more information about on-the-ground practices. See George I. Lovell, *This Is Not Civil Rights: Discovering Rights Talk in 1939 America* (Chicago: University of Chicago Press, 2012).

[46] Petition from the American Friends Service Committee et al. to Jack Carter (secretary of the Federal Home Loan Bank Board), reprinted in US Congress, House, Committee on the Judiciary, *Federal Government's Role in the Achievement of Equal Opportunity in*

Boundary Expansion

Fourth, if successful, these activities can contribute to *boundary redefinition or expansion*: they can change formal laws and administration, as well as convince providers to change their practices. A group's impact on policy processes and business practices is notoriously difficult to measure.[47] Slightly easier to detect is the contribution of boundary groups and movements to placing issues that earlier had been viewed by private actors as purely market issues onto the policy agenda, articulating new justifications for government action, and also reaching out to help reshape business's perceptions of profit. However, as many of the groups learned the hard way, success in moving boundaries seldom addressed all of their constituents' grievances in a single shot. Instead, the process of boundary detection, information, contestation, and expansion may recur as groups monitoring their earlier efforts come to find new challenges in the law, its implementation, and business practices.

It is important to note that boundary groups can wage these battles across multiple venues, political and market. In looking only at one venue – say, Congress, the courts, or business associations – scholars might miss the broader strategies groups employ. The ability to wage an attack across multiple fronts has been recognized by many boundary groups as one of their advantages. Organizations have also at times explicitly recognized the limitations of viewing policy change only in terms of legislative outcomes. A leader of one of the organizations involved in the women's movement for access to credit in the 1970s observed as much: "Federal policy involves much more than the development and passage of legislation, covering numerous executive branch operations from regulations to federal laws to executive orders, enforcement machinery, and program development. Hence, the range of possible intervention points is great."[48] Depending on their resources and perceptions of the likelihood of success or failure, groups may try to reach out and shape all of these venues simultaneously, or they may focus their

---

Housing: Hearings before the Civil Rights Subcommittee of the Committee on the Judiciary, 92nd Cong., 1st sess., 1971, 146.

[47] See, for example, Frank Baumgartner, Jeffrey Berry, Marie Hojnacki, David Kimball, and Beth Leech, *Lobbying and Policy Change: Who Wins, Who Loses, and Why* (Chicago: University of Chicago Press, 2009), chap. 10.

[48] Jane Roberts Chapman, "Policy Centers: An Essential Resource," in Irene Tinker (ed.), *Women in Washington: Advocates for Public Policy* (Beverly Hills, CA: Sage Publications, 1983), 178.

efforts on a single venue. The efforts of groups involved in shaping and contesting policies have often spanned the institutions that tend to divide political science scholarship.

The Logic of Collective Action against the Hidden State

The claim that boundary groups have helped to generate pressure for policy change should not come as a complete surprise to scholars of social movements. Resource mobilization theories of social movements have, since the late 1970s, taken seriously the idea that social movement actors aggregate problems into collective grievances and make tactical use of the social structures already in place.[49] It is well known that interest groups and social movements raise the salience of issues and raise new issues onto the public agenda; that they can operate across multiple venues – political, economic, and social – to secure their aims; and that their activities, and prospects for success, can vary at different stages in the policy process.[50] Finally, it is well known that interest groups and social movement organizations help to forge collective identities that may have not yet existed, and to politicize identities in new ways. Recent work by Sandra Levitsky and by Eileen Boris and Jennifer Klein document how organizations have worked to chip away at the barriers that have long prevented home care workers from forging collective identities and then channeling those into political demands. Work by Kenneth Kollman shows that advocacy groups possess a wide range of strategies and tactics that they can use, both inside and outside of formal government channels, to pressure elected officials to act on their demands. And work by Brayden King and Sarah Soule has shown that social movements can play an important role in the policy process, though their efficacy varies depending on the stage of the policy process.[51]

My aim is not to prove the already demonstrated point that boundary groups – which are a subset of advocacy groups and social movement organizations – raise the salience of issues, help citizens to see and articulate collective grievances, and mobilize across political venues for

[49] John McCarthy and Mayer Zald, "Resource Mobilization and Social Movements: A Partial Theory," *American Journal of Sociology* 82, no. 6 (1977), 1212–48.

[50] Brayden King and Sarah Soule, "The Stages of the Policy Process and the Equal Rights Amendment, 1972–1982," *American Journal of Sociology* 111, no. 6 (2006), 1871–1909.

[51] Levitsky, *Caring for our Own*; Ken Kollman, *Outside Lobbying* (Princeton, NJ: Princeton University Press, 1998); King and Soule, "The Stages of the Policy Process."

policy change.[52] Instead, it is to shed light on an issue that has received far less attention, namely, how these organizations interact with a state apparatus that is removed from public view, often deliberately. How, in short, do groups and movements operate in this particular kind of policy context, characterized by the invisibility of policy and policy-makers from the distributional issues at hand? A large body of scholarship has concluded that when the government delegates provision of social benefits to third-party providers that rely on market mechanisms, these arrangements tend to mobilize businesses and third-party providers into politics while demobilizing citizens from political activism, since they are apt to view their receipt of benefits – a student loan, perhaps, or an employer-provided pension – as secured through the market rather than through government policies.

This book challenges that narrative by showing how boundary groups not only are able to overcome some of the structural disadvantages to collective mobilization in this arena, but also, in doing so, manage to creatively use those same features that tend to hide the role of the government as tools to contest their constituents' positions.

CASES, SOURCES, AND ORGANIZATION

To recap, I have contended so far that the delegation of social benefit provision to third-party providers and other indirect market mechanisms produces a distinctive type of politics. This is characterized by the mobilization of groups whose constituents find themselves excluded from the benefits of the public–private welfare state. This dynamic has been largely overlooked by a literature that tends to stress how such indirect mechanisms help to hide the state from benefit recipients and, correspondingly, depoliticize their distribution. Instead, I argue that the same features of the delegated state that allow many of its beneficiaries to imagine their benefits as "privately owned and privately earned" have emerged as focal points by which outsider groups can recognize and contest their exclusion.[53] In contesting their exclusion, boundary groups engage in four main activities: boundary detection, information gathering, contestation, and boundary expansion (in other words, a shift in the terms on which citizens can access these goods in a way calculated to improve their members' access).

[52] Kollman, *Outside Lobbying.*
[53] Clemens, "Lineages of the Rube Goldberg State," 209.

Cases

To understand how outsider groups have grappled with their constituents' exclusion from the public–private welfare state in homeownership, I examine three cases: civil rights groups' efforts against racial discrimination that emerged in response to the FHA's policies in the 1930s; a feminist credit movement that, despite a longer history of sex discrimination in home mortgage lending, emerged in the early to mid-1970s; and, finally, an effort to bring homeownership to low-income households that began to gain momentum in the mid-1960s.

As Chapter 4, which looks at how civil rights organizations responded to the FHA's "color line," documents, racial exclusion in local real estate predated the FHA. However, through the development of the field of real estate valuation and appraisal, and the incorporation of their methods and theories into the FHA's own underwriting guidelines, exclusion became routinized, nationalized, and concretely tied to beliefs that the future value of a house was related to its neighborhood's racial homogeneity and the likelihood of changing racial (or "user group") characteristics over time. This belief in segregation as codified into real estate practices – combined with other provisions and self-fulfilling ideas about property values – contributed to the movement of capital out of black neighborhoods, with consequences that reverberate today.[54]

For women, the source of exclusion was not ideas about the determinants of *property* values, as it was for African Americans, but rather ideas about the *borrower*. Among other factors that Chapter 5 explores, women's exclusion from mortgage credit was built out of beliefs about what constituted stable employment and income over time and credit bureau reporting practices that generated just one report per household, eliminating a married woman's individual economic standing. Women did not begin to view homeownership as just out of their reach until the late 1960s, when a period of economic and social transformation rendered their position of exclusion from access to homeownership more obvious, and a wave of new feminist organizations helped to aggregate women's individual challenges in getting loans into a broader collective grievance, linked to public policy.

For the low-income households studied in Chapter 6, the barriers to access were more straightforward, in that those people tended to lack the

---

[54] Melvin Oliver and Thomas Shapiro, *Black Wealth, White Wealth: A New Perspective on Racial Inequality* (New York: Routledge, 2006).

cash for a down payment and to have incomes too low and unstable to meet underwriting guidelines. Slightly less straightforward was the conventional wisdom that the poor were neither capable nor desirous of homeownership, a wisdom seemingly confirmed by the lack of maintenance of public housing and the dilapidated state of much of the affordable private rental housing stock. In addition to wealth, income, and what I will call philosophical barriers are issues of intersectionality pertaining to the specific program whose development I trace, as the target groups were initially poor, African American, often female-headed households in rural Mississippi in the late 1960s. (The special challenges posed by bringing homeownership to citizens facing multiple overlapping sources of disadvantage are why I address this as the final case, despite its chronological placement between the two other cases.)[55]

Each of the three cases was selected for several reasons. First, they were all tied to a historically significant social movement, making them important to understand in their own right. Second, the cases track three of the most durable sources of social inequality in the United States over the twentieth century: race, gender, and class. Finally, the causes of each exclusion vary in crucial ways, providing insight into the commonalities that exist regardless of the causes of exclusion, along with the differences in strategies available to contest the constituents' positions. The different sources of exclusion are important, because they help to demonstrate that it is not so much the exact causes or nature of the boundary

[55] The temporal orientation of these cases raises questions about whether and how they relate to one another in a longer-term developmental story. Subsequent efforts to expand access to homeownership made deliberate use of existing policies aimed at bringing access to mortgage credit to earlier groups, making the case that those policies ought also to be used to extend access to mortgage credit to their own constituents. Civil rights groups made this argument in the 1930s through the 1950s when noting the extensive role of the federal government in bringing homeownership to the middle class while creating and enforcing a color line to keep it out of reach of African Americans. By the time women's advocates made their push for equal access to mortgage (and other forms of consumer) credit, civil rights advocates had succeeded in getting Congress to pass legislation to outlaw racial discrimination in housing through the 1968 Fair Housing Act. Feminist credit advocates then successfully pushed for the law to be amended to cover sex discrimination. Finally, low-income housing advocates in the mid-1960s successfully converted a low-income homeownership program initially designed for use on Native American tribal land to use by low-income residents of rural areas. In these ways, advocates seized on existing institutions (themselves generally the product of earlier groups' efforts for access to homeownership), hoping to revise them or use them as templates to bring greater access to their constituents.

that matter. Instead, political conflicts surrounding market access were shaped in each case by the existence of government-backed market boundaries that were in turn combated and challenged by organizations that represented those who found themselves on the other side of those boundaries.

Sources

This book relies on a variety of sources, including archival collections of business and citizens' organizations (as well as the personal papers of individual leaders), bureaucratic agencies, and presidents and their administrations; testimonies in legislative hearings; interest group and mass periodicals; real estate industry training manuals; and a large body of secondary literature. They help to establish, first, the motivations and core concerns of the policy-makers in charge of designing the public–private homeownership infrastructure during the 1930s; second, the distributional consequences of the public–private homeownership infrastructure as formal laws and industry practices began to inform each other in determining who should become a homeowner and on what terms; and third, the response by organizations whose constituents found themselves outside of the boundaries to access.

Through these sources, I demonstrate that organized groups came to recognize their constituents' exclusion as something that was politically (as opposed to market) generated and collectively (as opposed to individually) experienced; that they linked this exclusion to specific public policies and regulatory and private sector practices; that they engaged in research and communication strategies to contest the market basis of their exclusion; and that they also used the fact of a government role in homeownership as a basis for contesting the political logic of their constituents' exclusion. When engaging with businesses, boundary groups threatened the loss of position and economic competitiveness if the government pulled its benefits from exclusionary housing providers (or, worse, if the government entered the homeownership market directly). More optimistically, they also pointed to overlooked market opportunities. When engaging with government, they argued that the federal government had not only the authority but also the obligation to act. This obligation, they argued, extended to ensuring that their members were not affected by exclusionary language, policing the activities of private providers, and withholding regulatory benefits for noncompliers. An outcome was the expansion and transformation of the state's role in the delegated state, albeit an often partial one, subject to reversal.

All research designs involve trade-offs, and this analysis trades off the ability to answer several *why* questions (for example, under what conditions do movements succeed or fail to change the boundaries to access?) in order to identify *how* public–private policies change over time and how groups mobilize politically within this structure of benefit provision. Future researchers might want to determine whether the presence or absence of different factors – public opinion, media attention, divided government, etc. – seems to matter for a movement's success or failure. They might also want to understand what factors explain why movements finally emerged when they did and what factors helped to move citizens from quiescence with the status quo to rebellion against it. These are worthy questions, though in order to be able to ask these questions in the future, it is important to first demonstrate the existence of boundary group mobilization as a process that characterizes the politics of the public–private welfare state and is itself constitutive of American political development, thereby forcing a modification of earlier views about the public–private welfare state as hidden or out of sight.[56]

Contributions

In describing the process by which citizens' groups have recognized and contested exclusions built into government homeownership policies, this book contributes to several academic debates. First and foremost, it challenges scholars of the public–private welfare state to give greater consideration to people and groups who have been excluded from such arrangements. By focusing mainly on how beneficiaries of public–private policies understand the role of the government in their lives, scholars have missed an important source of activism that has come from citizens at the margins. In contrast to insiders, who often fail to view themselves as beneficiaries of government social policies, outsiders can detect and have detected the precise ways in which state power can be used to shape

---

[56] Dietrich Ruschemeyer, "Can One or a Few Cases Yield Theoretical Gains?" in James Mahoney and Dietrich Ruschemeyer (eds.), *Comparative Historical Analysis in the Social Sciences* (Cambridge: Cambridge University Press, 2003), chap. 9, 307.

citizens' market opportunities – precisely because they see the state's coercive power as being directed against them.

In addition, this book contributes to the public–private welfare state research agenda by exploring the origins and evolution of homeownership and credit policy as a core component of the public–private welfare state. Culturally, homeownership occupies an important place in the American imagination, signifying meritocratic capitalist achievement despite the often heavy hand of the government in making this achievement possible for many Americans. Materially, homeownership matters greatly to American households because it is how they build wealth and store it to use later, for their children or through retirement.[57] It is an important factor in understanding the intergenerational transmission of wealth. Homeownership also matters within the broader American political economy. Finance, insurance, and real estate together constitute roughly 20 percent of the American GDP today, up from 10 percent in 1947.[58] For these reasons, it is important that we understand the origins and consequences of the US government's decision to promote, indirectly, homeownership as a way to house citizens, to provide for their economic security, and to bolster the economy. Forged in the New Deal and reasserted at midcentury, decisions to emphasize homeownership over other types of housing tenure, and to promote the idea of houses themselves as assets and stores of value, also helped to raise the

---

[57] Americans are also strongly wedded to the idea of housing as an asset that appreciates in value. According to a Pew survey, in 1991, 84 percent of Americans strongly or somewhat agreed with the statement "Buying a home is the best long-term investment a person can make." In 2011, five years after the housing bubble burst, 81 percent of people still agreed with this sentiment strongly or somewhat. In addition, the negative correlation between national homeownership rates and welfare state generosity in industrialized democracies has generated a spirited debate over the possible trade-off between homeownership and welfare generosity, and its relationship to pensions. See Pew Research Center, "Home Sweet Home. Still" (April 12, 2011), at www.pewsocialtrends.org/2011/04/12/home-sweet-home-still/; Francis Castles, "The Really Big Trade-off: Home Ownership and the Welfare State in the New World and the Old," *Acta Politica* 33, no. 1 (1998), 5–19; Jim Kemeny, "'The Really Big Trade-Off' between Home Ownership and Welfare: Castles' Evaluation of the 1980 Thesis, and a Reformulation 25 Years On," *Housing, Theory and Society* 22, no. 2 (2005), 59–75; John Doling and Nick Horsewood, "Home Ownership and Pensions: Causality and the Really Big Trade-off," *Housing, Theory and Society* 28, no. 2 (2011), 166–82.

[58] Richard B. Freeman, "It's Financialization!" *International Labour Review* 149, no. 2 (2010), 163–83; Christopher Witko, "The Politics of Financialization in the United States, 1949–2005," *British Journal of Political Science* 46, no. 2 (2016), 349–70; Greta Krippner, *Capitalizing on Crisis: The Political Origins of the Rise of Finance* (Cambridge, MA: Harvard University Press, 2011).

stakes for those left behind, shaping the political responses documented in these pages.[59]

Finally, this book adds to a literature concerned with the sources and nature of American state building over the twentieth and twenty-first centuries. The boundary group politics described in this book constitute a politics of discovery that is prevalent across a variety of realms in the United States, from health care to the carceral state. Because the US government conducts so much of its activity through complex governing arrangements and market mechanisms, it creates a space in which activists may engage in particular forms of collective action – especially information gathering – to reveal, contest, and transform the scope of the American state.

A Look Ahead

The chapters that follow identify the boundaries that constrained some groups from accessing homeownership over the twentieth century and show how those boundaries developed – the evidence, ideas, goals, and idiosyncrasies that shaped them. They then show how citizens' organizations came to recognize their constituents' position at the boundaries of access to housing, and then link that exclusion not to the invisible hand of the market, but to the visible hand of the government. Finally, they describe how advocacy groups used the government's role in creating and then reinforcing barriers to access and the private sector's investment in continuing as a partner in the provision of services as tools in the groups' quest for greater access to homeownership.

Together, they provide a comprehensive description of the development of the public–private welfare state in homeownership, and of the political consequences of the patterns of exclusion it engendered. The view of boundary groups as catalysts for policy reform over time challenges perspectives that view the American state's complexity as inherently depoliticizing. Complex and indirect government policies do not

---

[59] The cultural and economic significance of homeownership also has a darker side, as several scholars have detailed its relationship to racial politics in the US. David Freund, *Colored Property: State Policy and White Racial Suburban America* (Chicago: University of Chicago Press, 2007); Brian McCabe, *No Place Like Home: Wealth, Community, and the Politics of Homeownership* (New York: Oxford University Press, 2016); Kevin Boyle, *Arc of Justice: A Saga of Race, Civil Rights, and Murder in the Jazz Age* (New York: Henry Holt and Company, 2004); Carol Anderson, *White Rage: The Unspoken Truth of Our Racial Divide* (New York: Bloomsbury, 2016).

allow the government to sidestep thorny issues of distributional politics. Instead, they proliferate a different kind of politics.

The first part of this book (Chapters 2 and 3) sets the stage for understanding boundary group mobilization for homeownership by tracing the historical development of the US's public–private homeowner- ship infrastructure, from its origins in the Great Depression and the New Deal to its postwar entrenchment as the dominant option for middle-class housing tenure and policy. This rendering reveals that policy-makers who designed the US's public–private homeownership infrastructure in the 1930s programs clearly recognized the construction of criteria for safe and risky lending as one of their challenges. The evolution of homeowner- ship into the dominant form of housing in the postwar United States would raise the stakes for those unable to obtain homes on an affordable basis, while the designation between safe and risky lending that policy- makers crafted in the implementation stages would become central to outsiders' efforts to contest the political and economic basis of their constituents' exclusion. The second part of the book (Chapters 4 through 6) then examines and compares the process by which different groups – each constrained from access in different ways – came to recognize and ultimately contest their constituents' exclusion from those earlier home- ownership programs.

The conclusion steps back to situate boundary group politics within a larger politics of discovery, whereby groups work to reveal the scope of the state, and the differential effects of state power on different groups of citizens. In revealing the scope of the state, actors make the state's role legible in outcomes that otherwise few people might trace to the state, in order to contest its scope. As government functions become ever more complex and difficult to trace back to the government, the politics of discovery – of rendering the state visible in order to contest it – has emerged as both a strategy and a mode of politics marginalized groups engage in to reform and expand the scope of the state.

2

Building a Government Out of Sight, 1932–1949

Great societal crises, such as war, depression, or the entry of a nation into modern development, are pivotal to understanding a society's economic development. Once in place, these "rules" of market-building and market intervention are keys to understanding how new markets develop in a society.

– Neil Fligstein, 1996[1]

The public–private welfare state in homeownership has its origins in the 1930s, when reformers in Congress, the Hoover and Roosevelt administrations, and the private real estate and lending industries sought policies that would fundamentally restructure the US mortgage market and increase the safety and availability of homeownership. They envisioned that the federal government would provide the infrastructure to promote these aims, but private enterprise would perform the day-to-day tasks of building, lending, and brokering. In other words, the indirect promotion of homeownership was not an accident of design.

Supporters of this approach touted a variety of potential benefits. Providers who had devoted decades to understanding their industries had valuable existing knowledge and expertise; indeed, the National Association of Real Estate Boards and the United States Building and Loan League were at times heavily consulted as the programs were being designed. They also staffed the agencies, once established. Just as important as what this structure could accomplish was what it might avoid: the high costs and risks (both political and economic) of either full

---

[1] Neil Fligstein, "Markets as Politics," *American Sociological Review* 61, no. 4 (1996), 656–73; 657.

33

government involvement (especially in public housing) or inaction.[2] Moreover, for some, having the borrower go through a private lender and not the government directly would help to minimize the moral hazard problems associated with its backing of the new loan contracts: had citizens thought of themselves as having borrowed from the government, they might take a more cavalier attitude toward repayment.

The "great societal crisis" of the Depression, then, prompted policy-makers to embrace a set of policies they believed would revive the housing market, stem the foreclosure crisis, and bolster employment in the construction sector, but in a way that would work in partnership with the private sector rather than as an alternative to it. This would be challenged in the post–World War II years by a competing vision for the nation's housing policy marked by skepticism of the idea that the profit motive could ever produce adequate housing at prices affordable to workers. For a time it looked as though the two competing visions for housing policy might be able to coexist; however, the public–private homeownership model gradually displaced its competitors, raising the stakes for those who found themselves excluded.

By the mid-twentieth century, few areas would better exemplify the United States' "government out of sight" than its quiet promotion of homeownership.

THE CHALLENGES OF PROVIDING MODERN HOUSING

Houses are difficult goods to provide on the market. They are expensive to build. They have high up-front costs, often amounting to many times a household's annual income. Few households have the cash to purchase a house outright. Mortgages attack this affordability problem by lengthening the amount of time people have to pay for their house. Yet mortgages carry their own risks for lenders. A borrower might not repay the loan if her financial circumstances change (say, due to unemployment). Or a borrower may decide he is unwilling to continue to repay the loan (for example, if the housing market crashes and the value of the house falls below what is owed). Furthermore, when profits are derived from interest rates charged to borrowers and paid to savers, then both inflation and fluctuating interest rates can threaten lenders' profitability and solvency. Another risk arises from the uncertainty over when a loan

---

[2] Memo on the National Housing Program, May 9, 1934, in Franklin D. Roosevelt Library, Harry Hopkins Papers (hereafter HH), Box 79, Folder: Housing 1934.

will actually be repaid, in particular whether a borrower will decide to pay off the loan earlier than anticipated.[3] Each of these factors makes it difficult for lenders to predict their future profits, which in turn can affect their willingness to extend loans to households.

Since the early twentieth century, these basic risks associated with home mortgage lending have not prevented a mortgage market from emerging in the United States, but they have variously shaped it.[4] To minimize uncertainty about the borrower's motives and prospects for repayment, lending was often kept local, which made it easier for the lender to know the borrower's reputation. Dating back to the 1830s, building and loan societies took this goal further. Their cooperative ownership structure required potential borrowers to first become members (and thus part owners), which incentivized borrowers to remain on good terms.[5]

Many lenders attempted to reduce their risk exposure by requiring high down payments from borrowers, usually on the order of 40–50 percent of the cost of the house. It was believed that by having more "skin in the game," borrowers would be less likely to default. Moreover, if a property did fall into foreclosure, then the high amount of equity already in the house would make it easier for the lender to recover its losses.[6]

---

[3] See also Mark Boleat, *National Housing Finance Systems* (London: Croom Helm, 1985); Douglas Diamond and Michael Lea, "The Decline of Special Circuits in Developed Country Housing Finance," *Housing Policy Debate* 3, no. 3 (1992), 747–77; Daniel Immergluck, *Foreclosed: High Risk Lending, Deregulation, and the Undermining of America's Mortgage Market* (Ithaca, NY: Cornell University Press, 2009); International Monetary Fund, *World Economic Outlook* (Washington, DC: International Monetary Fund, 2003), chap. 2.

[4] By the 1920s, a variety of lenders had emerged to offer households more options for home buying. This included building and loan societies (today known as savings and loan associations) and mutual savings banks, which held roughly 31 and 12 percent of mortgage debt outstanding on one- to four-family homes in 1925, respectively. Commercial banks, meanwhile, held about 11 percent and life insurance companies only 6 percent. Most of the remainder of mortgage debt – about 38 percent – was held by noninstitutional lenders. Kenneth Snowden, "Debt on nonfarm structures, by type of debt, property, and holder: 1896–1952," in Susan B. Carter, Scott Sigmund Gartner, Michael R. Haines, Alan L. Olmstead, Richard Sutch, and Gavin Wright (eds.), *Historical Statistics of the United States, Earliest Times to the Present: Millennial Edition* (New York: Cambridge University Press, 2006), Table Dc913–921/2; Kenneth A. Snowden, "Mortgage Banking in the United States, 1870–1940," Research Institute for Housing America Special Report, Paper 13129 (October 2013), 51.

[5] Stuart, *Discriminating Risk*, 90–1.

[6] Kenneth Snowden, "The Anatomy of a Residential Mortgage Crisis: A Look Back to the 1930s," in Lawrence E. Mitchell and Arthur E. Wilmarth Jr. (eds.), *The Panic of 2008:*

Lenders held borrowers to short repayment periods as another way to minimize risk. Contracts typically lasted from two to fifteen years, with the entire value of the loan to be repaid at the end of the term (in practice, loans were usually renegotiated and terms extended as they came due). Commercial banks tended to lean toward the lower end of this range, preferring the option to call back loans after one to three years with the expectation that they would probably be refinanced at that point. Building and loan societies by the 1920s tended to offer much longer terms – up to twelve to fifteen years. Finally, to tap into household demand for credit and to help manage risk, lenders had also begun to experiment with several new tools, such as issuing private mortgage insurance, offering bonds or participation certificates, and experimenting with early forms of securitization.[7]

These tools helped to protect lenders against some of the risks associated with lending, but posed challenges for borrowers. Households that could not afford large down payments often resorted to second and third mortgages, usually with high interest rates. Short repayment periods became a potential source of risk, as many borrowers did not have the funds to repay if the entire loan was called back at the end of the term. This was not much of an issue during the boom years of the 1920s, when borrowers could easily refinance their loans at the end of the term. However, this structure was theoretically vulnerable to a change in lenders' need for liquidity – a theory that would be tested after 1929.

THE CONSOLIDATION OF THE REAL ESTATE INDUSTRY

During the decades leading up to the Great Depression, the real estate industry worked concertedly to organize its constituents into national professional associations. These included, most importantly, the United States Building and Loan League (USBLL), established in 1893, and the National Association of Real Estate Boards (NAREB, today the National Association of Realtors), in 1909. In the early decades of the twentieth century, NAREB and the USBLL became prominent political players at the local, state, and, eventually, national levels. Other associations

Causes, Consequences, and Implications for Reform (Cheltenham, UK: Edward Elgar Publishing Ltd., 2010), chap. 2.

[7] Snowden, "Anatomy of a Residential Mortgage Crisis"; Richard Green and Susan Wachter, "The American Mortgage in Historical and International Context," *Journal of Economic Perspectives* 19, no. 4 (2005), 93–114.

founded in these years were less involved in homeownership directly, but eventually would become more involved in national debates about home-ownership and housing policy. They included the Mortgage Bankers Association of America, the American Bankers Association, and the Life Insurance Association of America.

NAREB and the USBLL worked tirelessly to bolster the status of their members. One of their most important tasks in the early years was to encourage their members to adopt shared professional identities around which they could mobilize (for example, real estate agents, or Realtors, taken for granted today). The two organizations also tried to standardize their respective industries. Although many financial organizations shared the mutual funding structure of a building and loan society, not all of them went by that name. The USBLL encouraged all of its members to identify themselves as "building and loan" societies. To standardize their professional practices, both organizations offered, among other things, boilerplate curriculum and training courses for members nationwide.

The two organizations standardized not only their members' professional identities, but also the larger housing market. Housing markets in the early twentieth century were highly localized, with wide geographic variation in costs and practices and few standard metrics of real estate market health. In the 1920s, NAREB began developing quantitative indicators for the housing market, releasing in 1925 (and regularly thereafter) "monthly index figures on real estate transfers and conveyances, new mortgage financing, residential rents, and foreclosures."[8] With the development of these new measures and their wide dissemination, NAREB played an outsized role in shaping how policy-makers, members of the industry, and the public would perceive the health of the US housing market.

A final task of the organizations at this time was to research and advocate for the adoption of new practices and techniques that they felt had the potential to transform the housing market. After World War I, the USBLL researched and briefly advocated for the adoption of a nation-wide mortgage discount bank that would allow building and loan

---

[8] In 1893, for instance, the USBLL surveyed its members, finding that they used dozens of different methods to calculate "dividends, loan premiums, and fees." David Mason, *From Buildings and Loans to Bail-Outs: A History of the American Savings and Loan Industry, 1831–1995* (New York: Cambridge University Press, 2004), 48–52; Josephine Ewalt, *A Business Reborn: The Savings and Loan Story, 1930–1960* (Chicago: American Savings and Loan Institute Press, 1962), 122–5; Pearl Janet Davies, *Real Estate in American History* (Washington, DC: Public Affairs Press, 1958), 154–5.

societies to expand the availability of funds into areas of the country that struggled to get credit. Though the plan was abandoned by the 1920s, it resurfaced during the Great Depression, and parts of it became law with the signing of the Federal Home Loan Bank Act of 1932.

For its part, NAREB formed divisions to study virtually every aspect of the housing market, even those tangential to the real estate brokerage business, that engaged its members on a daily basis. Its dozen or so divisions included one to study appraisals, one for mortgage finance, another for construction (this eventually became the National Association of Home Builders), and yet another for marketing. Through its work in these topic areas, NAREB concluded that some of the lenders' earlier practices and precautions could safely be eliminated or replaced. A 1923 report by NAREB's Mortgage Finance Division suggested that lenders had overestimated the risks of first mortgages. Instead, what appeared to drive default risk were the second and third mortgages that many middle-class borrowers often took out to help with the down payment.[9]

By 1930, NAREB was deeply concerned about how to reduce Americans' reliance on second and third mortgages, as its top leadership began to worry about the organization's gradual retreat from the "market for homes for persons of small means," in the words of its president. He elaborated that the doubling of homeownership costs in the fifteen years prior had "placed [homeownership] out of the reach of the great majority of our population."[10] (In 1930, just under 48 percent of families owned their home.) NAREB resolved to lower the costs of homeownership "to make homes not too costly for 80 percent of the American people to buy."[11] Both ideas – the need for affordable houses and mortgages, and the benefits of reducing borrowers' reliance on second and third mortgages – would gain currency in Washington by the mid-1930s as policymakers came to see borrowers' reliance on second and third mortgages as a contributing factor to the Depression's foreclosure crisis.[12]

---

[9] Davies, *Real Estate in American History*, 153–8.

[10] President Leonard P. Raume, Speech to the 1930 National Building Survey Conference, quoted in Davies, *Real Estate in American History*, 166.

[11] Ibid., 179.

[12] Ibid., 153–8, 177. See also Letters to Alexander Summer from Carrie Maude Jones, June 5, 1964, and from Alexander Summer to E. L. Ostendorf, June 9, 1964, both in National Association of Realtors Library and Archives, Subject Files A-C (hereafter NAR SFAC), Box 1, Federal Housing Administration. While the role of NAREB in crafting the legislation is clear, there are also indications of disagreements within NAREB over the

From their local and decentralized roots just a few decades earlier, by the 1920s and 1930s professional associations such as NAREB and the USBLL had made tremendous strides in organizing their members as experts with shared professional identities, and had contributed to the perception and contours of the US housing market with their research, curricula, and training materials.

THE FEDERAL GOVERNMENT AND HOUSING BEFORE THE GREAT DEPRESSION

The activism of the two major professional associations in the mortgage business contrasted starkly with the government's hands-off approach throughout the 1920s. To be sure, there were a few exceptions: a federal survey of housing conditions in 1893; the Federal Reserve Act of 1913, which indirectly promoted consumer credit expansion; and an effort during World War I to quickly build housing for war workers. Another exception was a national "own-your-own-home" marketing campaign – a collaboration between private sector housing providers and first the Department of Labor, then later the Department of Commerce under Herbert Hoover. Its main goal was to spur housing demand as a way to channel returning World War I veterans into construction jobs. It did not seek to address the issue that kept many people from owning: inadequate access to finance.[13]

Federal involvement with farms had a slightly longer history. Farmers had long experienced episodic but severe credit crises tied to a funding structure that required them to pay off or renegotiate loans every two to five years at high and variable interest rates. In response to rural unrest, Congress passed the Federal Farm Loan Act in 1916. The act created two federally chartered farm banks, the Joint Stock Land Banks and the Federal Land Banks, to be supervised by the newly created Federal Farm Loan Board. Both of the banks enjoyed an implicit subsidy via their tax exemption, though they differed in terms of ownership (the Federal Land Banks were nonprofit cooperatives owned by member associations, while the Joint Stock Land Banks were privately owned) and funding structure

proposal. See Letter to Alexander Summer from David B. Simpson, June 3, 1964, in NAR SFAC, Box 1, Folder: Federal Housing Administration.

[13] See, for example, Lendol Calder, *Financing the American Dream: A Cultural History of Consumer Credit* (Princeton, NJ: Princeton University Press, 2001); Jeffrey Hornstein, *A Nation of Realtors: A Cultural History of the Twentieth-Century* (Durham, NC: Duke University Press, 2005).

(the Federal Land Banks did not originate loans, but acted as an inter-mediary of sorts between member banks).[14] As Jonathan Rose describes, "[t]he goal of both systems was to provide affordable mortgage loans, particularly those with amortization over long terms (30–40 years) not generally offered by other lenders."[15]

Notwithstanding the government's lack of involvement in the home mortgage field, the existence of a farm mortgage infrastructure would prove significant. The farm mortgage programs were a template for the USBLL's demands for something similar following World War I, and then again during the Great Depression, as policy-makers looked for solutions to the housing and mortgage crises. Eventually, they adopted many of the same features that characterized the new farm mortgage contracts, including amortized long-term loans. The farm mortgage infrastructure also helped spur the development of new political players, in particular the Farm Mortgage Bankers Association, which formed in opposition to farm mortgage programs as they were being debated and eventually morphed into the Mortgage Bankers Association of America.

Ultimately, the existence of a farm mortgage infrastructure would come to provide a normative justification for similar interventions in the home mortgage field, though not without controversy.

THE GREAT DEPRESSION AND THE FORECLOSURE CRISIS

The housing and mortgage markets that developed by the 1920s were thrown into a free fall in the 1930s, with the onset of bank, unemploy-ment, and foreclosure crises. The Great Depression revealed several fun-damental weaknesses in the existing housing finance system and, more importantly, created a setting in which political, social, and economic pressure facilitated a fundamental restructuring of the mortgage market and the government's role within it. The Depression had its origins in a banking crisis, and banking's ties to housing – indeed to the health of the entire economy – quickly became apparent. As millions of Americans found themselves unemployed, many were unable to repay their mort-gages. The short-term funding structure of most mortgages, which, in

---

[14] Jonathan Rose, "A Primer on Farm Mortgage Debt Relief Programs during the 1930s," Federal Reserve Board of Governors Working Paper 2013–33 (April 22, 2013), 4; Lee Alston, Wayne Grove, and David Wheelock, "Why Do Banks Fail? Evidence from the 1920s," *Explorations in Economic History* 31, no. 4 (1994), 409–31; 415–16.

[15] Rose, "A Primer," 4.

some cases, called for the full value of the mortgage after only a few years, only exacerbated the crisis. Suddenly in need of funds, banks began calling back the full value of the loans rather than allowing borrowers to refinance, which meant that even borrowers who could have afforded the monthly loan costs were blindsided by having to repay the full value of the mortgage. Bank foreclosures fueled the problem by driving down neighborhood house values, leaving many mortgagees owing more than their houses were worth and creating a "downward spiral."[16] By 1933, 13.3 out of every 1,000 mortgage homes were in foreclosure – more than triple the rate in 1926 (3.6).[17] As of January 1934, almost half of all mortgaged owner-occupied dwellings in urban areas were in default.[18]

The plight of farmers was even more severe in many respects, since farmers relied on credit for their daily activities. As agricultural prices plummeted, farmers were unable to maintain their mortgage payments. By 1933, thirty-nine out of every thousand mortgaged farms were in foreclosure (more than double the foreclosure rate from 1926 to 1930). The federal government had a large stake in the farm credit system through its implicit backing of the Federal Land Banks and the Joint Stock Land Banks. By 1930, these two types of lenders held nearly 15 percent of the nation's farm mortgage debt. Without any remedial action, the land bank system was in danger of collapsing by 1933.[19]

Urban dwellers and farmers, as well as lenders and state governments, demanded that something be done. The response of citizens to the foreclosure crisis ranged from prayer gatherings at churches to petition- and letter-writing campaigns asking state officials to declare mortgage moratoriums to spontaneous organizations aimed at attacking the problem through political channels, and more radical forms of resistance.

One of the more radical citizens' groups was the Small Home Owners Federation, a mutual defense organization founded in Cleveland in 1932 by Hungarian homeowners. The federation developed a system whereby block captains would monitor local evictions and dispatch groups of members to an evicted member's house right after the bank

---

[16] Price Fishback, Jonathan Rose, and Kenneth Snowden, *Well Worth Saving: How the New Deal Safeguarded Homeownership* (Chicago: University of Chicago Press, 2013).

[17] Kenneth Snowden, "Mortgage foreclosures and delinquencies: 1926–1979," in Carter, et al. (eds.), *Historical Statistics of the United States*, Table Dc1255–1270.

[18] Fishback, Rose, and Snowden, *Well Worth Saving*, chaps. 2–3; David Wheelock, "The Federal Response to Home Mortgage Distress: Lessons from the Great Depression," *Federal Reserve Bank of St. Louis Review* 90, no. 3 (2008), 133–48; 138–9.

[19] Fishback, Rose, and Snowden, *Well Worth Saving*, chapter 4.

had taken possession and removed the family's belongings. Within a few hours of an eviction, the group could restore all of the residents' belongings from the front yard to the house. This type of activity forced lenders to call on the police and courts for protection, which overwhelmed the legal system and delayed foreclosure proceedings for weeks. The federation could dispatch members quickly, because it had a membership base of 14,000, as well an alliance with the local Unemployed Councils.[20] While there is no evidence in hearings or otherwise that this particular group shaped national-level responses to the crisis, there is evidence that they and other local movements may have helped shape political outcomes within their own areas.[21] Moreover, the spread of the organization to neighboring cities, as well the interest it elicited from organizers in other states, may have contributed to a general recognition in Washington of the demand for some form of relief for homeowners.[22]

Other more mainstream groups formed to appeal to homeowners' interests. Two of the more prominent ones were the Consolidated Home Owners Mortgage Committee (CHOMC) and the Home Owners Protective Enterprise.[23] Neither group came close to mobilizing the fourteen million homeowners whose interests they claimed to speak for, but they did conduct research on housing and mortgage needs, meet with elected officials, send letters and telegrams to elected officials, endorse candidates, and organize other types of drives. One stated concern of the CHOMC was that the eventual solution to the foreclosure crisis should balance the interests of homeowners and bankers (they feared that the latter had more

---

[20] Gregory Martin Stone, "Ethnicity, class and politics among Czechs in Cleveland, 1870–1940," PhD Diss., Rutgers University (1993), 179.

[21] An article in *The Nation* described a scene in Cleveland in August 1933 (shortly after the signing of the Home Owners' Loan Act) of 10,000 men, women, and children gathering for several days to protest one homeowner's eviction. The police – an estimated 300 officers – were called to break up the protest and wielded tear gas and batons unsuccessfully. The protest culminated two days later in the Cleveland Public Square with calls to the mayor, who (on his way to a luncheon) urged the banks to go more slowly on the foreclosures. A report in the *Cleveland Press* suggested that such riot would not have occurred if the city had a federal home loan office. It was announced the next day that Cleveland would receive an office. James Steele, "Home-Owners in Revolt," *The Nation* (September 1933), 266.

[22] US Congress, Senate, Committee on Banking and Currency, *Home Owners' Loan Act: Hearings before the Committee on Banking and Currency*, 73rd Cong., 1st sess., 1933, esp. 88–90, 128–9.

[23] Marie Obenauer, testimony in US Congress, Senate, Committee on Banking and Currency, *National Housing Act: Hearings before the Committee on Banking and Currency*, 73rd Cong., 2nd sess., 1934, 388–9.

influence). The American Federation of Labor supported the CHOMC's activities and stances, later praising the organization's agenda for home-owners' relief as "an economical and wise investment for our nation."[24]

Farm groups, however, surpassed the mobilization capacity of citizens' groups.[25] Farmers first mobilized at local and state levels, trying to convince Midwestern legislatures to adopt some sort of foreclosure relief. Farmers also organized into a handful of groups to exert pressure on local and state governments, including the Modern Seventy-Sixers, the United Farmers, County Councils of Defense, and county agricultural credit councils. Isolated reports of collusion between foreclosed farmers and their neighbors to hold down auction prices and repurchase their neigh-bors' belongings surfaced in newspapers at the time. By 1933, more farmers were resorting to violence and intimidation to halt foreclosure sales, according to a number of reports.[26] A story in *The Nation* said that one such mob of a thousand in Iowa

seized the attorney for an insurance company, dangled a rope before his eyes, and threatened him with immediate lynching. They held the judge of the district court a prisoner in his chambers and defied the county sheriff. And they got what they wanted – the withdrawal of foreclosure proceedings against one farmer and the defeat of a deficiency judgment against another. It was the opening engagement between an organized rural population and established authority – social revolu-tion in the cornfields of Iowa.[27]

This type of uprising was not unique to Iowa. In December 1932 and January 1933, farm newspapers in at least a dozen states reported instances of mobs of fifty to a thousand farmers intimidating sheriffs, county treasurers, district judges, and mayors. The mobs managed to declare effective mortgage foreclosure moratoriums even before state legislatures and governors had officially declared them.[28] Testifying

---

[24] Editorial, *The American Federationist* (May 1933), 459.

[25] In fact, an editorial in *The American Federationist* suggested that homeowners should try to replicate farmers' organizations, which had met with more success in making their grievances known and defending their neighbors against foreclosures. See Editorial, *The American Federationist* (March 1933), 232; Editorial, *The American Federationist* (May 1933), 459.

[26] Harlan Miller, "The Farmer in a Fighting Mood," *The New York Times* (February 12, 1933), 93.

[27] Charlotte Hubbard Prescott, "An Iowa Foreclosure," *The Nation* (February 1933), 198–9.

[28] Miller, "The Farmer in a Fighting Mood." Miller based his report on reports collected by farm newspapers in these areas, which consolidated reports of farmer unrest.

before the Senate Agricultural Committee in January 1933, the head of
the American Farm Bureau Federation warned: "unless something is done
for the American farmer we will have a revolution in the countryside in
less than twelve months."[29]

Meanwhile, lenders were also overwhelmed by the rapid deterioration
of the mortgage market in cities and farm regions alike. Beyond threats of
violence, many mortgage lenders were swamped with foreclosure proceedings and could not manage the number of foreclosures on their
books. As such, they had an interest in reducing or at least slowing the
foreclosure rate. On farms, life insurers (at the time the largest private
lenders to farmers) became so overwhelmed by the heavy load of foreclosures that they "voluntarily suspended foreclosures so that they could
avoid seizing and managing even more farm land than they already
had."[30]

Faced with these dire circumstances, state governments were already
beginning to act and declare foreclosure moratoriums. Between January
1932 and spring 1933, twenty-seven states had adopted some sort of farm
or house mortgage moratorium.[31] Plausibly, lenders felt more threatened
by populist pressures that demanded state-level action and undermined
the sanctity of contracts than by a uniform approach at the federal level
that upheld contracts and also protected banks from excessive losses.
Given that the Supreme Court later upheld one state's – Minnesota's –
mortgage moratorium law on the grounds that, in an emergency, "public
welfare" ought to take precedence over "individual rights," the banks'
concerns were well founded.[32]

These developments had three major implications for policy-makers
responding to the crisis. First, developments on farms, in cities, and in
state legislatures suggested that waiting for the foreclosure crisis to

---

[29] Special to *The New York Times*, "Democrats Offer $1,500,000,000 Bill to Aid Farmers,"
The New York Times (January 26, 1933), 1. The farmers' revolution was not mentioned
in the later hearings in April. By April, the main issues of discussion were technical,
with the attendees concerned about the challenges posed by loan renegotiation. See US
Congress, House, Committee on Agriculture, *Farm Mortgage Relief: Hearings before the
Committee on Agriculture*, 73rd Cong., 1st sess., 1933.

[30] Rose, "A Primer," 9–10; quote, 9.

[31] Miles Colean, *The Impact of Government on Real Estate Finance in the United States*
(New York: National Bureau of Economic Research, 1950), 40–1.

[32] "Mortgage Moratorium Is Upheld by U.S. Supreme Court," *National Real Estate Journal*
(January 1934), 16.

resolve itself was not a viable option from an economic, political, or social standpoint. The countryside seemed to be under threat of revolution, and radicalism was developing in some urban areas as homeowners banded together to defend against foreclosures. Beyond citizens' demands that something be done, the foreclosure crisis revealed coordination and information problems for lenders and state governments. The uncertainty over how state governments and businesses would respond to foreclosures also threatened to exacerbate the severity and duration of the crisis.

Second, the years and even decades of industry-level organization meant that some degree of industry involvement would be desirable in any federal government response to the crisis. Home mortgage lenders and real estate agents had an advantage over government policy-makers, since they had already devoted time and resources to studying different aspects of the mortgage market. Their organizational infrastructure would also enable the leadership to enlist the cooperation of members across the country to help administer new programs on the ground. And organizations had expertise that would be valuable in designing policy responses, providing some empirical support for the soundness of what often seemed like revolutionary proposals, and administering programs. To reiterate how these two points relate, the crisis pushed the government to look for novel solutions to the foreclosure problem, and decades of creating shared expertise in the mortgage market placed real estate–related organizations in an advantageous position to advise on possible government solutions.

Third, over time, policy-makers gradually came to recognize that the solution to the housing crisis would involve not only stabilizing the market, but also creating a new kind of housing market, one that would be characterized by a hybrid of government support and private enterprise. Before the Depression, organizations within the housing industry – in particular, NAREB – had researched and publicized the dangers and risks of the housing system, and the Depression materialized them for all to see. Bank runs, for example, exposed the risks of short-term lending, even for people who managed to remain employed. Policy-makers came to see a reorganization of the mortgage market as likely and desirable when the housing market failed to heal itself. Added to these factors, developments on farms and in rural areas required decisive government action to stanch the wave of foreclosures, which made it politically expedient to consider doing something similar for homeowners.

CONSTRUCTING A NEW MORTGAGE MARKET

Consequently, between 1932 and 1938, Congress established four land-mark programs that took aim at these problems. In doing so, they fundamentally restructured the mortgage market and the government's role within it.

The Federal Home Loan Bank Act

Congress's first response to the housing crisis came in 1932 with passage of the Federal Home Loan Bank Act. The act created the Federal Home Loan Bank System (FHLBS), consisting of twelve regional banks and a five-member supervisory Federal Home Loan Bank Board (FHLBB) in Washington, DC. Modeled after the Federal Reserve System and the Federal Land Banks, the FHLBS allowed member institutions to borrow funds from regional banks to lend within their local markets, in turn using their existing mortgage holdings as collateral (this is what is known as a mortgage discount bank).

The logic behind the FHLBS was that it would free up more funds to loan to more households, which would stabilize mortgage lending and housing prices and, in turn, housing demand.[33] Proponents of the federal home loan banks, which included NAREB and the USBLL, reasoned that many foreclosures occurred because commercial mortgage lenders were forced to call back the full value of the mortgages as short-term contracts expired.[34] This caught borrowers off-guard, even those in good standing, as they could usually expect to renegotiate a mortgage at the end of the term. In theory, building and loan societies would have been happy to take on that group of borrowers. But with a business model that tied up funds for eight to twelve years, most were unable to take on new borrowers, however low the risk. By freeing up funds to loan out, the system of federal home loan banks presumably would address this challenge. In return, borrowers would enjoy the security and stability of longer

---

[33] Fishback, Rose, and Snowden, *Well Worth Saving*, 33–5.

[34] A similar system had been proposed by the United States Building and Loan League after World War I, when the organization argued that it would stabilize the home loan system. At the time, it also argued that the system would facilitate the flow of mortgage funds from the capital-rich North to the capital-poor West and South, but it was dropped after 1920 due to lack of interest. When the proposal resurfaced in the 1930s, its proponents (primarily the leadership of the USBLL) retrofitted it to a new set of circumstances, proposed as a solution to the foreclosure crisis.

repayment terms. Mortgages that would be eligible as collateral would have to be amortized over a longer term (e.g., fifteen years) and could not exceed $20,000. Eligibility was limited to building and loan societies. The new legislation also contained a provision that authorized the new home loan banks to make direct loans to ailing homeowners.

Yet for all the discussion about how the FHLBS would ease the housing crisis, the legislation was ineffectual once enacted. This seemed to confirm opponents' suspicion of the building and loan industry's motives. The USBLL had lobbied hardest for the legislation and managed to secure language that treated its industry favorably, while excluding other types of lenders. Facing charges that the legislation was really just for the enrichment of the building and loan industry, the USBLL leadership countered that the structure of the FHLBS made it inherently unsuited to tackling the crisis. Because membership was restricted to financial institutions in good standing, the FHLBS was precluded from assisting lenders and homeowners most in need of foreclosure relief. Meanwhile, the one provision that might have benefited struggling homeowners – the direct loan provision – was repealed a year later, with no loans ever made.

The FHLBS's failure to help struggling homeowners grew into a political liability for Hoover. The home loan banks became criticized as the "Home Loan Bunk" in the lead-up to the election that turned over the presidency to Franklin D. Roosevelt.[35] At the same time, the nature of the USBLL's involvement in shaping the system foreshadowed the development of a government out of sight in homeownership – just not through the same means of the FHLBS.

The Home Owners' Loan Act

The next major effort to stabilize the housing market came in the form of the Home Owners' Loan Act, enacted during FDR's first hundred days. Designed for homeowners who were unable to repay their mortgages, the act created the Home Owners' Loan Corporation (HOLC), which would purchase and refinance underwater mortgages from banks and offer homeowners more favorable repayment terms, including delayed

---

[35] Democratic National Campaign Committee, 1932, "The Home Loan Bank" (campaign advertisement), in FDR-L, Democratic Party National Committee Papers, Library and Research Bureau Papers, 1928–1933, Box 403, Folder: Publicity, Campaign, Home Owners and Farmers, Rand, James H. Jr. (Speech).

payment on the principal for a year, an extension of the repayment period, and the option for self-amortizing loans. The latter two features also meant that homeowners could enjoy lower monthly payments.

HOLC was a massive improvement over the Federal Home Loan Bank System as well as earlier ad hoc efforts to deal with the foreclosure crisis. For one thing, it was able to intervene in communities across the country simultaneously. While in theory banks already could – and did – independently renegotiate loan terms with individual borrowers, it was unlikely that sporadic individual renegotiations could stabilize the housing market overall in the midst of a nationwide housing crisis.[36] Second, after further amendments, HOLC became appealing to private lenders and investors. HOLC lured them into the program with government guarantees for the interest and principal of the loans they purchased. Lenders who participated were compensated generously, with interest rates approaching those of high-quality corporate bonds and (after revisions to the law in 1934) "equivalent to Treasury bonds."[37] At its peak, HOLC held 10 percent of all residential mortgages. Moreover, it accomplished this through the voluntary participation of lenders, and while not profitable, it operated without great cost to the government.[38]

HOLC was phased out in 1951. By then, it had already left its imprint on the housing market. It had demonstrated to private lenders the viability of more liberal loan terms, encouraging the widespread adoption of long-term, high loan-to-value, self-amortizing loan contracts, which could make monthly payments more affordable for more households.[39] Another important contribution of HOLC was its role in coordinating research into and statistics on the housing market for general use by the government and private housing providers. Before HOLC, the government data that did exist was fragmented and inconsistent. Finally, and most infamously, as the next chapter discusses, HOLC contributed to the development of a hybrid public–private housing market by standardizing residential real estate appraisal criteria. While initially created so that HOLC would be able to determine the value of the properties it refinanced, both government underwriters and private appraisers quickly

---

[36] Moreover, as Fishback, Rose, and Snowden point out, there were other reasons why banks might have been reluctant to offer loan modifications; see Fishback, Rose, and Snowden, *Well Worth Saving*, 42–9.

[37] Ibid., 49–51.   [38] Ibid., 114–15.   [39] Ibid., 101.

discovered the utility of standardized appraisal criteria for making decisions about whether to issue a mortgage (or insurance) on a property in the first place.

The National Housing Act and the Creation of the Federal Housing Administration

As successful as HOLC may have appeared in addressing the foreclosure crisis, it was not suited to remedy a different crisis related to the housing market: the massive falloff in construction employment during the Depression. By 1934, two million construction workers remained out of work, even as employment had begun to rebound in other sectors. Officials at the Department of Labor and from the American Federation of Labor estimated that getting those two million unemployed construction workers back to work would, through the magic of multipliers, translate into an added 5.5 million jobs in the economy.[40]

The decline of construction demand as a result of the Depression was staggering: 490,000 permits for new residential construction were issued in 1925, the peak of the housing boom. Eight years later, that number had plunged to 26,000.[41] Yet many saw a latent demand for construction, in particular for housing modernization. The problem was financing, which was impossible to come by in the frozen credit market.[42] Commercial banks had been through years of failures, and those still standing were in no position to lend. Building and loan societies suffered fewer casualties during the Depression, but those that did survive could not make many new loans.[43]

---

[40] Testimony of William C. O'Neill, Secretary-Treasurer, Building Trades Department, American Federation of Labor, Washington, DC, in US Congress, Senate, Committee on Banking and Currency, National Housing Act, 412. This was also quite costly for the unions, as O'Neill mentions in his testimony, since local unions also dispersed relief aid to members (ibid., 413–14).

[41] US Congress, House, Committee on Banking and Currency, National Housing Act, 64.

[42] On demands for construction financing, see, for example, ibid., 158, 194, 199, 416. On the lack of demand for houses, see, for example, ibid., 183. On housing demand (for approximately 800,000 single-family homes), see Telegram to M. J. McDonough (President, Building Trades Dep't, AFL) from James Caffery (Ohio Real Estate Boards), in US Congress, House, Committee on Banking and Currency, National Housing Act, 408–9.

[43] See, for example, "Home Financing Attacked," *The American Building Association News* (March 1934), 101. Part of the industry's concern had to do with the inability of thrifts to attract many new funds to lend as smaller borrowers retreated to the safety of banks under the newly created FDIC. For this reason, Title IV of the National Housing Act proposed creating a Federal Savings and Loan Insurance Corporation (FSLIC) to

In May, FDR's National Emergency Council circulated a proposal for a National Housing Program, identifying "the great deficiency and lag in mortgage lending and home-improvement financing" as "the most serious problem that the American industrial system has to grapple with." Yet it also saw in this problem the nation's

greatest industrial opportunity – namely, the field of modern housing. The sound development of this field affords the opportunity for (a) the secure investment of capital and credit that is now idle, (b) the economic use of our immense industrial equipment and abundant natural resources, and (c) the long-continued employment of that part of our industrial population which has been most seriously affected by the failure of the so-called heavy industries to share in the recent economic recovery proportionately with the consumption-goods industries.[44]

The centerpiece of the National Housing Program was a proposal for the federal government to provide mortgage insurance to private lenders. In exchange, lenders would be required to offer much more liberal mortgage terms than most were previously accustomed to, including long-term, fixed-rate, self-amortizing contracts with 20 percent down payments. As the proposal explained, the "[US] Treasury would stand behind this home-mortgage insurance," yet would still protect itself "against ultimate loss, even under extremely adverse circumstances."[45]

The proposal for loan insurance was incorporated into Title I and Title II of the National Housing Act of 1934. Title I created the Federal Housing Administration (FHA) to provide loan insurance to private lenders for home repairs, and Title II extended the insurance to cover home purchases. Unlike the Federal Home Loan Bank System, which was limited to savings and loans, any lender could apply for FHA insurance. Like the FHLBS and HOLC, the FHA established basic standards that loans had to conform to: mortgages for single-family homes would have to be for twenty years, at fixed interest rates, self-amortizing, and economically sound (the enacting legislation was vague about what that last condition meant, as the next chapter will examine in further detail).

---

attract small depositors back to the savings and loans with the offer of similar depository insurance. The provision received strong support from the members of the building and loan industry as well as the FHLBB representatives invited to testify. Moreover, even those who were opposed to the idea of depository insurance in principle had many reservations about expanding something that was already available to other types of banks to building and loans in order to put them on more equal footing.

[44] Memo on the National Housing Program, May 9, 1934, in HH, Box 79, Folder: Housing 1934.

[45] Ibid.

The Federal National Mortgage Association (Fannie Mae)

Private providers were not universally, or especially, eager to actually participate in the FHA program. Most lenders were unaccustomed to lending on such liberal terms, and the dust had barely settled from the last housing market crash, which did not necessarily bolster their confidence about the safety of such lending. Even the promise of government mortgage insurance to shield lenders from potential losses associated with the new products was not necessarily sufficient to overcome a related problem: the lengthier repayment terms offered by the FHA were at odds with lenders' preference for short-term liquidity. Anticipating these reservations from lenders, the NHA proposed the creation of a new market for these types of loans. The idea was to convince investors to buy government-backed mortgages, freeing lenders from long-term constraints and also enabling them to turn around and extend more FHA-backed loans to borrowers. Meanwhile, investors would have the security of a government guarantee that was "subject to strict Federal supervision." National mortgage associations, as they were called, would constitute "a new type of financial agency in the home-mortgage field" – a secondary market indirectly supported by the government, by virtue of its power to charter the associations and its oversight of them.[46] Plans for a secondary market were incorporated into Title III of the National Housing Act of 1934.

Presumably, private investors would be drawn to forming national mortgage associations because of the safety of the investments and the favorable tax treatment provided by the National Housing Act, but that assumption was not realized. In fact, no applications for national mortgage association charters came during the FHA's first year of operation. Would-be investors were uneasy about forming national mortgage associations for many reasons, including uncertainty about the FHA's future (the program was initially set to expire in 1937), an inability to come up with the $5 million in capital required to form a national mortgage association, and prohibitively stringent requirements for obtaining a charter.[47]

---

[46] Ibid.

[47] Letter from Gov. Wilbur L. Cross to Franklin D. Roosevelt, April 2, 1935, in FDR-L, Presidential Papers Official File (hereafter FDR PPOF), OF 1091misc, Folder: Federal Housing Administration 1935; Letter James Moffett to Stephen Early, April 9, 1935, in FDR PPOF, OF 1091misc, Folder: Federal Housing Administration 1935.

The lack of interest in the secondary market was a barrier to the construction employment revival, which still hinged on the revival of lending and, hence, on the FHA's success. As Wilbur Cross, the governor of Connecticut, explained to a letter to FDR in April 1935, mortgage money was key to reviving home building, and yet "[t]he existing financial institutions are unable to make additional long-term amortized mortgage loans without the opportunity to sell a substantial number of such loans to others."[48] As a stopgap, Congress voted to allow the government's Reconstruction Finance Corporation to create its own national mortgage association in 1935.[49]

The hope was that the RFC Mortgage Company would demonstrate its desirability and viability for private investors; i.e., "get the thing started and then ... withdraw from the field," in the words of one of its officials.[50] Ultimately, this did not happen, and no new associations formed.[51] Owing to private investors' lack of enthusiasm for secondary mortgage associations, in 1938 Congress amended the National Housing Act, once again expanding the role of the RFC Mortgage Company and renaming it the Federal National Mortgage Association (FNMA). Its expanded role allowed the fledgling FHA program to finally get off the ground, as investors immediately began to flock to Fannie Mae (as FNMA was nicknamed).[52] However, Fannie Mae's success also helped to further discourage private competitors, leading the FHA to announce,

[48] Letter from Wilbur L. Cross to Franklin D. Roosevelt, April 2, 1935, in FDR PPOF, OF 1091misc, Folder: Federal Housing Administration 1935.

[49] Charles M. Haar, *Federal Credit and Private Housing: The Mass Financing Dilemma* (New York: McGraw Hill, 1960), 75–9; Letter from Stewart McDonald (Acting Administrator, FHA) to Col. Marvin H. McIntyre, July 26, 1935, in FDR PPOF, OF 1091, Folder: Federal Housing Administration July–Aug. 1935.

[50] Haar, *Federal Credit and Private Housing*, 76.

[51] The reasons for this are not entirely clear, though scholars have pointed to the uncertainty caused by the National Housing Act's sunset provisions, as well as the RFC's haste to buy the best stock, which in turn forced would-be private associations to pick up the potentially more profitable, but also riskier, remainder. At the time, no private associations seemed willing to take the risk. There is also some evidence that would-be entrants were unable to shake their worry of future government expansion and competition in this area, which could crowd out private investors. Haar, *Federal Credit and Private Housing*, 80; Telegram from James Moffett (Federal Housing Administrator) to Franklin D. Roosevelt, November 23, 1934, in FDR PPOF, OF 1091, Folder: Federal Housing Administration: Nov.–Dec. 1934.

[52] Kenneth A. Snowden, "Mortgage Banking in the United States, 1870–1940," Research Institute for Housing America Special Report, Paper 13129, October 2013, 82. See also letter from Franklin D. Roosevelt to Jesse Jones (Chairman, RFC), February 7, 1938, in FDR PPOF, OF 3110, Folder: Federal National Mortgage Assoc. 1934–42.

in May 1938, that it "would no longer consider applications for add-itional mortgage associations."[53] By 1938, Fannie Mae was synonymous with the secondary mortgage market, and it remained so more or less until the late 1960s.

The modern mortgage market was now in place. It consisted of a discount bank for the thrifts through the FHLBB, loan insurance for private lenders through the FHA, and a secondary market for government-insured loans provided by Fannie Mae. Developments following World War II further consolidated this system. The VA home mortgage provisions in Title II of the Servicemen's Readjustment Act of 1944 (the GI Bill) further bolstered this modern mortgage market by providing World War II veterans with a loan guaranty structurally similar to the FHA's. Finally, while HOLC was phased out after it served its purpose of allaying the foreclosure crisis, it left its imprint on the mortgage market by demonstrating the viability of amortized loans (which would be more affordable to a larger number of citizens) and helping to standardize appraisal techniques.

CREATING A NEW HOUSING MARKET: CONCERNS AND CONTROVERSIES

The public–private welfare state in housing was forged by the end of the 1930s, but not without ambivalence, friction, and concern from the start. Even at the time these changes were being debated, policy-makers and members of the housing industry were aware that the proposals consti-tuted a sea change in housing – perhaps revolutionary, but also perhaps dangerously untested. Many worried about the implications of the government's entrée into the home mortgage market, and on such a scale. In debates over each of these four policies, some skeptics questioned the appropriateness of the proposed interventions. Supporters pointed to the federal government's support for commercial banks and farm

---

[53] See, for example, letters from Frank Elbridge Webb to Franklin D. Roosevelt, February 17, 1938, and from Franklin D. Roosevelt to Jesse Jones, February 7, 1938, in FDR PPOF, OF 3110, Folder: Federal National Mortgage Assoc. 1934–42. Webb, a prospect-ive investor, was complaining to FDR about the impossibility of entering the market now that Fannie Mae had taken over more of it. See also Snowden, "Mortgage Banking in the United States," 82.

mortgages that dated back to 1913 and 1916, respectively.[54] During the hearings for the Federal Home Loan Banks, a twenty-eight-year veteran of the building and loan industry from Durham, North Carolina, offered his support for the measure on the basis of federal support for farms and commercial banking:

Now coming back to the bill, the whole theory that those of us who are for the bill have in mind is that these millions of owners of small homes are entitled to exactly the same aid from the Government that commercial paper is entitled to and that the farmer is entitled to.

I am also a large farmer myself, and represent a great many farm people. In other words, the purpose of this bill, as I understand it from its provisions, is to put these millions of small home owners on exactly the same basis as the farmers and as the commercial institutions who borrow money, whose paper can be discounted at the Federal reserve [sic] on statements, whereas here is something that is real, in front of the eyes, that you cannot discount anywhere as a general proposition.[55]

Morton Bodfish, the executive vice president of the USBLL (and one of the chief advocates for the FHLBS), testified along similar lines: "I see no reason why the Government should not take the same attitude in creating this system which is to help the home financing institutions for city people that it has taken in connection with the system that is [sic] created for the farm lending institutions and for the general banking institutions."[56]

Not everyone agreed that the federal government's reach into farms and commercial banking warranted similar action toward people's homes. Michigan Senator James Couzens responded to Bodfish's logic skeptically:

The farm land bank was proposed for productive purposes; that is, the land on which we lend the money is used to produce foodstuffs. I see a clear distinction between these two activities and the Government engaging in capital investments. Certainly a home is a capital investment; I mean that that is not a producer unless

---

[54] A year earlier, Federal Home Loan Bank Act proponents raised a similar argument in favor of creating the home loan bank system, pointing to government institutions already in place to stabilize commercial and farm mortgage banking. To the FHLBS's proponents, their existence suggested that government involvement in mortgage lending was not only possible, given its history, but also warranted in the name of fairness. (Those who opposed the building and loans' reasoning pointed to the fundamentally different productive aims that the FRB and Federal Land Banks served, contrasting this to homeownership.) US Congress, Senate, Committee on Banking and Currency, *Creation of a System of Federal Home Loan Banks: Hearings before the Committee on Banking and Currency*, 72nd Cong., 1st sess., 1932, 67, 91, 190.

[55] John Sprunt Hill testimony, in ibid., 48.   [56] Morton Bodfish testimony, in ibid., 91.

the production of families may be included in the category; but certainly it is not producing commodities and it is not aiding commerce in the same sense that the Federal reserve and the Federal land banks do. ... I think there is a distinction.[57]

As with the other Depression-era homeownership policies, the matter of whether it was appropriate for the government to intervene in the housing market – and, if so, on what basis – remained unsettled. Congress passed the Federal Home Loan Bank Act despite those fundamental disagreements, not because they had somehow become resolved during the hearings.

For others, the concern was not so much the theoretical validity of government involvement in the mortgage market, but rather the practical wisdom of the approach. Most agreed that the policy proposals contained components that placed the government in the position of providing benefits that the market alone would not provide. FHLBS supporters argued that lenders would not offer any comparable program without government nudging (here, in the form of appropriations to help capitalize the banks).[58] HOLC's proposed status to act as a bad bank – by definition, taking on risks that no reasonable lender in the market would want to assume – fundamentally cast it as an entity that could not exist or survive without government support. "[T]here is no question ... that no private institutions, and no combination of private institutions, would ever have tackled this job, or will tackle it now," a FHLBB representative testified in support of HOLC during the NHA hearings.[59] And in the case of the National Housing Act, there was recognition that the government would need to facilitate credit in order to revive construction and help unthaw a frozen credit market.[60] This included creating the FHA and then "creat[ing] a market for that kind of mortgage" through Title III, which eventually became Fannie Mae.[61]

Where some saw, and accepted, the necessity of government involvement to create and reshape the housing market, others questioned whether the basic fact that the private sector could not or would not generate these solutions on its own was precisely a sign that they ought

---

[57] James Couzens, quoted in ibid., 91.   [58] I. Friedlander, testimony in ibid., 183–4.

[59] John Fahey, testimony (in response to HOLC) in US Congress, House, Committee on Banking and Currency, *National Housing Act*, 34.

[60] Winfield Riefler, testimony in US Congress, Senate, Committee on Banking and Currency, *National Housing Act*, 48–64.

[61] Ibid. See also, for example, Fannie Mae's first circular: Federal National Mortgage Association, *Circular No. 1: Information Regarding the Activities of the Association* (Washington, DC: Government Printing Office, 1938), April 15, 1938.

not to be implemented. If private enterprises were already unwilling to take on these activities as unsound risks, then why should one expect that a new, noncoercive law would create sufficient countervailing incentives? It was not immediately clear that banks were willing to accept the terms of membership in the FHLBS, that financial institutions would be willing to accept the bonds that HOLC proposed to offer, that private lenders would look to an FHA that required them to offer terms that some lenders considered inherently dangerous, or that investors would rush to form national mortgage associations when none had done so in the past.[62]

Addressing this reluctance by further liberalizing the terms of access for private enterprise raised concerns about the government's exposure to undue risk. Perhaps, some worried, any terms generous enough to entice private providers were too generous to mitigate their risks. As proposals to create the FHA were under debate, the general counsel of the Federal Home Loan Bank Board (and a longtime building and loans industry member) opined that such a proposal encouraged lending practices that had been "wholly discredited by all lending experience in the past," and that it "encourages speculative, promotional enterprise and discourages the practice of conservative home financing."[63] Some in Congress also worried about the consequences of the program's structure. They were skeptical of the national mortgage associations' structure as "mongrel institutions" – neither public nor private. Speaking in a hearing, Representative Robert Luce remarked, "You are advocating a hybrid institution of the same type of the joint-stock land bank; not fully a Government

---

[62] Testifying at the HOLC hearings, a NAREB representative doubted that financial institutions would be willing to accept the bonds that HOLC proposed to offer. In a sense, he was right. HOLC drew a large share of investors only after it made its terms on offer more generous. Similarly, the early experience with the FHA seemed to confirm skepticism among several policy-makers and members of the housing industry that the program could create a successful private market. The legislation that created the FHA was not able in the end to incentivize the emergence of a private secondary market to purchase FHA-backed debt. This stifled the development of the FHA in its early years. In the end, the government ultimately filled this role by creating Fannie Mae. The fact that most of the New Deal housing programs struggled to get off the ground makes it somewhat remarkable that members of Congress were willing to rewrite the incentives in various legislative amendments rather than throwing in the towel. See, for example, Walter Schmidt testimony in US Congress, Senate, Committee on Banking and Currency, *Home Owners' Loan Act*, 55.

[63] Memo to the Federal Home Loan Bank Board from Horace Russell, March 1934. Reprinted in Horace Russell, *Savings & Loan Associations* (Albany, NY: Matthew Bander & Company, 1956). Russell at the time had left his post in the USBLL and was working for the FHLBB.

agency and therefore not fully supervised; not, on the other hand, a fully private agency, where the investor knows he must take the risk, but a crossbreed with the two, a mongrel."[64] The suggestion that safeguards would prevent this from happening circled back to policy-makers' earlier reservations, in a seemingly intractable loop: if the "intention is that they [the banks] shall confine their operations to legitimate loaning operations," a representative asked during National Housing Act hearings, then "why should they be subsidized at all by society?"[65]

Beyond exposing the *government* to risks, others wondered whether it was really advisable to encourage ordinary citizens to take on the risks associated with longer repayment terms – terms that would have been unimaginable even to many private lenders just a few years earlier. The proposals, especially for HOLC and the NHA, seemed to cut against values of thrift, as one senator remarked during HOLC hearings: "I am still old-fashioned enough to believe in thrift. ... And you do not encourage it by inviting a man to go in a house and give him 30 years or 40 years to pay for it. I do not subscribe to any such theory as that."[66]

Despite these reservations, the proposals had three factors in common that favored the eventual acceptance of a greater role for the government in the home mortgage market. The first was the context of the Great Depression and its extenuating circumstances. The combination of a banking crisis, a credit crisis, a foreclosure crisis, and an unemployment crisis led many (both members of Congress and witnesses testifying in committee hearings) to at least begrudgingly support the programs. Even those who stated a preference for seeing these solutions developed and carried out by private initiative alone conceded the supporters' point that such a scenario was implausible in the current climate. As one NHA supporter reasoned, with private lenders "unable, or unwilling, to utilize their funds ... then there is no authority to meet the situation except the Government."[67] Many agreed.

---

[64] Robert Luce, in US Congress, House, Committee on Banking and Currency, National Housing Act, 164.

[65] Fahey, testimony in ibid., 26–7.

[66] James Couzens, in US Congress, Senate, Committee on Banking and Currency, Home Owners' Loan Act, 63.

[67] John Fahey, testimony in US Congress, House, Committee on Banking and Currency, National Housing Act, 26–7.

Related to this was the second factor that helped build support for New Deal housing policies: in each of these cases, the government was already undertaking similar activities on farms. To recall, the farm precedents from the early 1900s were now salient to the housing market of the 1930s. As Fishback, Snowden, and Rose pointed out in the context of HOLC, there was ample indication that elected officials recognized the political risks of helping farmers while doing nothing for the plight of urban homeowners.[68] Similarly, supporters of the Federal Home Loan Bank Act and the National Housing Act pointed, respectively, to the existence of a vast farm mortgage infrastructure similar to what was being proposed by supporters of the Federal Home Loan Bank and the Farm Credit Act signed in 1933.

Finally, federal officials had decided that homeownership carried a special status. Officials did not accept the logic that farms and commercial banks were interchangeable with home mortgages. Instead, they argued that homeownership itself was worthy of safeguarding. Summing up both the crisis and the moral status of homeownership in justifying an intervention like HOLC motives, FDR remarked,

Implicit in the legislation which I am suggesting to you is a declaration of national policy. This policy is that the broad interests of the Nation require that special safeguards should be thrown around home ownership as a guaranty of social and economic stability, and that to protect home owners from inequitable enforced liquidation, in a time of general distress, is a proper concern of the Government.[69]

The argument that the federal government both can and should intervene to safeguard homeownership in times of crisis would resurface a year later in discussions over the FHA. In the longer term, *crises* would no longer be the only context in which government officials, members of the public, and businesses would argue for an expansion of the government's role in homeownership. The idea that government had not only the authority but an obligation to intervene in multiple areas that affected homeownership would be affixed to a number of different circumstances beyond economic crises. At the same time, homeownership's special status could be gleaned by the limits policy-makers drew around the new programs, deliberately confining them to support for homeownership and housing finance,

---

[68] Fishback, Rose, and Snowden, *Well Worth Saving*, 38–9. See also US Congress, Senate, Committee on Banking and Currency, Home Owners' Loan Act, 50.

[69] Fishback, Rose, and Snowden, *Well Worth Saving*, 37; see also FDR's Memo on The National Housing Program, May 9, 1934, in HH, Box 79, Folder: Housing 1934.

rather than supporting financing for mortgages for a variety of purposes, as some in the lending industry had requested. [70]

This last point was bolstered by the practical purposes that the so-called moral value of homeownership fulfilled. In his 1933 book on real estate appraisal, Philip Kniskern noted that owner-occupiers tended to have a special tie to their mortgages, making them reliable as repayers. There was a "certain sacredness" to which they would hold their property and obligations, and they were strongly motivated also by the "disgrace and humiliation from public knowledge that accompanies foreclosure."[71] In hearings, witnesses and policy-makers also described owner-occupancy as a natural hedge against risks.

In short, then, this combination of crisis, precedent, and the elevated status of homeownership commingled to help produce the public–private homeownership infrastructure that dominated the postwar landscape. The crisis required expedience in response, yet policy-makers knew that whatever institutions they designed to deal with Depression-era exigencies would likely be permanent. The institutions that ultimately emerged reflected these circumstances – as well as participants' concerns about introducing risk and instability into the system – more than being part of a comprehensive master plan. The out-of-sight policy framework for homeownership was forged.

HOW THE NEW DEAL TRANSFORMED THE HOUSING MARKET

Though voluntary, the Depression- and New Deal–era housing programs transformed not only the government's role in the housing market, but also the housing market itself. The conditions placed on private providers for participation encouraged many to change their loan contracts; for others less interested in availing themselves of FHA insurance, the experimental products of the FHA and HOLC still reverberated.[72] In six short years, with its four programs, the federal government had ushered in a revolution in American mortgage finance and established an architecture

---

[70] Horace Russell, testimony in US Congress, Senate, Committee on Banking and Currency, *Home Owners' Loan Act*, 10–11; Barkley, in ibid., 50; Letter from NAREB Committee on Real Estate Finance to Stewart McDonald, December 10, 1935; Herbert Nelson's Confidential Secretary's Letters, from February 1934 through December 1935 in NAREB (on-site electronic collection).

[71] Philip Wheeler Kniskern, *Real Estate Appraisal and Valuation* (New York: The Ronald Press Co., 1933), 139–40.

[72] Green and Wachter, "The American Mortgage," 97.

and infrastructure for mortgage lending that would persist roughly unchanged for decades to come.

For example, its programs had demonstrated that long-term, low-down-payment mortgages could be marketed safely and profitably. The length of loan terms increased markedly after 1934 across two categories of lenders (Figure 2.1). The shift was less pronounced for the savings and loans (which historically offered longer repayment terms than the other two types of lenders and which could draw on the FHLBB for indirect support), though they too began to offer longer average loan terms, particularly after 1936. In addition, all three types of lenders saw an increase in the loan-to-value ratio they offered after 1933 (Figure 2.2). This was not fully attributable to the FHA (or later the VA housing program, which through the Servicemen's Readjustment Act of 1944 offered a similarly structured though more generous program to veterans).[73] Even at their height, both agencies accounted for only half of all mortgages loaned, and their share declined even as the standards they promoted became more

---

[73] US homeownership rates saw their fastest growth between 1940 and 1960. No single factor can explain this rise. Rising incomes following the Depression and World War II would have made housing more affordable for citizens regardless of other policy changes, and rising incomes along with changing marginal tax rates might also have made the home mortgage interest deduction relatively more attractive to prospective buyers. This period also saw a change in patterns of family formation, which may have increased the demand for homeownership. Yet scholars have also found that government policy mattered, in particular policies to lower down payments and to extend the length of time borrowers had to repay. Looking specifically at the VA, Daniel Fetter has estimated that the loan guaranty program accounted for about 7 percent of the overall increase in homeownership rates between 1940 and 1960. Looking at the FHA, Matthew Chambers, Carlos Garriga, and Don Schlagenhauf estimated that FHA loan insurance, by increasing the length of mortgage terms, likely accounted for 12 percent of the overall increase in homeownership between 1940 and 1960. The indirect spillover effects of the policies have also been noted but are more difficult to estimate with precision. These include the diffusion of FHA-style mortgage terms into the non-FHA and non-VA mortgage markets, the shift in cultural norms about homeownership that may have attended the rise of FHA and other government supports, and the programs' encouraging the construction of large-scale suburban projects, which, along with the general growth in housing demand, "may have allowed builders to take advantage of economies of scale." See Daniel K. Fetter, "The Twentieth-Century Increase in US Home Ownership: Facts and Hypotheses," in Eugene N. White, Kenneth Snowden, and Price Fishback (eds.), *Housing and Mortgage Markets in Historical Perspective* (Chicago: University of Chicago Press, 2014), chap. 10, 342; Matthew Chambers, Carlos Garriga, and Don E. Schlagenhauf, "Did Housing Policies Cause the Postwar Book in Home Ownership?" in White, Snowden, and Fishback, *Housing and Mortgage Markets*, chap. 11; Kenneth Jackson, *Crabgrass Frontier: The Suburbanization of the United States* (Oxford: Oxford University Press, 1987); Daniel K. Fetter, "How Do Mortgage Subsidies Affect Home Ownership? Evidence from the Mid-Century GI Bills," *American Economic Review: Economic Policy* 5: 2 (2013), 111–47.

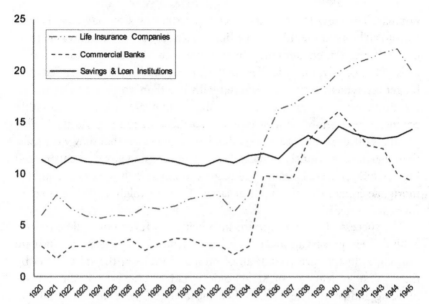

FIGURE 2.1 Average nonfarm home mortgage contract length (in years), by type of lender

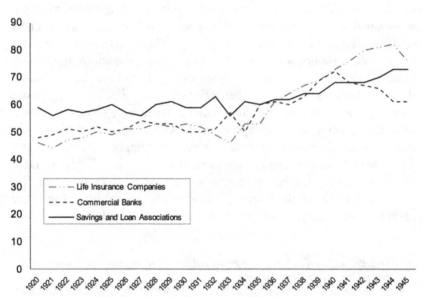

FIGURE 2.2 Average loan-to-value ratio on nonfarm home mortgages, by type of lender

Source: Snowden, "Terms on nonfarm home mortgages, by type of mortgage and holder: 1920–1967," in Carter, et al. (eds.), *Historical Statistics of the United States, Earliest Times to the Present*, Table Dc1192–1209.

popular. The New Deal homeownership programs also may have helped transform how non–FHA or VA-affiliated lenders viewed what was in their own self-interest, encouraging them to liberalize their own lending standards.[74] Previously, many lenders balked at the idea of loans extended over longer repayment terms and offered with less than 50 percent down. For the borrower, new loan terms also meant that a household's monthly payments now more closely approached those of renting. As these new products diffused into the market, lenders began to see that they were safer than they had previously thought. And by purchasing government-backed loans from lenders, Fannie Mae helped to expand the pool of available mortgage credit by freeing up funds that otherwise might have been tied up for years or decades.

The success of these programs also helped to forge political coalitions behind their preservation and expansion. Not everyone in the private housing industry agreed with all of these programs at the start.[75] Yet by the 1940s, a clear set of stakeholders had emerged from the private building industry. The FHLBS became a mouthpiece for the building and loan industry, and drew criticism from its opponents in the mortgage banking and commercial life insurance industry. The FHA brought builders, manufacturers, raw materials dealers, building trades representatives, real estate agents, commercial lenders, and life insurers into a new coalition that would remain pro-FHA (or, at least, anti–public housing) for decades. Members of these housing market coalitions testified at hearings, took policy positions in their own publications, and mobilized their members when they saw their position under attack. They also lent their expertise to these programs, staffed government agencies, helped to write the agencies' new regulations and procedures, and detailed in their training manuals how members could use and comply with the different agencies and various institutions created by the New Deal. As these agencies became fixtures of the policy landscape over the next few decades, elements of the housing industry came to accept and in many cases even embrace the new principles of real estate lending.

---

[74] George Break, *The Economic Impact of Federal Loan Insurance* (Washington, DC: National Planning Association, 1961).

[75] R. Earl Peters to Marvin H. McIntyre, March 12, 1936, in FDR PPOF, OF 1091, Folder: Federal Housing Administration Jan.–May 1936; Memorandum to Stewart McDonald from Jay Keegan, March 18, 1938, and letter from Stewart McDonald to Henry Morgenthau, March 1, 1938, both in FDR-L Papers of Henry Morgenthau (hereafter HM), Box 88: Correspondence, Fed. Housing Administration, Folder: Federal Housing Administration May 1936 thru 1938.

THE QUIET POLITICS OF THE DELEGATED WELFARE STATE?

Up to this point, the evolution of the public–private mortgage market would seem to confirm the "submerged state" view that such a hybrid advances business interests while it occludes citizen awareness and activism. But that would be a partial view. Mass citizens' groups – ostensibly the population that was to benefit from these new housing programs – were indeed conspicuously absent from earlier debates over homeownership policy. Throughout the 1940s, only two had made inroads into the broad issue of homeownership and the public–private housing system. The first, organized labor, had been involved from the beginning, though primarily motivated by a desire to stabilize construction employment. The second, veterans' groups (led by the American Legion), had also become important players in this arena, though their interest in homeownership policy was limited to veterans' issues and lagged (rather than drove) the inclusion of homeownership provisions in the GI Bill.[76] Two other groups were formed in the 1930s for the sole purpose of representing home-owners' political and economic interests, the Consolidated Home Owners Mortgage Committee and the Home Owners Protective Enterprise, but they largely vanished by the end of the decade. Homeownership policy, it appeared, was the domain of real estate, construction, and banking groups more than labor or citizens' groups.

A lack of citizen input ostensibly confirms suspicions of some scholars of the public–private welfare state, who argue that citizen and nonbusiness groups are deterred, if not stupefied, by such technical issues. However, the post-1949 policy history (as we will see) suggests that these technical issues clearly *were* within the purview of citizens' groups that eventually mobilized to be included in public–private homeownership programs. Another hypothesis – that citizens somehow lacked the capacity to mobilize over housing issues – is debunked by developments of the 1930s, when distressed farmers and underwater homeowners (and their neighbors) formed protest groups and made demands on the state and private industry.

Neither the technical nature of housing finance nor the notion that citizens lacked the capacity to mobilize around homeownership issues explains why citizens' voices were missing from debates on the creation of Depression-era housing programs. Instead, the historical record lends

---

[76] Thurston, "Policy Feedback in the Public-Private Welfare State."

support to Jacob Hacker's account of the parallel development of public and private social policy alternatives, which tend to attract different constituencies. Privatized approaches to social policy, Hacker reasons, tend to draw support from "conservative politicians and private industry leaders, who in other areas of social policy are staunch opponents of government intervention or spending," indeed a very different constituency than that usually associated with the support of social policies.[77]

In other words, citizens and countervailing groups were not absent from housing policy debates so much as they were otherwise engaged, actively trying to shape policy in a different housing arena: public housing. Gail Radford and others have shown that labor groups, low-income advocates, urban planners, social workers, and mayors all had tremendous doubts that their housing interests could ever be served by a program such as the FHA. They argued that the private sector had never been able to provide affordable housing at any socially adequate level. Throughout the 1930s and 1940s, groups that represented these citizens offered their own plans for public and cooperatively owned housing that they believed could meet the demands of their lower-income constituents.[78] For the most part, public and private housing coalitions had warring ideas about what the housing problem was, and how it would be solved.

THE BATTLE OVER POSTWAR HOUSING PRIORITIES

For a time it appeared that the urban coalition's focus on the public and cooperative housing debates would pay off. At roughly the same time that the federal government was debating how to bolster private homeownership, it was also discussing measures to address urban housing problems and creating the nation's first public housing program as a part of the National Industrial Recovery Act. Led by Harold Ickes, the new Public Works Administration (PWA) housing program consisted of publicly constructed and owned low-rent housing of reasonably high quality (compared with later public housing construction) and, until a reform in 1936, was not means-tested. In its four years of operation, the PWA Housing Division built fifty-eight developments with a total of twenty-five thousand housing units.[79]

---

[77] Hacker, *Divided Welfare State*, 279–86.
[78] Gail Radford, *Modern Housing for America: Policy Struggles in the New Deal Era* (Chicago: University of Chicago Press, 1996).
[79] Ibid, chapter 4.

The PWA program ended in 1937, though Senator Robert Wagner (a Democrat from New York) had already proposed a replacement public housing bill the previous year, with the backing of organized labor, mayors, the Labor Housing Conference, and the National Public Housing Conference. The 1937 Wagner Act created the US Housing Authority, directing it to channel funds to local housing authorities for the construction of low-rent housing, though not before opponents in the private housing industry managed to win concessions, including stipulations on maximum income limits and construction costs that effectively limited public housing to low-income groups.[80]

Despite these setbacks, the Wagner Act would prove advantageous to public housing advocates in that control over the program was housed in the new US Housing Authority, allowing it to develop on a parallel track to the FHA. Several of the coalition's leaders held chief positions within the public housing agency, enabling them to develop their own capacities parallel to those in the private housing arena.[81] In sum, while discussions of homeownership policies attracted little attention or input from citizens (outside of those who worked in the housing industry), that does not imply that citizens were fully disengaged from housing policy. Instead, most who were active in these issues were engaging in housing policies along the parallel track of public housing.

The United States' entry into World War II jolted the plans of public and private housing advocates alike. Materials and credit controls stymied private housing construction as the government funneled new construction into strategically important defense areas through special FHA insurance programs. Funds previously appropriated for public housing were diverted to help fund the rapid, desperately needed construction of 850,000 housing units for war workers between 1940 and 1945. This left the government owning a sizeable housing stock after the war. Both public and private housing advocates also faced an administrative challenge, as FDR's Executive Order 9070 of February 1942 placed all of the government housing agencies (including the FHA, the US Housing Authority, and the FHLBB) under the auspices of a single National Housing Agency, which would help to shape postwar conflicts between public and private housing advocates.[82]

---

[80] Alexander von Hoffman, "A Study in Contradictions: The Origins and Legacy of the Housing Act of 1949," *Housing Policy Debate* 11, no. 2 (2000), 299–326; 302–3.

[81] J. Bradford Hunt, "Was the U.S. Housing Act a Pyrrhic Victory?" *Journal of Planning History* 4, no. 3 (2005), 195–221; 211–12.

[82] See Franklin D. Roosevelt, Executive Order 9070 Establishing the National Housing Agency, February 24, 1942, online in Gerhard Peters and John T. Woolley, the American Presidency Project, www.presidency.ucsb.edu/ws/?pid=16225.

The war effort offered both public and private housing advocates the chance to develop and prove the feasibility of their respective programs, while also pitting the two housing concepts directly against each other, particularly after the war ended. Coverage in both the American Federation of Labor (AFL)'s journal, *The American Federationist*, and the National Public Housing Conference (NPHC)'s newsletter, *Public Housing Progress*, suggests that public housing groups and their allies were optimistic that their contributions to the war housing effort would give them a stronger voice in the development of postwar housing policy.[83] In their member newsletters, both the NPHC and the AFL wrote that they hoped to apply the lessons learned from the war housing experience to create more affordable postwar housing. Gradually, public housing advocates began to lose hope in a postwar détente with the private housing industry.[84]

In sum, rather than being oblivious to the role of the government in promoting housing, housing and labor groups were simply skeptical that the private sector was up to the task, and instead occupied the public housing arena during the years when the FHA grew.[85] In contrast to the silence of most citizens' groups on the creation of the Depression-era homeownership programs, hearings on postwar housing policy turned out dozens of interest groups.[86]

THE HOUSING ACT OF 1949

In this context, debates surrounding the Housing Act of 1949 represent a watershed for the politics of housing policy and, more generally, for the

[83] Harry C. Bates, "Housing War Workers," *The American Federationist* (May 1942), 6–7; John Blandford, "The War Housing Program," *The American Federationist* (December 1942), 20–1; "Post-War Housing News," *The American Federationist* (June 1944), 32; "Housing Program for Peacetime Is Endorsed," *The American Federationist* (December 1944), 15; Harry C. Bates, "The Challenge of Housing," *The American Federationist* (September 1945), 16–17, 31. On public housing advocates, see "Convention Elects Hovde, Paves Way for Post-War Plan," *Public Housing* (March 1943), 1, 3; "Arizona Names Committee to Push Post War Plans," *Public Housing* (April 1943), 1, 3; "NPHC Weighs Legislation for Future Housing," *Public Housing* (May 1943), 1–2.

[84] See, for example, "Arizona Names Committee"; "NHA Sees Less Public Housing After War," *Public Housing* (March 1944), 2, especially inset entitled "Believes U.S. Will Stay Out of Postwar Public Housing"; Charles Abrams, "Real Estate's Radicals," *Public Housing* (April 1944), 6.

[85] Editorial, *The American Federationist* (June 1934), 578–9.

[86] "Housing Policy and Programs, 1945–1964," in Congressional Quarterly, *Congress and the Nation, 1945–1964* (Washington, DC: CQ Press, 1965), vol. 1, chap. 4.

public–private welfare state. For years, the Truman administration had sought a bill to comprehensively address both public and private housing. In 1945, three senators – Wagner, Allen Ellender (Louisiana), and Robert Taft (Ohio) – unveiled a bill to revive the public housing program, introduce urban renewal and slum clearance funds, liberalize FHA loan terms, and declare a basic government commitment to ensuring that all Americans had access to decent housing. The AFL had requested these public housing and urban renewal proposals in its ten-point housing plan, drafted by the organization's Housing Committee. The two Democrats, Wagner and Ellender, found an unlikely ally in Taft. A Republican and stalwart opponent of FDR's and Truman's social programs, Taft's visits to the slums of Cincinnati nonetheless left him with the impression that public housing was the only way to provide the poorest citizens with decent housing.[87]

Over several years, the three senators mustered enough votes to get the bill through the Senate, only to watch it get buried in the House Banking and Currency Committee, chaired by Jesse Wolcott, a Republican from Michigan and a staunch opponent of public housing and the New Deal. In 1948, a frustrated President Truman called a special session of Congress to reprimand congressional Republicans for their inaction and urge them to reconsider the Taft-Ellender-Wagner bill. The special session served a dual purpose. Truman was embattled in a reelection campaign against New York Governor Thomas Dewey and had decided to run on a domestic platform, with his criticism of congressional inaction on housing as a focal point. The special session provided Truman with an opportunity to reach out to his support base by appealing to an issue they cared about, while also chiding the Republicans for obstructing the housing reform bill "at the behest of the real estate lobby."[88]

Truman's maneuver helped force Congress's hand. In August 1948, Congress managed to pass a housing act, but it was a much weaker version than the Taft-Ellender-Wagner proposal, with provisions mainly to bolster the private housing industry.[89] The Housing Act of 1948 liberalized the FHA and VA mortgage insurance programs, but contained no provisions for public housing or slum clearance. Its main effort to promote low-cost housing was language that directed Fannie Mae to

---

[87] von Hoffman, "A Study in Contradictions," 317.
[88] Harry S Truman, quoted in Richard Davies, *Housing Reform in the Truman Administration* (Columbia: University of Missouri Press, 1966), 109.
[89] Ibid., chap. 7.

"purchase mortgages under $10,000," while also prohibiting the agency "from purchasing mortgages that covered rental properties."[90] The act left the issue of public housing unresolved and did little to address housing affordability more generally. Truman registered his disappointment in a statement he made after the bill was passed, decrying Congress for producing an "emasculated housing bill." He announced that, although he approved of any bill to ease the present housing shortage, "the people of this country should understand clearly that it falls far short of the legislation which could and should have been enacted."[91]

Emboldened by his reelection and the regaining of Democratic control of Congress, Truman pressed on with his housing agenda in 1949, this time hoping to pass the full Taft-Ellender-Wagner proposal. Predictably, public housing issues remained controversial. Throngs of interest groups lobbied for and against the act, waging letter-writing campaigns to members of Congress and advertising campaigns, issuing press releases, testifying at congressional hearings on the 1949 bill (a total of seventy-five witnesses), and passing resolutions. Organized labor groups, public housing advocates, and civic, religious, and professional groups, including social workers and planners, favored the bill. Groups representing veterans, farmers, and African Americans also mobilized in favor of the bill, though generally on the basis of support for particular components.[92]

The main opponents of the act were business groups (including the Chamber of Commerce), banking groups (including the USBLL and Mortgage Bankers Association of America), realtors, home builders, lumber manufacturers, and the National Small Business Association. By this time, significant changes in business strategy were under way. Groups such as the National Association of Manufacturers, the National Association of Home Builders, and the National Association of Real Estate Boards had realized the power of direct mail to mobilize their members and waged letter-writing campaigns, urging their members to contact their representatives to oppose "the most dangerous piece of legislation of our generation."[93] Many targeted their disapproval at Taft, accusing

[90] Kathleen Frydl, *The GI Bill* (New York: Cambridge University Press, 2009), 287.

[91] Harry S Truman, "Statement by the President Upon Approving the Housing Act," August 10, 1948, online in Peters and Woolley, the American Presidency Project. http://www.presidency.ucsb.edu/ws/index.php?pid=12975.

[92] Congressional Quarterly, "Housing Policy and Programs," 479; Davies, *Housing Reform*, 101–15.

[93] Congressional Quarterly, "Housing Policy and Programs," 479; Davies, *Housing Reform*, 101–15; *Headlines*, quoted in Davies, *Housing Reform*, 109.

the Republican senator of being a "fellow traveler," in the words of NAREB.[94] In June 1949, Truman wrote to House Speaker Sam Rayburn to express his dismay at the "extraordinary propaganda campaign that has been unleashed against this bill by the real estate lobby."[95] He continued:

I do not recall ever having witnessed a more deliberate campaign of misrepresentation and distortion against legislation of such crucial importance to the public welfare. The propaganda of the real estate lobby consistently misstates the explicit provisions of the bill, consistently misrepresents what will be the actual effect of the bill, and consistently distorts the facts of the housing situation in the country.[96]

The bill finally made it out of the House Banking and Currency Committee and through the Rules Committee, and was reported to the House floor, where, on June 29, the Wagner-Ellender-Taft Act finally passed the House with a vote of 227–186.

The final legislation was similar to what had been proposed in 1945. It declared the government's commitment to "a decent home and a suitable living environment for every American." Among other provisions, it also provided for federal grants to localities for slum clearance, the construction of 810,000 units of low-income public housing (with preference given to veterans and families displaced by urban renewal), wage floors for builders of public housing, increased authorization for farm housing grants and research, the reauthorization of the FHA for six weeks, and an increase in the FHA mortgage fund by $500 million.

The 1949 Housing Act may have seemed to broker a compromise between conflicting visions of the government's role in housing, but it provided few mechanisms to actually execute the public housing portions of the proposal. It would take twenty years to reach the act's public housing construction targets.[97] And while the act was initially hailed by labor and public housing advocates as a legislative victory, within five years of its passage, the locus of activity for housing middle-income citizens would shift decisively into the arena of homeownership, insured

---

[94] Quoted in Frydl, *The GI Bill*, 283.

[95] Letter from Harry S Truman to Sam Rayburn, June 17, 1949, in Public Papers of the Presidents: Harry S Truman, online at http://presidency.ucsb.edu/ws/index.php?pid=13212.

[96] Ibid.

[97] On the labor lobby's importance in mobilizing for the Taft-Ellender-Wagner Act, see Hilary Botein, "Labor Unions and Affordable Housing," *Urban Affairs Review* 42, no. 6 (2007), 799–822; 803.

though the FHA and VA and sold to Fannie Mae, and housing obtained through the thrifts, supported by the Federal Home Loan Bank Board.

A "DECENT HOME" – BUT FOR WHOM?

As he signed the Housing Act of 1949 into law, Truman remarked that the national objective of providing decent housing for every American and the policies to achieve this goal "are thoroughly consistent with American ideals and traditions. They recognize and preserve local responsibility, and the primary role of private enterprise, in meeting the Nation's housing needs. But they also recognize clearly the necessity for appropriate Federal aid to supplement the resources of communities and private enterprise."[98] The statement seemed to reflect a broad commitment to promoting housing through indirect public–private channels and more direct public channels, appeasing both groups of housing advocates. Instead, as the public housing programs struggled to reach the objectives laid out in the 1949 Housing Act, and as homeownership expanded, the original mandate of the 1949 law to ensure a "decent home and suitable living environment for every American" was repurposed as a justification for pursuing policies to further expand access to homeownership – consolidating a political economy centered around homeownership in the US, while also raising the stakes of exclusion for those left behind.

But even as these new policies that began during the Great Depression and solidified after World War II were dramatically transforming the mortgage market, key questions remained about the precise limits of government involvement and the latitude and discretion accorded to private lenders. Those details – and especially the lines initially drawn in the 1930s between safe and unsafe lending, as we will see – would influence the shape and character of the housing market, and would themselves be shaped by public policy and private practices. They are the subject of the next chapter.

---

[98] Harry S Truman, "Statement by the President Upon Signing the Housing Act of 1949," July 15, 1949, online in Peters and Woolley, the American Presidency Project, www.presidency.ucsb.edu/ws/?pid=13246.

3

"To Create and Divert"

If the power to tax involves the power to destroy ... then conversely the
power to grant credit involves the power to create and divert.
                                              – Charles M. Haar, 1960[1]

To win over skeptics during hearings on the National Housing Act,
Winfield Riefler, a witness from the Federal Reserve Board, touted the
fundamental safety of the mortgages the proposed Federal Housing
Administration would insure: "These will be model home mortgage
instruments, and not distress instruments." He went on to explain that
only high-quality lenders, borrowers who met strict credit standards,
properties sure to hold their value, and a mortgage contract itself that
contained all of the latest safeguards would be eligible for insurance
under the new program. "The standards are designed to be the highest
type."[2]

"Where do you draw the line?" New York Senator Robert Wagner
responded. "What is eligible and what is not?"[3] The text of the proposed
legislation offered only vague guidance. After the National Housing Act
was signed into law in August 1934, officials of the newly established
FHA faced the gargantuan task of writing rules that would allow the
agency to function as Riefler had promised. Importantly, they had to
specify just what kinds of borrowers, what kinds of lenders, and

---

[1] Charles M. Haar, *Federal Credit and Private Housing: The Mass Financing Dilemma*
(New York: McGraw Hill, 1960), 2.
[2] Riefler, testimony in US Congress, Senate, Committee on Banking and Currency, National
Housing Act, 52.
[3] Robert Wagner, testimony in ibid., 55.

what kinds of properties would be of the quality that the government deemed insurable.

To some extent, all public policy must contend with questions of access and exclusion. Whether by deliberate design aimed at "target populations" or by happenstance as formal policies and regulations interact with on-the-ground conditions (producing, for example, policy drift), policies contain barriers that can systematically make them easier or more difficult for some groups to access than others. This quest to develop policy standards (not to mention the quest for standards at the firm or market level), then, can have major consequences for the distribution of opportunities in a society.[4] Yet political scientists often overlook that side of policy-making, focusing instead on the factors that precipitate a policy's passage.[5]

This chapter has two aims. The first is to examine *how* government mortgage policies have delimited access to mortgage credit over time and, in particular, to understand *why* it was that certain decisions about access were made (or not made) in the phase of implementation, leading to easier access for some groups of Americans, or some types of housing, but not others. Out of the New Deal housing programs (and, in particular, the FHA) came many new ideas about who should have access to these programs and what terms of access would ensure the soundness the government sought. In turn, this helped to reshape the overall housing market.

A second aim of this chapter is to elaborate on the idea of boundaries, in a manner applicable to other policy areas characterized by the interplay of public power and market incentives. There is no straightforward way of identifying all of the boundaries to accessing a policy or a good whose provision is shaped by that policy. One could count the number of public laws pertaining to a specific issue area, yet this number would conceal administrative details, and also leave itself open to questions of reliability (especially in the areas of concern here, where a remote bank regulation could have spillover effects on housing access). Scrutinizing the text of laws for inclusions and exclusions seems more promising at first glance,

[4] See King and Stears, "How the U.S. State Works."

[5] Two notable exceptions are Eric Patashnik, *Reforms at Risk: What Happens After Major Policy Changes Are Enacted* (Princeton, NJ: Princeton University Press, 2008); Eric Patashnik and Julian Zelizer, "The Struggle to Remake Politics: Liberal Reform and the Limits of Policy Feedback in the Contemporary American State," *Perspectives on Politics* 11, no. 4 (2013), 1071–87.

yet could lead to the omission of groups whose status vis-à-vis the policy is either assumed, and unmentioned, or ignored, and also unmentioned.

To answer these challenges, this chapter examines boundaries from three vantage points: first, as they come about in formal legislation; second, as they are further defined when laws are translated into implementable rules and regulations; and finally, as they are understood by people on the ground – in this case, by professional associations, individual lenders, real estate agents, buyers, and sellers. Examining these three different vantage points also serves to highlight how these different domains, rather than existing independently or in a clear hierarchy, often influence each other. Rules and regulations can shape how private market actors behave, while practices in the market can shape public laws and regulations, both because policy-makers have relied on industry insiders to help write the rules, and because shared beliefs and practices of an industry can come to constitute common knowledge about how a market functions. Together, the interplay of these three levels illustrates why and how access to credit has been promoted or constrained to different groups over time sometimes even, long after a policy's passage.

HOW PUBLIC LAWS ENABLE (OR CONSTRAIN) ACCESS

In creating new agencies or writing new laws, the government often weighs in on questions of access by stipulating what types of financial institutions may participate in such programs and under what conditions participation or membership can be revoked. For example, the FHLBB's enacting legislation restricted membership to building and loan societies, while also empowering the central Federal Home Loan Bank Board to monitor member agencies and remove those deemed financially unsound. Formal legislation also stipulated the nature of the contracts to be insured or otherwise protected by the government. Before the 1930s, to reiterate, loan terms were often individually negotiated and lasted anywhere from two to fifteen years, and those that were not amortized (the majority) required the entire balance to be repaid at the end of the term. After 1932, Federal Home Loan Bank members could only use loans of eight to fifteen years' duration as collateral. Likewise, HOLC and the FHA specified repayment terms of twenty years, with amortized contracts that fixed interest rates, established statutorily. Finally, formal legislation also weighed in on questions such as how much the minimum down payment should be for a borrower to be able to use the programs, or what the maximum value of an eligible house or loan should be. The FHLBS and HOLC's enacting legislation set these numbers at 20 percent down payment and houses valued at $20,000. The FHA held to the same down payment requirements but had a lower price ceiling of $16,000, which covered an estimated 85 percent of owner-occupied housing at the time.

It is important to emphasize that formal laws do not always (or even often) reflect a basic consensus about the best way to delimit access. For instance, discussions leading to HOLC's $20,000 price ceiling were based on concerns that the program might subsidize well-to-do homeowners. Early proposals argued that the limit should be set at houses valued at $10,000 or less, which would cover about three-quarters of the nation's owner-occupied houses. Some questioned the fairness of such restrictions. As one witness during HOLC hearings testified: "I see two neighbors, one with a $14,000 house, one with a $10,000 house, adjoining. I see one saved by the Government, the other one loses his home. He does not understand why. I think the social unrest, that very feeling, must be considered."[6] The final legislation did not adopt this witness's suggested solution, which was to remove limits altogether, but did raise the limit to $20,000 after members from New York made the case that the lower $10,000 limit would exclude homeowners of modest means who just happened to be living in an expensive real estate market.[7]

FHA limits reflected concurrent concerns about meeting various social goals (including generating employment in the construction sector, promoting homeownership on affordable terms, and reducing borrowers' reliance on second and third mortgages) while protecting the government from excessive risk. As such, the National Housing Act of 1934 stipulated the terms of the loan contract that would qualify as insurable, placed a ceiling on maximum loan values, and required borrowers to pay 30 percent down. Moreover, the enacting legislation stipulated more generous terms for new construction than for existing construction. Supporters argued that this would better stimulate construction employment, and that newer houses would be subject to the FHA's minimum construction standards, which would make them easier to appraise (and less risky from an insurance standpoint) than older houses.[8]

---

[6] D. E. McAvoy, testimony in US Congress, Senate, Committee on Banking and Currency, Home Owners' Loan Act, 29.

[7] Russell, testimony in ibid., 6.

[8] Watson, testimony in US Congress, House, Committee on Banking and Currency, National Housing Act, 150.

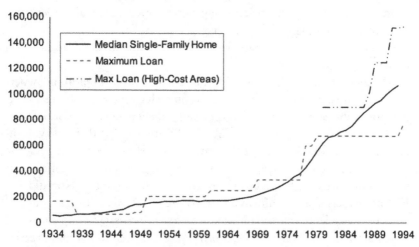

FIGURE 3.1 FHA loan limits and median single-family house prices
Source: Vandell, "FHA Restructuring," 303–6.

It is also difficult (if not impossible) for the law to specify every possible contingency, or to foresee feedback effects that would undermine its initial aims. An immediate response to the National Housing Act's $16,000 ceiling on loans that qualified for FHA insurance was to induce builders to increase the supply of housing that fell just short of that limit, undermining the middle market objectives of the program (most households could not afford more than $4,000–$6,000) and threatening to inject more instability into the housing and construction markets. (A year later, Congress addressed this unintended consequence by lowering the ceiling to $4,000.) Similarly, laws may lag behind changing conditions on the ground. Over time, inflation has continually elevated median house prices above the FHA's statutory limits, as Figure 3.1 shows has occurred throughout its history. This reality has dictated that the program either update its limits or "drift" away from the goal of supplying housing to those in the middle of the market.

WHAT LAWS LEAVE OUT: IMPLEMENTATION AT THE AGENCY LEVEL

Moving down a level from law to implementation, bureaucrats at the agency level confront and grapple with many of the limitations of formal laws as they attempt to operationalize what can often consist of vague directives – for example, the 1949 Housing Act's statement of a government commitment to ensuring decent housing for all Americans. As with decisions made at higher levels, even seemingly minor decisions at the agency level can influentially shape the boundaries of access to a policy.

This was certainly the case with the four Depression-era homeownership programs, each of which included somewhat vague legislative directives about the economic soundness of either the lenders they worked with or the properties they insured. The FHLBB interpreted this policy mandate most liberally: it retained the power to expel member banks that the board deemed to have engaged in unsound practices, but for the most part it did not specify what constituted an unsound practice. Nor did the FHLBB prescribe any uniform underwriting standards until the 1960s.

Other agencies developed much more extensive criteria to implement the economic soundness directives set forth by law, as well to put into practice other concepts stipulated, but not actually defined, by the enabling legislation. HOLC was created to help "distressed" homeowners, which required HOLC bureaucrats to develop a set of standards by which to classify homeowners as distressed and, importantly, to weed out those who simply wished to take advantage of the agency's generous refinancing terms. HOLC's definition of "distress" automatically disqualified nearly one-quarter of the 150,000 applications it received in its first few months of operation.[9] The degree of distress was not the only factor in determining a borrower's eligibility. By May 1934, HOLC officials had also determined that the "moral character and past record for honesty and integrity of the applicant" be taken into account as an "element of eligibility" and advised that a home "openly used for illegal or immoral purposes" should be disqualified.[10]

Another question generally left to agencies was how to determine the value of a property that was being considered as FHLBB member collateral, for HOLC refinancing, or for FHA insurance. This was especially important, given that the enacting legislation for each agency stipulated maximum eligible loan or house values. As with other examples, the agencies' approaches varied. The FHLBB only required that an appraisal be made in order for a member bank to pledge that property as collateral. Similarly, HOLC, whose legislation stipulated that only

---

[9] Memo from John Fahey (FHLBB), November 25, 1933, in FDR PPOF, OF 644, Folder: Federal Home Loan Bank Board.
[10] William H. McNeal, "Home Owners' Loan Corporation," Bulletin #118, May 21, 1934. In FDR-L, John Fahey Papers (hereafter JF), Cont. 7, Folder: Home Owners Loan Corp.

houses up to $20,000 in appraised value were eligible for the insurance but never specified an appraisal method, initially accepted any form of appraisal. HOLC changed its approach after a suspicious number of appraisers set the value slightly below the $20,000 limit. It responded by requiring a second appraiser to render an independent opinion, and ultimately by developing its own uniform, generically applicable appraisal standards.[11]

As vexing as the appraisal problem may have been for HOLC, the FHA faced an even more formidable task in implementing a sparse legal framework. The FHA's mission went well beyond saving homeowners already under distress, to expanding the pool of homeowners and borrowers. Almost as soon as the National Housing Act was signed, administrators of the newly established FHA set out to write the specific rules that would translate the broad brush strokes of the law into actionable on-the-ground regulations, in particular for Titles II and III.[12]

As had the law's designers, those devising its regulations wanted to make the terms of access enticing enough to lure private providers without exposing the government to undue risk.[13] The FHA's concerns about the risk of the agency's new investments culminated in a 260-plus-page *Underwriting Manual*, first issued in 1936. The *Manual* contained uniform guidelines to help the FHA determine whether a proposed transaction was of insurable risk. To actually measure this concept, the *Manual*'s designers broke risk into four component parts. First, the *Manual* required a rating of the features of the property and the degree of mortgage risks attributable to the property itself. Second, it rated the "degree of mortgage risk attributable to location." As it explained, the "rating is a prediction of the degree of mortgage risk likely to be experienced at such location during a period of about the next twenty years." Third, underwriters were asked a number of questions to rate the borrower, whose "conduct and performance will determine whether the mortgage insurance transaction with the Federal Housing Administration will merely create a contingent liability or result in the actual issuance of the debentures and certificate of claim of the Federal Housing Administration to the mortgage in accordance with the terms and conditions of the mortgage

---

[11] Ibid.

[12] Letter from James Moffett (Federal Housing Administrator) to Marvin H. McIntyre, September 4, 1934, in FDR PPOF, OF 1091, Folder: Federal Housing Administration: Nov.–Dec. 1934.

[13] Ibid.

insurance contract." Finally, underwriters were asked to rate the "mortgage pattern," or the economic soundness of the proposed loan contract itself. Each of these categories was further subdivided into quantifiable and rateable categories. There was also a "Reject" category for each. One "Reject" typically meant that the entire application had to be denied, regardless of eligibility in other areas.[14]

WHO DETERMINES RISK AND VALUE? PRIVATE ASSOCIATIONS AND THE DEVELOPMENT OF SCIENTIFIC VALUATION PRINCIPLES

By their own estimation, the FHA's procedure for determining mortgage risk followed "the most advanced and technically correct methods of mortgage analysis available."[15] Administrators' confidence in this assertion came from the fact that their underwriting criteria drew on the advice of industry experts as well as the latest academic research. (They also looked to social reformers such as the Better Homes Movement for guidance.[16]) The close tie between industry-sponsored and academic research and the programs' regulatory design was also evident in the implementation of the FHLBB and HOLC.[17]

Many of the concerns underlying the FHA and HOLC's postwar underwriting criteria actually predated those programs by years and had been shared by others in government, business, academia, and social reform for some time, such that a bit of history is in order. For each of these different actors, the accurate valuation of houses was of the utmost importance. Local governments needed to value properties in order to tax or condemn them, and lawyers needed to valuate property in order to determine the assets of estates for wills and inheritance. And then there was the lending industry, which needed to know the value of a house in

---

[14] FHA, *Underwriting Manual* (Washington, DC: Government Printing Office, November 1936), Part II, sec. 102, 202, 302, 402.

[15] L. C. Chappell, "Judging a Mortgage's Soundness," *Insured Mortgage Portfolio* 1, no. 1 (1936), 12.

[16] James Greer, "The Better Homes Movement and the Origins of Mortgage Redlining in the United States," in Novkov and Nackenoff (eds.), *Statebuilding from the Margins*, chap. 7.

[17] In justifying its proposal to fundamentally reorganize the market, the National Emergency Council explained that nationwide appraisal standards would help to protect "future home-financing from a recurrence of the abuses that have characterized the prevalent haphazard and disorganized methods of appraisal." Memo on the National Housing Program, May 9, 1934, in HH, Box 79, Folder: Housing 1934.

order to glean a mortgage contract's risk. Yet the value of a house was, as many recognized, not a straightforward concept. Houses have long been difficult goods to valuate, because they are not standardized and because the appeal of a neighborhood can change over time in ways that affect buyers' willingness to pay.

In spite of the manifest importance of determining the value of a house, most people making appraisals (the professional category of appraiser barely existed) still relied on subjective judgment and improvised standards to determine those calculations.[18] By the 1920s, pressure had developed to move away from subjective judgment and instead apply the scientific method to problems of real estate valuation. Frederick Babcock (a future designer of the FHA's *Underwriting Manual*) wrote in one of the earliest books on the subject that although "values are a social phenomenon dependent on human behavior," it is nonetheless possible "to discover the principles which tend to govern values."[19] Babcock and others felt that discovery of those principles would reduce errors in the estimation of value and enable lenders to estimate the maximum safe mortgage that would still allow them the protection of being able to sell the property in case of foreclosure. Finally, it was thought that these principles would help protect the industry's clients – buyers and sellers of property.[20] Officials of the National Association of Real Estate Boards had these considerations in mind when they designed their first real estate appraisal course in 1926.[21] NAREB's outline for the course documented

---

[18] On the development of scientific appraisal to replace the use of "business hunch," see Arthur May, *The Valuation of Residential Real Estate* (New York: Prentice-Hall, 1942), foreword. On the lack of an appraisal profession, see also James D. Henderson, *Real Estate Appraising: A Practical Work on Appraising and Appraisal Methods* (Cambridge, MA: Banker & Tradesman, 1931), foreword, and Frederick M. Babcock, *The Appraisal of Real Estate* (New York: Macmillan Company, 1924), 11–12.

[19] Babcock, *Appraisal of Real Estate*, 2–11; Henderson, *Real Estate Appraising*, 5–8.

[20] Philip Wheeler Kniskern, *Real Estate Appraisal and Valuation* (New York: The Ronald Press Co., 1933), 123. Not everyone agreed that real estate valuation could be approached scientifically. In another widely circulated text, Stanley McMichael and Robert Bingham wrote, "The valuation of residential properties depends so much on the ability of the appraiser to correctly balance various elements of value that it is manifestly impossible to establish definite rules that may be applied with certainty. Fad and fancy operate here to influence the buyer almost as much as in the merchandising of women's wearing apparel, for women for the most part have the final decision in home buying." In Stanley McMichael and Robert Bingham, *City Growth Essentials* (Cleveland: Stanley McMichael Publishing Org., 1928).

[21] National Association of Real Estate Boards, Department of Education and Research, "Session by session outline of a course in real estate appraisals" (Chicago: National Association of Real Estate Boards, 1926), 1.

the organization's frustration with past appraisal procedures, which considered as satisfactory an appraiser's "general judgment as to its value." The course would promote their revised view that "while general judgment always plays a part in the final evaluation of property it can no longer be used as a cloak for ignorance of underlying principles."[22]

The need for better appraisal methods was felt even more keenly during the Depression, as many in the housing industry blamed haphazard appraisal methods for the 1920s housing bubble and its collapse. Some in the lending and real estate industry also believed that a lack of confidence in appraisal might further stymie the housing market recovery. In October 1932, 120 real estate appraisers formed the American Institute of Real Estate Appraisers as an offshoot of NAREB. Their *Journal of the American Institute of Real Estate Appraisers* was founded the same year and conveyed the viewpoints of members of the financial industry, government agencies, the real estate industry, and the newly developing field of real estate appraisal. Not to be outdone, the United States Building and Loan League set up its own division to concentrate on appraisal procedures. It became the Society of Residential Procedures in 1934, quickly grew to nine hundred members, and issued the periodical *Residential Appraisers Review*.[23]

It was not just a more scientific determination of the value of the house itself that attracted such attention and came to matter, but a more scientific evaluation of the borrower himself. In the early decades of the twentieth century, this knowledge was less important, because the required large down payments gave lenders a buffer in case of default: the house could always be resold. For those financing their houses through the building and loan system, the cooperative membership structure under which it operated acted as another kind of hedge against repayment risks. A survey of 215 New Jersey savings and loan associations around this time found that fewer than one in four made regular credit inquiries for their borrowers.[24] But as down payment requirements were relaxed and loan terms lengthened in the 1930s, methods to determine the suitability of the borrower became more imperative.

These new methods were especially important to the FHA in the postwar years, as its new mortgage contracts required an assessment of

[22] Ibid.
[23] Josephine Hedges Ewalt, *A Business Reborn: The Savings and Loan Story, 1930–1960* (Chicago: American Savings and Loan Institute Press, 1962), 124–5.
[24] Stuart, *Discriminating Risk*, 90–1.

the borrower's risk. FHA officials looked to developments in installment lending for guidance. Guy Stuart describes that local credit reporting bureaus emerged as repositories for individual credit information, on the underlying logic that credit history would be a good predictor of future repayment. Supporting this local credit-reporting infrastructure were the National Retail Credit Association and its division, the National Consumer Credit Reporting Corporation, which facilitated the sharing of credit bureau information across localities. Among other things, the NCRA helped to construct a profile of the ideal borrower, taking into account his character, reputation, business dealings, and repayment history.[25]

The FHA relied on the NCCRC's expertise when it wanted to determine which borrower characteristics correlated with a loan's economic soundness. According to Stuart, of the three private organizations the FHA contracted with to help design its credit reporting criteria, the NCCRC was the best equipped and seems to have played the most direct role. NCCRC's influence was certainly present in the FHA's first "Standardized Factual Data Report," which the agency "produced in conjunction with the NCCRC" and included categories that pertained to the borrower's age, racial descent, marital status, dependability, general reputation, habits and morals, domestic difficulties ("Does his wife lend encouragement to him?"), attitude toward contractual obligations, reputation of living within his means, employment and ability to pay, level of ambition, and reputation of social associates.[26] The Standardized Factual Data Report also suggested amplifying any unfavorable information as well as asking the same questions about a female applicant's husband's or father's reputation.[27]

Federal agencies such as the FHLBB, HOLC, and the FHA situated themselves at the forefront of this new data-driven approach to real estate valuation and risk determination, though private institutions and academics were also increasingly studying these issues, either individually or in cooperation with the FHA.[28] Better information about the market as a whole, it was believed, would make it easier to determine maximum safe loan values, and to predict fairly accurately the safety of the investment and probability of repayment. This was an advancement on earlier

---

[25] Ibid., 84–9.   [26] Ibid., 91–3.   [27] Ibid.
[28] Edgar A. Lodge, *A Mortgage Analysis: A Twenty-Eight Year Record of the Mortgages of Home Title Insurance Company, 1906–1934* (Brooklyn, NY: Home Title Guaranty Company, 1935), 1–2, 74–5.

subjective approaches to mortgage risk assessment. As one of the earliest
studies of long-term lending risk pointed out: "The institution which
relies upon rule of thumb methods is apt to find itself at a considerable
disadvantage in competing with other institutions which have set up
informative mortgage experience tables."[29]

Yet subjective judgment was never fully removed from the equation.
Federal agencies, professional associations, and authors of training
manuals all exercised judgment when they determined which factors to
consider as relevant to lending risk in the first place. They lacked solid
data to link characteristics such as, for example, the sex, marital status, or
social reputation of the borrower, or the homogeneity of the neighborhood to repayment risk or a decline in property values. They included
these factors based on their own assumptions about the relationship
between these characteristics and lending risk. Lenders and underwriters
also exercised judgment as they undertook evaluations of individual
borrowers and properties.[30]

MARKET PRACTICES ON THE GROUND

Government lending agencies not only reflected but also reinforced private sector practices. To make use of FHA and VA insurance and guarantees, lenders needed to conform their practices to the respective
agency's guidelines.

This mutual reinforcement and infiltration of public practices in the
private sector is evident in how practices found their way into textbooks
and manuals to train the real estate community and all types of lenders,
not just those who planned to use the FHA's mortgage insurance. The
American Bankers Association's American Institute of Banking issued its
first edition of *Home Mortgage Lending* in 1937. The publication's
lessons on how to gauge a borrower's repayment prospects largely

---

[29] Ibid., 74–5.

[30] For example, as late as 1971, the FHA's materials coached underwriters about the need to
exercise judgment, even in the context of an underwriting procedure that appeared to
reduce all of the elements of risk to a single formula: "The HUD-FHA system requires
constant exercise of judgment. It is not a formula. However, when properly applied it will
guide judgment, eliminate widely divergent conclusions on the same matter by different
competent persons, and thus make possible a maximum degree of accuracy and consist-
ency." US Department of Housing and Urban Development, "HUD-FHA Underwriting
Analysis," October 1972 (Washington, DC: Department of Housing and Urban Development, 1972), 4020.1, sec. 3–18.

reflected what had already been outlined by the FHA *Underwriting Manual*, which was itself derived from the credit reporting industry. The textbook held in common with these two sources the idea that it was important to know a borrower's "attitude and behavior" in order to gauge whether he was likely to repay. "It is obvious that if he had conducted himself properly in public and if his known habits are such that they create a good impression, a favorable conclusion might be reached. The borrower's actions are largely the expressions of his thoughts and hence are important evidences of the quality of his character."[31] Likewise, the text singled out "pride of ownership" as an important incentive to motivate a potential borrower.

Even those lenders who ostensibly operated independently of the most constraining government lending programs found their practices largely shaped by the dictates of government policy, which had helped to remake industry norms. The FHLBS had no underwriting standards for its members in the savings and loan industry until the 1970s. Yet it still wanted to develop a more standardized and professionalized cadre of appraisers. The Society of Residential Appraisers (which began as a part of the USBLL) helped to expand the use of professional appraisers in the savings and loan industry. The Society of Residential Appraisers, in turn, was influenced by the American Institute of Real Estate Appraisers (the NAREB group that helped design the FHA's *Underwriting Manual*) and the FHA.[32]

Often, these changes were durable. As recently as the 1970s, training materials still emphasized the same basic elements of mortgage risk: a combination of the soundness of the security (real estate), the borrower's credit and personal characteristics, and the terms of the loan. A section on the character of the borrower in an American Savings and Loan Institute textbook from 1971 could well have been written in the 1930s, advising lenders: "From personal references, the investigator looks for information on the applicant's nonfinancial background and habits. It may turn out that the applicant is Joe Average in his personal life, that he has managed major medical or other bills with a degree of responsibility that doesn't show up in the coded facts and figures on a credit report, or that he drinks heavily and has serious marital difficulties."[33]

---

[31] American Institute of Banking Section of the American Bankers Association, *Home Mortgage Lending*, 1st ed. (New York: American Institute of Banking, 1937), 97.

[32] Stuart, *Discriminating Risk*, 62.

[33] American Savings and Loan Institute, *Lending Principles and Practices*, 1st ed. (Chicago: American Savings and Loan Institute Press, 1971), 73.

Yet even as professional associations and government underwriting requirements were homogenizing loan underwriting standards in the broader home mortgage industry, other factors still allowed for industry-wide variation in practice. For one thing, the training was not always current with changes in federal guidelines. Nearly two decades after the FHA removed explicit racial criteria from its own *Underwriting Manual*, the American Savings and Loan Institute textbook still mentioned the changing racial and ethnic makeup of a neighborhood as a relevant factor to consider when determining a property's likelihood to hold value.[34] Surveys of mortgage lenders in the 1970s found that many were basing their policy of discounting a working wife's income on federal guidelines that had since been updated, the news of which had not reached many lenders.

Finally, whether or not they were relying on federal underwriting, many lenders used their own informal rules to help them reach a decision. One was known as the "rule of 65," stipulating that the age of the borrower plus the loan term should not exceed sixty-five years. A survey of 421 savings and loan banks in 1972 revealed that 7.2 percent of them still followed this rule, with 14 percent of respondents saying that in general they would require a co-signer for a loan made to a senior citizen.[35] Another rule pertained to the debt service–to–monthly income ratio, which since the 1920s many lenders had felt should not exceed 25 percent of the borrower's monthly income. While the FHA tried to discourage its use, many lenders continued to rely on this informal criterion to guide their decisions for decades.[36]

HOW LAWS, REGULATIONS, AND MARKET PRACTICES INTERACT TO PRODUCE BOUNDARIES TO ACCESS

Formal statutes, agency regulations, and ground-level practices did not exist in isolation. They interacted in ways that shaped who could and could not access homeownership, and on what terms. Constraints on credit in turn demarcated the boundaries of the public–private welfare state in homeownership. On the ground level, where the law and its

[34] Ibid., 93–5.
[35] United States Savings and Loan League, "Survey on Credit to Women," May 1972, in CACSW, Reel 12, Frame 38.
[36] For example, a survey from the 1980s found that sixteen out of eighteen lenders questioned continued to apply "some version of the rule of thumb to screen mortgage applications." Stuart, *Discriminating Risk*, 80.

TABLE 3.1 *Homeownership rates by region and select characteristics of household head*

	1920	1930	1940	1960	1970	1980	1990	2000
Overall	46	47	44	62	63	65	68	69
Region								
Northeast	38	45	38	56	58	60	67	66
Midwest	54	54	49	67	68	69	72	74
South	42	41	41	62	64	68	69	70
Race								
White	48	50	46	64	65	68	70	72
Black	23	25	23	38	42	45	48	49
Sex								
Male	46	47	43	65	67	71	74	75
Female*	46	49	45	49	48	49	55	57
Marital Status								
Married	45	47	42	67	70	78	80	81
Single	42	42	39	34	29	26	33	36
Divorced/ Separated	34	33	29	31	33	41	49	55
Veteran			47	66	71	79	82	82

Source: US Census, from Steven Ruggles, J. Trent Alexander, Katie Genadek, Ronald Goeken, Matthew B. Schroeder, and Matthew Sobek, *Integrated Public Use Microdata Series: Version 5.0* (Minneapolis: University of Minnesota, 2010). (Note: Sample consists of household heads who do not live in group quarters. For "race," I use the single race identification variable. Data from 1950 are unavailable.)
* The categorization of gender and household head status is not consistent across census years. Until 1970, the man was regarded as the household head unless no man was present. Moreover, a sizeable number of household heads in 1920 were married women, which may reflect the lack of a designated category for separated women that year.

bureaucratic translation played out in people's lives, multiple boundaries to access applied, some involving the property, others involving the borrower, and still others involving the neighborhood. Table 3.1 presents US Census data on homeownership rates over time, broken down by several of the categories in which access has been bounded.

Dwelling- and Place-Based Constraints on Access

One of these boundaries pertains to property costs, themselves related to location and construction features. For example, maximum loan limits have indirectly delimited access to credit. A statutory maximum of $20,000 was included in the FHLBS and HOLC's original legislation, and $16,000 in the FHA's, as a safeguard for the government.

A maximum loan limit may seem like a trivial barrier, especially when compared to barriers rooted in discriminatory assumptions about a borrower's race or sex, yet at times it has become quite politically significant. Maximum loan limits means that higher priced metropolitan areas have often fallen through the program's net, which led the government eventually to adopt higher limits for certain parts of the country. Moreover, by signaling what kinds of housing private industry should construct, loan and price ceilings also produced feedback effects that have undermined earlier policy goals. For instance, after the FHA was created, policymakers initially found that rather than being incentivized to construct middle-class housing, builders instead focused on the higher end of the FHA's $16,000 limit in an effort to maximize their profits. Accordingly, Congress decreased the limit to incentivize more production of middle-market housing. Finally, statutory limits can drift into irrelevance as they fail to keep up with changes in nominal house prices. Indeed, policymakers have occasionally failed to update FHA loan limits as a politically expedient and passive way to contain the program's growth (see Figure 3.1).[37]

In addition to costs, terms of access have historically varied based on the types of housing different agencies, regulations, and private providers have favored. Most FHA insurance went toward purchasing newly constructed single-family suburban homes.[38] Mortgage insurance was also available for older homes and multifamily housing, but those programs tended to be less generous, since the original policies were intended to revive the construction industry. The other justifications for differential treatment were, first, that the appraisal of older houses entailed more risk and was less certain, and, second, that single-family owner occupancy tied borrowers to their houses in a way that made them more likely to repay. This belief predated the federal housing agencies. As members of the housing and lending industries began to shift from basing their decisions upon improvised rules to adopting scientific lending principles, many reached the conclusion that single-family (or small multifamily) owner-occupied homes were one of the safest bets for repayment. Owners were much more likely to pay for a house that they were living in than one they were renting out for a profit, and were also reluctant to face the moral

---

[37] Kerry Vandell, "FHA Restructuring Proposals: Alternatives and Implications," *Housing Policy Debate* 6, no. 2 (1995), 299–393; 330–1.

[38] Jackson, *Crabgrass Frontier*, chap. 11.

shame of foreclosure, even if the option was conceivably available. Larger-scale apartment construction projects, on the other hand, were usually done on speculation, and the borrower was perceived to have a less profound stake in the property or its future.

Minimum construction standards could also clash with the architecture of existing cities and communities, making it more difficult to get housing in some places than in others. In some instances, lenders viewed entire neighborhoods suspiciously. This was a potential risk for urban neighborhoods with a row house style of construction. In Baltimore, for example, the standard sixteen-foot width of row houses was too narrow to meet the FHA's requirements. According to Kenneth Jackson, requirements like minimum lot sizes, setbacks, and widths "effectively eliminated whole categories of dwellings" – including, possibly, Baltimore's narrow row houses.[39] In more remote, less densely populated areas, the problem might be the absence of basic FHA-required infrastructure, such as plumbing and electricity.[40] Aside from the FHA's interest in construction standards, the rise of scientific appraisal and changes in the lending market gradually made these dwelling and property characteristics an important consideration. Even lenders uninterested in FHA insurance would want to ensure that they were lending on a sound property, because it protected their investment.

Geographic constraints were also written into law: thrifts were required by law to limit their lending to within a fifty-mile radius. And Fannie Mae required any loan that it purchased to be made by a lender who was within a hundred miles of the property in question. In some cases, lenders and government agencies lacked a physical presence in an area of the country and consequently were unavailable to its residents.

---

[39] Ibid., 208.

[40] Not every potential homeowner wanted these amenities. Some coming from remote rural areas preferred to stay in their areas, even if it meant they would not have access to amenities now considered basic in the suburbs. Indeed, these concerns were on the minds of American Legion officials as some government officials weighed shifting the administration of the VA mortgage guarantee program out of the VA, which was overwhelmed by the initial difficulties of getting the program off the ground, to the more experienced FHA. Worried that such a shift could write off the roughly two-thirds of the country that did not meet the FHA's economic soundness and construction criteria, the head of the American Legion testified: "In other words, the veteran who desired to obtain a loan but who wished to build where electricity and sewers were not available would not be eligible. We of the Legion are, of course, interested in the boys who live at the fork of the creek." John Thomas Taylor, testimony in US Congress, Senate, Committee on Finance, *Amendments to the Servicemen's Readjustment Act of 1944: Hearings before the Subcommittee of the Committee on Finance*, 79th Cong., 1st sess., 1945, 114.

This was a problem most common in remote rural areas where financial institutions found it unprofitable to set up business.[41]

All of these constraints affected access to credit insofar as they precluded potential borrowers from getting loans for certain types of dwellings, whether due to cost, the nature of the property itself, or its proximity to lending institutions.

Borrower Constraints on Access

Lenders and the federal government were also concerned with characteristics of the borrower that might affect his or her repayment abilities. They addressed this in several ways: they ensured that borrowers put enough equity into the house up front and scrutinized their repayment history, reputation, character, and future income potential.

Down payments were a potential constraint levied on borrowers rather than the properties themselves. The FHA's 1934 legislation required a 30 percent down payment, which was relaxed in subsequent years to 20 percent (it hit zero percent for certain categories of borrowers in the 1990s).[42] Down payment requirements (along with other underwriting standards, including income reporting) effectively barred households that either earned too little or were unable to save enough to cover the down payment. In practice, this would most often disqualify low-income households – as was the case for the poor rural families described in Chapter 6. However, in more recent decades, rising house prices have also required middle-income households to have more money set aside for a down payment than they may be able to accumulate. By the 2000s, many proponents of eliminating down payment minimums for FHA insurance argued that young families, African Americans, and immigrants were systematically excluded from access to homeownership based on the fact that house prices in the modern market have tended to require large sums of money up front in 'order to make the down payment, and that these groups have been unable to accumulate enough assets to make homeownership a possibility.[43]

---

[41] Henry J. Aaron, *Shelter and Subsidies: Who Benefits from Federal Housing Policies?* (Washington, DC: Brookings Institution Press, 1972), 146.

[42] Vandell, "FHA Restructuring," 303–6.

[43] By the 2000s, lenders and members of Congress had adopted the language of exclusion in pressing for the deregulation of credit markets. See, for example, US Congress, House, Committee on Financial Services, *Promoting the American Dream of Homeownership through Downpayment Assistance: Hearing before the Subcommittee on Housing and*

Beyond asking borrowers to pay a certain amount of money up front, lenders and the federal government have also considered whether potential borrowers had a history of timely repayment. A borrower's credit history would play an important role in determining his or her future likelihood of repayment. While the idea of perusing a borrower's past history of repayment to gauge future risk may seem uncontroversial, the way that credit reports were issued presented specific challenges for people who were unable to establish a history. Until the 1970s, for example, most credit bureaus issued only one credit report per household; women who were divorced or widowed typically found themselves with no credit history to speak of, regardless of their financial contribution to the family or their timely repayment of debts (the same was not true of men in these circumstances).

A borrower's social reputation and character have also at different times factored into a lender's estimation of his or her repayment prospects. In the 1930s, it was not uncommon for a lender to conduct confidential interviews with an applicant's associates, as well as to factor in the applicant's standing in his community. The American Institute of Banking's 1937 *Home Mortgage Lending* went even further, suggesting that an applicant's associates could also provide valuable clues about his repayment prospects: "Usually persons with similar interests, ideals, and habits associate with one another. It is, therefore, possible to draw conclusions regarding the mortgagor by obtaining information concerning the people with whom he constantly and voluntarily associates."[44]

A borrower's *future* income prospects also became increasingly important to his or her ability to qualify for a loan. Before low-down-payment, long-term mortgages became the industry standard, a borrower's equity in the house was a more important hedge against risk than his or her future income. As mentioned earlier, as down payment requirements were relaxed, lenders and government underwriters became more concerned about an applicant's future income, ability, and willingness to pay. It was not just the amount of income that mattered, but its susceptibility to fluctuation. Underwriters valued income derived from long-term, standard forms of employment more highly than income from less stable forms of employment or self-employment. They also tended to prefer the

Community Opportunity of the Committee on Financial Services, 108th Cong., 1st sess., 2003, esp. 1, 3, 7, 12–13, 50, and "Statement of Michael I. Petrie, President of P/R Mortgage and Investment Corporation," in ibid., 29.

[44] American Institute of Banking, *Home Mortgage Lending*, 97.

income of professional workers and government employees over that of unskilled workers, who were "more apt to suffer layoffs than professionals and government employees."[45]

Assumptions about gender and family structure also shaped lenders' predictions of future income. As recently as the 1970s, lenders regularly dismissed or discounted a wife's income when determining a married couple's loan eligibility, on the assumption that her income was less stable than her husband's. This was due to a combination of legal uncertainty (whether real or imagined) over married women's property in the case of divorce and assumptions that a wife might become pregnant and leave her job.[46] A woman's occupation also came into consideration, with federal underwriters (and private lenders) until the mid-1970s more willing to count a working wife's income if she was a professional (for example, a lawyer, nurse, or teacher) rather than a clerical worker:[47] "If the wife works, her income is another uncertain factor, depending upon her age, type of employment and the number and ages of any children. Even if she can be expected to continue working, expenses arising from her employment – such as housekeepers, transportation and additional taxes – should be deducted. All the probabilities must be weighed."[48] A working wife would have difficulty getting her income counted toward a loan limit unless she could provide additional certification as to the stability of her work and the unlikelihood of pregnancy.[49] As Chapter 5 details, this could entail a letter from her employer attesting to the continued stability of her employment, or from her physician certifying that she was using birth control.

Lenders also questioned what to consider as income in the first place. Stable salaried income seemed straightforward enough (though lenders might still take into account the likely stability of the job), but it was more difficult to know how to handle income generated from part-time, temporary, or overtime work. Nonemployment income also proved vexing. Underwriters were unsure whether or not they ought to consider alimony, welfare payments, child support, dividends, and pensions as income, even

---

[45] American Savings and Loan Institute Press, *Lending Principles and Practices*, 76.

[46] See, for example, Margaret Gates, "Credit Discrimination against Women: Causes and Solutions," *Vanderbilt Law Review* 27, no. 3 (1974), 409–42.

[47] See, for example, US Commission on Civil Rights, "Mortgage Money: Who Gets It? A Case Study of Mortgage Lending Discrimination in Hartford, Connecticut" (Washington, DC: Government Printing Office, 1974).

[48] American Savings and Loan Institute Press, *Lending Principles and Practices*, 76.

[49] James C. Hyatt, "No Account Females," *The Wall Street Journal* (July 18, 1972), 1.

if these could be considered stable and predictable. During the Equal Credit Opportunity movement of the mid-1970s, groups representing senior citizens, welfare recipients, and women pressured both private lenders and the federal government to have these forms of income counted on loan applications.

Race, Place, and Access

Nothing better exemplifies all the ways that public laws, bureaucratic implementation, and private practices converge to shape and mutually reinforce on-the-ground conditions than the matter of racial residential segregation. Historically, the racial composition of a neighborhood has had an important influence on citizens' ability to access credit.[50] The earliest appraisal manuals maintained that neighborhood conditions played a crucial role in determining property values and their longer-term stability, often disaggregating the concept of "neighborhood stability" into a list of criteria that appraisers could use to determine whether a neighborhood was likely to pose a risk to the future house prices. This prompted those at the forefront of the scientific appraisal movement to establish general rules about neighborhood development. One of those rules was that homogeneity of residents was desirable. Homogeneity was even contained in the definition of "neighborhood" itself, with one influential textbook defining neighborhoods as "certain districts where the inhabitants have a sameness of income level, or racial and national traits, and (to a lesser degree) of religious affiliations."[51] Underlying this claim was an assumption that people preferred to cluster with others similar to themselves. A related assumption was that shifts toward greater diversity threatened future house values in a neighborhood.

While it was not the only characteristic that mattered (factors such as proximity to industry could hurt property values, while proximity to high-end shopping centers could help), a neighborhood's racial composition was often one of the factors considered in early appraisal manuals, with the assumption being that diversity – and especially changing racial and ethnic compositions – was a harbinger of declining property values.

The first major effort to create government appraisal criteria incorporated these assumptions about neighborhood in its standardized

---

[50] Federal Housing Administration, *Underwriting Manual* (Washington, DC: Government Printing Office, 1938), sec. 937.

[51] Arthur May, *The Valuation of Real Estate* (New York: Prentice Hall, 1953), 86.

appraisals. When HOLC set out to determine the values of formerly underwater properties that it held in its portfolio in the 1930s, it incorporated the racial composition of neighborhoods into its beliefs about values more generally. HOLC residential security maps created color-coded districts, rated "A" through "D," which largely overlaid the racial characteristics of neighborhoods. Yet for all of their infamy, HOLC's appraisal practices were confined to determining the values of properties for agency accounting purposes, not for making decisions about whether or not to refinance a house. In practice HOLC refinanced properties across neighborhood grades.[52]

The same could not be said of the FHA, which built the criterion of a neighborhood's racial composition into front-end considerations about whether to grant insurance. Federal underwriters were required to consider the presence of "inharmonious racial groups" and "protection against infiltration" by racial and ethnic minorities in the first few editions of the *Underwriting Manual*. These rules were directly informed by the nascent appraisal industry. The FHA hired two prominent appraisal textbook writers, Frederick Babcock and Ernest Fisher, to help develop a system of standardized underwriting procedures that would allow the agency to operate on a large scale, while minimizing foreclosure risks that would imperil its financial soundness.[53] Hence the use of an underwriting grid, which broke down the different elements of risk into more tractable categories that underwriters could then evaluate. This took discretion away from underwriters, allowing the FHA to hire and train more people to implement the program on the ground. By disaggregating residential real estate risk into several underlying factors, as Babcock explained, an underwriter would be able to "separate the factors so that those factors can be analyzed quickly, the results can be weighed, and a clear picture of the soundness of the mortgage produced."[54]

Quickly, the idea that the racial composition of a neighborhood could influence its property values moved from a theory into a set of practical guidelines that could be applied when calculating the risk of underwriting any property. These guidelines also proved remarkably resilient. Even

[52] Amy Hillier, "Redlining and the Home Owners' Loan Corporation," *Journal of Urban History* 29, no.4 (2003), 394–420.

[53] See, for example, Jennifer Light, "Discriminating Appraisals: Cartography, Computation, and Mortgage Insurance in the 1930s," *Technology and Culture* 52, no. 3 (2011), 485–522; 488.

[54] Ibid., 488.

after the FHA removed mentions of racial composition of neighborhoods from its own guidelines, it relied on the term "user groups" to convey similar ideas about the necessity of neighborhood stability. The 1955 *Underwriting Manual* advised:

The tendency of user groups to seek compatible conditions can sustain and enhance, diminish or destroy neighborhood desirability. ... If a mixture of user groups is found to exist it must be determined whether the mixture will render the neighborhood less desirable to present and prospective occupants. If the occupancy of the neighborhood is changing from one user group to another, or if the areas adjacent to the immediate neighborhood are occupied by a user group dissimilar to the typical occupants of the subject neighborhood or a change in occupancy is imminent or probable any degree of risk is reflected in the rating. It is to be noted that additional risk is not necessarily involved in such change.[55]

The manual was already a fixture of modern appraisal textbooks, and removing mentions of race from it had less effect on private training practices. A 1971 training manual of the American Savings and Loan Institute echoed earlier sentiments about neighborhood composition: "As a rule, people buy property in areas where others have comparable incomes and backgrounds." It then cautioned lenders that transition areas leave the future situation of a neighborhood unclear, and included the neighborhood's ethnic composition (and stability) among the criteria to consider in its example residential appraisal form.[56]

As Jennifer Light points out, once off the ground, the FHA was overwhelmed by demand for the program and began to run out of qualified potential appraisers to implement the new criteria on such a large scale. Looking for new ways to streamline the process and make do with fewer employees, Homer Hoyt, another FHA staffer, whose background was in real estate valuation, began to press the agency to condense its neighborhood risk criteria into maps, which could be used to quickly judge whether a property was of sufficient economic soundness to justify FHA underwriting. Hoyt's interest in maps predated his time at the FHA. As a graduate student in economics at the University of Chicago, Hoyt's dissertation used mapping (then a new tool of the social sciences) to try to uncover patterns in Chicago land values over time. His 1933 book, *One Hundred Years of Chicago Land Values*, delved further into these topics, and also mentioned that the racial breakdown of a neighborhood should

[55] Federal Housing Administration, *Underwriting Manual* (Washington, DC: Government Printing Office, 1955), sec. 1320 (1–2).
[56] American Savings and Loan Institute Press, *Lending Principles and Practices*, 95.

influence its residential rental prices. He included in his book a ten-point ranking of ethnic and racial groups, from most desirable ("English, Germans, Scots, Irish, Scandinavians") to least ("Mexicans").[57]

Hoyt's belief in the power of mapping motivated him to push for the large-scale creation and adoption of neighborhood risk maps by local FHA branches, and his belief in the role of race in determining value motivated his specific instructions for creating those maps. Hoyt debuted his plan in Springfield, Massachusetts. He instructed mapmakers to begin with a blank map of the city and, from there, draw lines around the central business district and industrial areas, then around larger apartment buildings. The remaining areas were to consist of single-family and small multifamily dwellings (potentially suitable for FHA-insured housing), and were to be designated into neighborhoods on the basis of average monthly rents. "Having completed the rental map," Hoyt wrote, "you are now to draw a blue pencil around all blocks in which there are more than 10% negroes or race other than white; also indicate areas in which there are a considerable number of Italians or Jews in the lower income group."[58] Hoyt explained that these maps, in turn, would form the basis for neighborhood ratings:

Usually areas in the lowest rental scale where a considerable number of the buildings need major repairs, where there is a mixture of races other than white, will be undesirable for loan purposes. On the other hand, where the rents are high, the percentage of owner occupancy is high, the conditions of the buildings good, and there is no race other than white, there will be found areas that rate high for loan neighborhoods.[59]

In this and other documents, Hoyt explained how maps could determine "reject" neighborhoods, or entire neighborhoods in which "no mortgage will be accepted for insurance in any block in this area." Areas where banking institutions already refused to make loans and areas with "an intermixture of races and nationalities" were candidates for reject neighborhoods.[60]

---

[57] Homer Hoyt, *One Hundred Years of Land Values in Chicago* (Chicago: University of Chicago Press, 1933), 316.

[58] Homer Hoyt, "Instructions for Dividing the City Into Neighborhoods," n.d., in NARA RG 31, Division of Research and Statistics UD-UP 6 (hereafter RS), Box 18, Folder: Neighborhood Risk Technique – Misc.

[59] Hoyt further explained the need for protection against infiltration as well: "Before making a final neighborhood rating, you must consider the possibility of the infiltration of undesirable elements or the decay or obsolescence of a good neighborhood." Ibid.

[60] Homer Hoyt to Ernest Fisher, "Instructions as to Procedure in Rating Neighborhoods," July 22, 1935; Homer Hoyt, "Instructions for Dividing the City Into Neighborhoods";

Yet despite this superficial methodological precision and the manuals and instructions to implement mapping on the ground, sources of value were ultimately a guessing game. This could be seen especially in the instructions of how to designate "The Best Neighborhoods," which blatantly relied on the value judgments of those doing the evaluations. Beyond having in place "zoning and restrictions against such adverse influences as infiltration of other races other than the predominant race," the best neighborhoods, according to Hoyt, would include those considered a "good address and [where] the residents take pride in the fact they live in such a neighborhood," with an "attractive shopping center fairly close to the neighborhood" and "attractive schools and churches."[61] Such criteria also appeared in the questionnaire designed for use with each neighborhood under study. Question three asked about the presence and percentage of nonwhite races in the neighborhood, with a sub-question asking about the presence and percentage of "any nationalities that are considered undesirable, such as certain groups of Italians or Jews."[62] Moving to more positive "best neighborhoods" criteria, question twenty asked, "Do residents take pride in the neighborhood? ... Is it considered a good address?"[63]

After the procedure was tested in Springfield, FHA headquarters began to offer assistance to local branches that wanted to utilize the maps to streamline their own procedures, and this further disseminated Hoyt's process. It is here, Light suspects, that early ideas about residential value became further embedded in both public and private practice, not only reverberating through the private real estate industry, but also directly informing public policy-makers' decisions about things such as the allocation of federal funds for certain neighborhoods and the determination of areas for slum clearance.[64] Architects of FHA underwriting procedures knew that their proposals were preliminary, had not been evaluated systematically, and would require further refinement as more data became

Homer Hoyt, "Tests of a Reject Neighborhood," n.d.; Springfield Chamber of Commerce (prepared by Homer Hoyt), "Springfield, Massachusetts," n.d.; "Questions to be Answered for Each Neighborhood," n.d., all in RG 31 RS, UD-UP 6, Box 18, Folder: Neighborhood Risk Technique – Misc.

[61] Homer Hoyt to Ernest Fisher, "Instructions as to Procedure in Rating Neighborhoods," July 22, 1935.

[62] "Questions to be Answered for Each Neighborhood," n.d.   [63] Ibid.

[64] Homer Hoyt, n.d., "Real Property Inventory of Cook County," NARA, RG 31 Division of Research and Statistics UD-UP 6, Box 19, Folder: Technique for Real Property Survey – Misc. See Jennifer Light's article for a more far-reaching discussion of the consequences of the mapping.

available; nonetheless, the maps largely, if prematurely, enshrined the early criteria. Once these decisions were made, there is no evidence of any large-scale effort to adjust the maps to reflect the evolution of underwriters' thinking about location ratings.[65] This may have been due to the considerable time and labor involved in making the maps in the first place.

It is also not clear that those responsible for the early underwriting criteria would have perceived any need to update the FHA's treatment of neighborhood racial diversity as more data became available. If anything, new data on house prices and neighborhood characteristics might have seemed to have confirmed underwriters' earlier beliefs about the relationship between race and house values. A study of Peoria, Illinois, for example, found that the percentage of nonwhite residents in a neighborhood was indeed a significant predictor of the overall price of housing in that neighborhood.[66] Yet this points to another shortcoming of the earlier criteria: even further study of residential values in the years that followed was only ever able to establish neighborhood racial composition as a correlate, not a cause, of residential values. Since nonwhites tended to be relegated to segregated areas with overcrowded and substandard housing, it was hardly surprising that their presence was correlated with lower overall housing values. Although less a true causal factor of neighborhood house values and more an artifact of residential segregation, discrimination, and other social inequalities, race (more specifically, the presence of nonwhite residents) came to be treated as a root cause of declining neighborhood house price values, with long-standing consequences for residential segregation and the wealth gap between black and white households in the United States.[67]

THE ENTANGLEMENT OF THE STATE AND THE MARKET: SOME CONSEQUENCES

As this chapter has shown, federal policies encouraged and diffused a new type of mortgage, characterized by low down payments and long repayment terms, that helped to put homeownership within the reach of millions of American households. Yet as these new programs were being debated and designed, policy-makers also recognized an urgent need to devise criteria that would allow the government, and the private lenders with

---

[65] Light, "Discriminating Appraisals," esp. 515.   [66] Ibid.
[67] See, for example, Oliver and Shapiro, *Black Wealth, White Wealth*.

which it partnered, to distinguish between safe, government-insurable and unsafe, uninsurable lending. Where these lines ultimately were drawn did not uniformly reflect a settled consensus on the innate characteristics of safe and risky loans. And where the consensus seemed more settled – for instance, on the need to preserve neighborhood racial homogeneity – it could be rooted in self-fulfilling beliefs more than underlying evidence. Specific terms of access were the product of contestation between academics, industries, and policy-makers. The specific terms of access were also forged out of political expediency. Scholars, practitioners, and policy-makers realized that their procedures might not perfectly capture the correlates of risk and value. But those procedures could at least be applied systematically and at a large scale, and could eventually be readjusted.

The give-and-take between private market actors and public policy-makers has had several consequences, chiefly that it has made it difficult to determine whether government rules about who can access mortgage credit (and on what terms) simply mirror the housing market or actively shape it. Neighborhood house prices might reflect local residents' preferences and willingness to pay, calibrated by some impersonal market logic of supply and demand. Or they might reflect values embedded in public policies, then adopted by private actors. Lenders asked to justify why they rejected loan applications could point to government underwriting criteria. Bureaucrats asked why their criteria excluded some applicants over others could point to concerns about market acceptance. It is not always possible to know where one ends and the other begins, which adds to the political challenge of contesting exclusion from homeownership on political and policy grounds.

A second consequence is that the quality of the rules and regulations is only as good as the quality of the evidence and analysis used to justify them in the first place. Research on the determinants of property values was nascent when FHA officials began drawing up their underwriting criteria – recall, only a few years prior, the ad hoc and haphazard practices of appraisers were blamed for exacerbating the Great Depression's foreclosure crisis. There was very little time to reverse course before the appraisal field's ideas about property values were codified into practice. Yet once codified, ideas can develop into self-fulfilling "laws" of the marketplace.

Finally, it is significant that, to some extent, the distinction between prime and subprime (in this case, safe, government-insurable lending and risky, uninsurable lending) represented a political settlement at a particular period in time rather than innate market attributes unambiguously dividing safe from risky mortgages. This is not to suggest that no line between safe and risky lending exists, but rather that the government's role in promoting access did require it ultimately to define, and then defend, a line between the two. While the government was figuring out where to draw that line, the housing policy landscape was coalescing around homeownership as Americans' main option for housing. This development would not be lost on those left on the outside, as the next few chapters document.

4

Breaching the Blockades of Custom and Code

After the National Housing Act of 1934 was signed into law, the *Chicago Defender* published a note praising the "opportunity afforded by the Federal Housing Administration" and encouraging those who were interested to apply for FHA-backed loans. The article reassured its largely African American readership that "[i]t is believed that there will be no discrimination in local communities, and if such should be found to be the case you are advised to take up the matter with the officials at Washington through the congressman in your district."[1]

The *Defender* had reason to be hopeful. The hearings for the legislation that created the FHA contained no explicit discussion of race as a possible basis for inclusion or exclusion.[2] True, the National Housing Act's deference to the private housing sector may have dampened the optimism of civil rights advocates, since many had long been aware of that sector's discriminatory practices. But federal involvement was initially enticing as

---

[1] "The Housing Loan," *Chicago Defender* (September 1, 1934), 14.

[2] In several regards, no explicit discussion was needed. The decentralized administration, and the dominance of the FHA by private housing interests, would allow for the continuation of discriminatory private market practices. Moreover, no explicit discussion was needed because many of the creators and defenders of the FHA had already rationalized segregation, creating a racialized housing market. On how historical racial preferences in the private housing industry prior to 1934 shaped the implementation of the National Housing Act, see David Freund, *Colored Property*, chap. 3; and Kevin Fox Gotham, "Racialization and the State: The Housing Act of 1934 and the Creation of the Federal Housing Administration," *Sociological Perspectives* 43, no. 2 (2000), 291–317. On race and the decentralized administration of New Deal programs, see Ira Katznelson, *When Affirmative Action Was White: An Untold Story of Racial Inequality in Twentieth Century America* (New York: W. W. Norton Press, 2006), 29–30, 38–42.

a possible reprieve from the ravages of private discrimination, especially in northern cities whose populations had exploded as a result of the Great Migration.[3]

Soon after the FHA's inception, it became clear that African Americans' hopes for more equitable access to housing had been misplaced. To be sure, black homeownership rates increased steadily through the 1930s, 1940s, and 1950s, as they did for whites. Even so, there remained a persistent and growing gap between rates for black- and white-headed households, with homeownership rates for whites reaching 64 percent in 1950, versus 36 percent for blacks. The gap between black and white homeownership rates grew from 23 percentage points in 1920 to 28 points by 1960.[4]

Nor was the increase in homeownership rates accompanied by a substantial change in the housing available to blacks. Developers hoping to build homes for African American or mixed occupancy continued to see their loan applications rejected. Prospective homeowners continued to find their options confined to secondhand (often deteriorating) houses in segregated neighborhoods. Segregation – and the way that it restricted competition on the basis of quality and quantity of housing – also ensured that even low-quality housing would remain expensive, at least more than comparable housing in white neighborhoods. Studies in the 1940s and 1950s corroborated that blacks still faced difficulties in securing good housing. In 1945, the American Council on Race Relations identified the "arbitrary limitation of land area available for occupancy by Negros" as one of the chief explanations for the poor housing conditions of African Americans.[5] In a 1955 report, the American Friends Service Committee found that between 1935 and 1950, only 2 percent of FHA loans went to

---

[3] For a wider-ranging discussion of how African Americans' unrealized hopes that a stronger federal government could counter segregation, see Desmond King, *Separate and Unequal: African Americans and the U.S. Federal Government* (New York: Oxford University Press, 2007), chaps. 1 (esp. 31–3) and 6.

[4] See, for example, William J. Collins and Robert A. Margo, "Race and Home Ownership from the End of the Civil War to the Present," *The American Economic Review: Papers and Proceedings* 101, no. 3 (2011), 355–9.

[5] "Draft Blueprint for Action for the Negro Organization in the Field of Housing," attached to letter from Robert Weave to Lester Granger, 6/26/45, 1, in Library of Congress Manuscripts Division, Records of the National Urban League (hereafter NUL) I: C2, Folder: Housing Activities Department, General Department File, American Council on Race Relations 1944–1947.

nonwhites, even as the FHA backed nearly two-thirds of all newly purchased houses.[6]

DISCRIMINATION BY THE MARKET, THE GOVERNMENT – OR BOTH?

Much contemporary scholarship places the blame for the black-white homeownership gap on government housing policies, which were implemented in such a way as to expand housing opportunities available to whites while restricting blacks from the same opportunities.[7] Yet, in the moment, the racial housing gap seemed mostly an extension of the same familiar, restrictive housing practices that had developed since the turn of the century to prevent African Americans from securing adequate housing or credit. Even explicit complaints that seemed to implicate the FHA were interpreted initially by the NAACP as locally rooted, not centrally coordinated.[8]

It made sense to attribute discrimination to private providers because there was already such a long history of it.[9] Local governments, real estate agents, and white homeowners initially justified racially restrictive practices, including deed restrictions, zoning, and real estate appraisal, as the preference of whites to live in homogeneous neighborhoods. As David Freund argues, in the early twentieth century, "northern whites justified exclusion by invoking a mythical racial hierarchy, claiming that blacks made poor neighbors because they had little in common biologically and, contingent upon this, economically and culturally, with people of European descent."[10] Then, beginning around 1910, a parallel, but related, logic of racial exclusion based on the perceived presence of blacks in a neighborhood also emerged. In their 1913 appraisal text, *City Growth and Values*, Stanley McMichael and Robert Bingham put forth the logic

---

[6] American Friends Service Committee, "Equal Opportunity in Housing," Report prepared by the Community Relations Program, March 1955, 7, in NUL I: C2, Folder: American Friends Service Committee.

[7] Katznelson, *When Affirmative Action Was White*, 162–6; Freund, Colored Property, chaps 3–4; Charles Lamb, *Housing Segregation in Suburban America since 1960: Presidential and Judicial Politics* (Cambridge: Cambridge University Press, 2005), 11–24; Douglas Massey and Nancy Denton, *American Apartheid: Segregation and the Making of the Underclass* (Cambridge, MA: Harvard University Press, 1993), chap. 2; Jackson, *Crabgrass Frontier*.

[8] Roy Wilkins to Stewart McDonald, October 12, 1938, in NAACP II-L-17, Housing – Federal 1938–39.

[9] Freund, *Colored Property*, chap. 3.   [10] Ibid., 8.

that land values were depressed "where negroes congregate."[11] In light of this "natural" phenomenon, they advised that

rigid segregation seems to be the only manner in which the difficulty can be effectively controlled. The colored people certainly have a right to life, liberty and the pursuit of happiness but they must recognize the economic disturbance which their presence in a white neighborhood causes and forego their desire to split off from the established district where the rest of their race lives.[12]

When the FHA's *Underwriting Manual* was under development nearly two decades later, the private real estate industry and white homeowners had already internalized such ideas about the danger of integration to residential harmony, and ultimately to property values. These ideas were also used to justify a variety of restrictive private practices, from considering an applicant's race in credit applications, to steering black applicants to older housing in black neighborhoods, to using racial covenants to ensure that a neighborhood's racial (or religious) characteristics would remain stable over time, to white neighborhood associations committing outright violence against black families who dared to breach the color line. Finally, these explanations were largely accepted – and furthered – by members of the private real estate industry, as well as government officials, including staff of the newly established FHA.[13] Indeed, industry associations codified these beliefs into their member guidelines, and local real estate agents and lenders into their practices on the ground.[14] For these groups, racial disparities in homeownership were considered natural.[15]

African Americans, of course, could reject these underlying assumptions while still attributing them to their persistent – and at times violent – exclusion from local housing markets. Yet it mattered in the

---

[11] McMichael and Bingham, *City Growth and Values*, 177.   [12] Ibid., 181–2.

[13] Writing in response to a query by FDR about the lack of uptake by African Americans, FHA Administrator Stewart McDonald explained: "It is difficult for the majority of Negroes to enjoy the benefits under Title II, as they are unable to furnish the necessary small, cash down-payment to build or buy a new home and, furthermore, as a rule their personal credit ratings are poor. And this, after all, is the crux of the matter as far as the banks, life insurance companies, and other lending institutions are concerned." Memo from Stewart McDonald to Franklin Roosevelt, July 7, 1936, in in FDR-L, PPOF, OF 1091, Folder: Federal Housing Administration June–Dec. 1936.

[14] The National Association of Real Estate Boards' code of ethics provided for the sanctioning of its members for attempting to integrate neighborhoods. Elsewhere, many mortgage lenders freely refused to lend to African Americans or charged them higher interest rates than whites. Massey and Denton, *American Apartheid*, 187–8.

[15] Freund, *Colored Property*, chap. 1.

1930s whether they came to view their limited opportunities in the housing market as the continuation of long-standing practices within the private real estate market or as a new development now actively shaped by federal government power. Viewing the problem through the former lens offered limited strategies for redress, as market discrimination was considered a private matter outside the purview of the state.

On the other hand, viewing credit and housing access as a problem created (or at least aided, abetted, and reinforced) by the federal government might open up different legal and political venues for contestation. For example, in contrast to the difficulty of influencing racial segregation in the private market, the NAACP prevailed in the 1917 *Buchanan v. Warley* decision. *Buchanan* emerged in response to a residential segregation ordinance adopted by the city of Louisville, Kentucky, in 1914. The following year, William Warley, the president of the local NAACP branch, arranged to purchase property in a white-zoned district from a white realtor, Charles Buchanan. Douglas Massey and Nancy Denton explain: "In a pre-arranged scenario, Buchanan accepted Warley's offer, but Warley refused to make payment on the grounds that he would not be able to occupy the property because of Louisville's racial segregation law; Buchanan then sued Warley for breach of contract in order to initiate a civil test of the law."[16] The Supreme Court ruled unanimously against the city's residential segregation ordinance, a sharp repudiation of the "growing movement toward legal separation in American cities."[17] The effort may have been the "cheapest case ever won by the NAACP," an attorney from Las Vegas wrote to Thurgood Marshall in 1939.[18] The effort was aided largely by the fact that it was the federal government that was directly implicated by zoning.

Buchanan did not extend to other forms of discrimination in the housing market and did not outlaw private practices such as restrictive covenants, racial steering, block busting, and general refusals to lend or sell to African Americans on equal terms. And *Buchanan* said nothing about *indirect* or *implicit* government involvement in segregation or housing discrimination. In fact, restrictive covenants flourished in the wake of the ruling, becoming the "primary means by which

---

[16] Massey and Denton, *American Apartheid*, 187–8.   [17] Ibid., 188.
[18] Arthur McCants to Thurgood Marshall, October 23, 1939, in NAACP I-C-404, Folder: Segregation – Residential Jan. 6–Nov. 18, 1939.

neighborhoods maintained racially segregated housing patterns."[19] In contrast to its ruling of racial zoning carried out by local governments as unconstitutional, the Supreme Court's 1926 *Corrigan v. Buckley* ruling held that the Fifth and Fourteenth Amendments "applied only to actions taken by states or governmental entities and did not apply 'to actions by individuals in respect to their property.'"[20] While the state could not directly segregate neighborhoods, it was free to allow private individuals to self-segregate, to allow private industry associations to enforce segregation, and to uphold contracts (e.g., restrictive covenants) that provided for neighborhood segregation.

SEEING THE STATE IN THE MARKET

In the years following the passage of the FHA, civil rights organizations shifted how they viewed the causes of segregation. Initially they had viewed segregation as rooted in market and social practices that, however unjust, were difficult to contest legally. Within a few years of the FHA's introduction, they had come to view residential segregation and blacks' limited homeownership opportunities as directly – and then indirectly – shaped and sanctioned by the federal government, in particular through the FHA.

What transpired was a decades-long fight against private discrimination, but discrimination crucially shaped and abetted by the power of public agencies. Advocacy organizations, including the NAACP, the National Urban League, the American Council on Race Relations, and the National Committee Against Discrimination in Housing, as well as allied groups, such as the Quaker American Friends Service Committee, were crucial actors in this campaign. The black press also helped to collect and publicize information about restrictive housing practices. The most prominent of these was the *Chicago Defender*, a weekly founded in 1905. The *Defender*'s editorial staff took advantage of its location in a northern city to tackle social and economic issues in a manner that may have been impossible in the South, and nearly two-thirds of its readers came from outside of the Chicago area. Cumulatively, this network of black civil rights groups, newspapers, and allied cooperative groups was able to detect restrictive housing practices as they occurred, to research the scope

[19] Leland Ware, "Invisible Walls: An Examination of the Legal Strategy of the Restrictive Covenant Cases," *Washington University Law Quarterly* 67, no. 3 (1989), 737–72; 739.
[20] Ibid., 740.

and causes of those problems, and to mobilize for solutions, in both the private and public sectors.

The public–private hybrid of the government's housing programs created an opening for civil rights groups to contest the legal basis of their exclusion. The existence of the FHA in and of itself highlighted the government's role in exclusion, while also providing civil rights organizations with firmer ground on which to challenge racial exclusion in private housing markets. Initially viewed as a problem of private market discrimination, civil rights groups came to link black-white differences in access to homeownership to the federal government, both directly and indirectly. They responded by appealing to government agencies and elected officials, and to businesses, with the carrot of potential profits and the stick of government intervention into their industries. A common theme in their appeals was that the state's role in building and then patrolling the boundaries to African Americans' access made the state culpable in the ensuing discriminatory outcomes and private lenders vulnerable, due to their relationship not only with the FHA, but with federal banking and housing regulators generally.

THE NAACP AS A REPOSITORY FOR COMPLAINTS

As Chapter 2 describes, it took a couple of years, along with minor policy tweaks and major institutional advances (in particular, the creation of Fannie Mae), to make the FHA fully operational. As the program's promise to provide an affordable route to homeownership was finally becoming realized in 1937 and 1938, the NAACP – with four hundred branches across forty states by 1938 – began to receive a trickle of complaints.

Some of the complaints did not mention the FHA outright, instead describing the overall difficulties that African Americans in a locality seemed to have in obtaining suitable housing – including homeownership options. In a handwritten note to the president of the Brooklyn, New York, branch, dated June 1937, a woman from Venice, Florida, reported that in her town there were 150 "or more Negroes here living in old dingy shacks. We can't rent house to live in an colored people can't by [sic] land here."[21] The letter made it to the national office, but not directly. Its writer, Martha McClaine, first gave it to a Pullman porter working the Florida–New York line, who then handed it to the president of the

---

[21] Letter to NAACP, June 9, 1937, in NAACP I-C-307, Housing: June–Sept., 1937.

Brooklyn branch of the NAACP when he got off his shift.[22] "Please advise me what to do," requested McClaine.[23] The branch president forwarded her query to the national executive director, Walter White.[24]

Other letters inquired more directly about the FHA. A developer in Norwalk, Connecticut, wrote the NAACP on behalf of a client, asking "if there is anything you can do for a colored couple of good character with a very good credit rating in their particular community who are desirous of building a house but cannot seem to have it financed because of their color."[25] The developer had already reached out to the FHA headquarters in DC to find out whether "the F.H.A. plan was for a privileged group or class. They informed me it was for everyone who could meet their standards and forwarded me the names of institutions in their locality only one of which would accept their application, however, they could only grant a fifty percent loan on the cost of the house."[26] In another letter, a woman from Austin, Pennsylvania, wrote to the NAACP to ask whether the organization had received any complaints about the FHA, relaying her own family's experience. Her husband (an engineer) and two colleagues (a forester and a superintendent) decided around the same time to build homes in a nearby town, each purchasing a lot and applying to the local bank for a construction loan. The forester's and superintendent's loans were approved. Her husband's was turned down, despite his having the same salary as the forester, and despite having a solid credit recommendation and (according to her contractor) being in a more sound financial situation than the others. The difference: "The other two men are white and we are Negroes and we know that the reason we can't get this loan is because of their prejudice and I am wondering if other Negroes are having this same trouble, and if so, what are they doing about it."[27]

Many of the letter writers wanted to know whether the NAACP had received other complaints of a similar nature. Clearly, the NAACP had.

---

[22] Letter from Alexander Miller to Walter White, June 17, 1937, in NAACP I-C-307, Housing: June–Sept. 1937.

[23] Letter to NAACP, June 9, 1937, in NAACP I-C-307, Housing: June–Sept. 1937.

[24] Letter from Alexander Miller to Walter White, June 17, 1937, in NAACP I-C-307, Housing: June–Sept. 1937.

[25] Merritt Builders to New York City Branch of NAACP, September 9, 1940, in NAACP II-A-310, Housing – General 1940.

[26] Ibid.

[27] Mrs. Herbert Walker to Walter White, March 10, 1940, in NAACP II-A-310, Housing – General 1940.

But initially, as the organization later conceded, it did not link the anecdotes from across the country to a systematic pattern of discrimination coordinated by the FHA. By 1938, it did.

THE NAACP AND THE BATTLE OVER THE FHA'S *UNDERWRITING MANUAL*

"For some time now, the National Association for the Advancement of Colored People ... has been receiving complaints that the Federal Housing Administration is restricting the opportunities of Negro citizens to purchase or build homes," wrote Assistant Secretary Roy Wilkins to the FHA administrator in October 1938. "At the outset," continued Wilkins, "we felt that perhaps these complaints were merely isolated instances of local prejudice, but the complaints have increased in volume and they come from widely separated areas of the country." Yet through compiling and investigating complaints, as well as an important anonymous tip, their assessment had changed. "The conclusion is inescapable that the Federal Housing Administration has a general procedure with respect to guaranteeing mortgages on property purchased or built by Negroes."[28]

One of the earliest investigations into the racial consequences of FHA policies came out of an inquiry made to the NAACP by Frank Summers, a black attorney from East St. Louis, Illinois.[29] In 1937, Summers had applied for a loan to buy a newly constructed house with an estimated value of about $12,000. The FHA denied insurance on the rationale that although the house and borrower met its insurance standards, the location did not: the surrounding buildings were old and in an "extreme state of dilapidation."[30] At $12,000, the house's estimated value also made it a notable outlier in a neighborhood where, the agency claimed, other houses were valued at $1,000–$2,500 (Summers disputed these numbers). Viewing this as "a clear case of discrimination ... wholly on the basis of color," the NAACP asked the FHA to open an investigation.[31] When pressed on the matter, the FHA denied that race had

---

[28] Roy Wilkins to Stewart McDonald (Director, FHA), October 12, 1938, in NAACP II-L-17, Housing – Federal 1938–9.

[29] Frank Summers to Walter White, June 7, 1937, in NAACP I-C-307, Folder: Housing June–Sept. 1937.

[30] Clyde Powell to Walter White, July 8, 1937, in NAACP I-C-307, Folder: Housing June–Sept. 1937.

[31] Walter White to Harold Ickes, June 18, 1937, in NAACP I-C-307, Folder: Housing June–Sept. 1937.

factored into the decision. The agency pointed out that any property so overvalued relative to other houses in the neighborhood would fail to secure approval.[32]

Unsatisfied with this explanation, Thurgood Marshall responded that the strict application of such a rule was inherently discriminatory. Since blacks at all income levels were relegated to neighborhoods that would not meet the FHA's criteria,

[i]t seems to us that the strict application of the rules of the Federal Housing Administration is, in effect, not only sanctioning segregation in housing facilities, but is also forcing Negroes to live in sub-standard homes in these segregated areas and, therefore, creating virtual 'Ghettoes.' We do not believe that the Federal Government should become a part of this move to restrict Negroes in segregated areas by enforcing this rule which you set out in your last letter.[33]

The NAACP initially made little headway with this argument, although it would draw from this case later.

A few states away, the NAACP's Jamaica, New York, branch was also investigating complaints. In April 1938, a developer, Efficient Homes, approached the branch for its assistance in securing FHA financing.[34] The branch's leadership was initially disturbed by Efficient Homes' marketing campaign. The company had posted a sign that read: "Merrick Park Garden Corporation – Homes for select colored people – Inspired by the F.H.A."[35] Upon further investigation, the NAACP learned from the developer that the FHA had initially refused financing due to the racial heterogeneity of the neighborhood, elaborating that banks in the city were unwilling to extend FHA loans in racially mixed areas. The project was approved only after the developer appealed to FHA headquarters in Washington.[36]

Shortly after this development, the Jamaica branch began an investigation into a second set of practices. Hearing complaints from potential homeowners attempting to buy in racially mixed neighborhoods, branch officials began to suspect that the FHA had designated some

---

[32] Clyde Powell to Walter White, July 8, 1937, in NAACP I-C-307, Folder: Housing June–Sept. 1937.

[33] Thurgood Marshall to Clyde Powell, August 5, 1937, in NAACP I-C-307, Folder: Housing June–Sept. 1937.

[34] A. Gibbons to Walter White, April 25, 1938, in NAACP II-L-17, Housing – Federal 1938–39.

[35] John Singleton (President, NAACP Jamaica, NY, Branch) to Walter White (Exec Sec NAACP), October 18, 1938, in NAACP II-L-17, Housing – Federal 1938–39.

[36] Ibid.

neighborhoods as "cushion areas," or buffers, between all-white and predominantly black neighborhoods where no FHA insurance was to be granted.[37] The FHA's form rejection letter provided little guidance as to what happened. "This property does not meet the general requirements of the Federal Housing Administration" was all it said.[38]

Piecing together the multiple complaints it had received, the Jamaica branch and national officials of the NAACP came to suspect that the FHA was acting to restrict blacks' access to its loan insurance in a much more systematic and coordinated way than initially suspected. The FHA, they surmised, had a general policy of refusing loan insurance to African Americans trying to buy houses (regardless of the racial composition of the neighborhood), and refusing to insure developments for mixed occupancy and properties in mixed-race buffer zones and black neighborhoods.[39]

The other development that helped to guide them to this view was a tip received in spring 1938 from a white acquaintance of Assistant Secretary Wilkins, who, according to Wilkins, had some knowledge of the FHA's operating procedures. The source mentioned to Wilkins that the local branch of the FHA "unofficially ... is making as one of its requirements for guaranteeing mortgages that the builders insert in the deed a clause prohibiting sale, rental, or occupancy by persons of African descent."[40] However, the source also advised the NAACP against a "frontal attack or a direct inquiry to the FHA," suggesting instead that the organization investigate this through alternative channels.[41]

Initially, Wilkins seems to have followed the advice to investigate through alternative channels, writing to an ally in the Department of the Interior, Robert C. Weaver, to see if he had any leads (Weaver would go on to become the first HUD secretary).[42] NAACP officials also continued

---

[37] Letter to Harry Neier, December 17, 1938; George Briggs to John Singleton, December 21, 1938; John Singleton to James Foley, January 10, 1938; John Singleton to Roy Wilkins, January 12, 1939 in NAACP II-L-17, Folder: General Office File, Housing – Federal 1938–39.

[38] Samuel Ragovin to George and Emma Briggs, December 17, 1938, in NAACP II-L-17, Folder: General Office File, Housing – Federal 1938–39.

[39] Roy Wilkins to Stewart McDonald, October 12, 1938, in NAACP II-L-17, Housing – Federal 1938–39.

[40] Roy Wilkins to Robert Weaver, June 11, 1938, in NAACP II-L-17, Housing – Federal 1938–39.

[41] Roy Wilkins to Gertrude Stone, June 11, 1938, in NAACP II-L-17, Housing – Federal 1938–39.

[42] Roy Wilkins to Robert Weaver, June 11, 1938.

with their investigation into the lending practices in the Jamaica area, learning from banks and developers that lenders in the New York City area seemed to be aware of an FHA policy and rejected loans in anticipation of it, as well as an FHA practice of requiring restrictive covenants on the properties it insured.[43]

In October 1938, NAACP officials decided to take a more direct approach with the FHA. Thurgood Marshall wrote the agency, asking for "a copy of the official rules governing loans under the jurisdiction of the Federal Housing Administration"[44] He received in return a copy of the National Housing Act and "The FHA Plan of Homeownership" and "Property Standards," none of which contained any instructions to consider the racial composition of a neighborhood as part of an underwriting assessment.[45]

Unsatisfied with the FHA's initial responses to questions about its role in race restriction, and sensing that they were not being provided the actual documents they had requested, NAACP officials persisted, and in November 1938 finally procured a copy of the FHA's *Underwriting Manual* from a local FHA field office.[46] Section 233 confirmed their suspicions. It stated:

The valuator should investigate areas surrounding the location to determine whether or not incompatible racial and social groups are present, to the end that an intelligent prediction may be made regarding the possibility or probability of the location being invaded by such groups. If a neighborhood is to retain stability it is necessary that properties shall continue to be occupied by the same social and racial classes. A change in social or racial occupancy generally leads to instability and a reduction in values. The protection offered against adverse changes should be found adequate before a high rating is given to this feature.[47]

It also seemed clear to the NAACP that the FHA was deliberately trying to conceal this information, which it had failed to provide in response to Marshall's earlier request. In a follow-up letter to the federal housing administrator sent on December 23, White quoted the offending Section

[43] Roy Wilkins to Stewart McDonald, October 12, 1938.
[44] Thurgood Marshall to Stewart McDonald, November 18, 1938, in NAACP II-L-17, Housing – Federal 1938–39.
[45] John G. Rouse (Deputy Administrator, FHA) to Thurgood Marshall, November 19, 1938, in NAACP II-L-17, Housing – Federal 1938–39.
[46] "Exposes 'Color Law' in Federal Housing Plans: Manual on Mortgages Outlines Jim Crow Ruling on Loans," *Chicago Defender* (December 31, 1938), 1.
[47] Walter White to Stewart McDonald, December 23, 1938, in NAACP II-L-17, Housing – Federal 1938–39.

233, observing that that the *Manual* was "serial numbered and evidently is not used for general distribution."[48] White saw this as proof of the FHA's direct involvement in the "establishment and maintenance of 'racial' areas." In the same letter, he also relayed something he had learned a day earlier from an official in the Long Island FHA office: that the particular office had indeed established separate "Negro," "white," and "cushion" districts, that no applications from blacks were to be accepted in white areas (and vice versa), and no applications for FHA insurance from blacks or whites would be accepted in cushion areas.[49]

For African Americans with the financial means to buy or build a moderately priced house, such policies left them with few options: "There is practically no land available in the so-called 'Negro' district, but there is much land available in the so-called 'cushion area.'" If the FHA was only willing to insure lending to blacks buying in the "Negro area," White reasoned, then "the F.H.A. has actually set up a system which denies to the Negroes of Jamaica, L.I., an opportunity to receive assistance from the Federal government." He followed with a searing denunciation of the agency: "It is almost unbelievable that the Federal Housing Administration distributing Federal funds, and set up and maintained by the Federal government should not only take an active part in maintaining segregation, but should also inject patterns of segregation unknown to certain areas in this country." White concluded by calling for the agency to rescind the offending underwriting guidelines, and for the Washington office to instruct its field officers "that there shall be no distinction because of race or color of applicant."[50] The NAACP also pushed its case by publicizing the administration's "Jim Crow Housing Policy" in news releases and the black press.[51]

The NAACP took its new evidence to the White House, sending a memo to FDR in January 1939.[52] Writing back a week later, the president parroted the FHA's defense that its status as an agency that "lends no Government money but simply insures mortgage loans made by private financial institutions, such as banks, life insurance companies, etc.," obligated it to certify that "no mortgage shall be accepted for insurance unless the Administrator finds that the project with respect to which the

---

[48] Ibid.   [49] Ibid.   [50] Ibid.
[51] NAACP Press Release, "Federal Housing Authority Has Jim Crow Rules for Mortgage," December 23, 1938, in NAACP II-L-17, Housing – Federal 1938–39.
[52] Memo from NAACP to Franklin D. Roosevelt, January 14, 1939, in NAACP II-L-17, Housing – Federal 1938–39.

loan is executed is economically sound."[53] FDR also reiterated the logic offered by the FHA about the need for its insurance principles to reflect that

real estate values are determined by the market which in turn is established by the demands of the buying public. In other words, the Federal Housing Administration does not and cannot in any way prescribe the mortgage area nor set the market price in reverse of public demand. To attempt to do so, of course, would cause lenders to lose faith in the stability of the Federal Housing Administration Plan and in the end defeat its objectives.[54]

The NAACP found itself caught in a feedback loop: Public policies were interfering to encourage discriminatory policies, practices, and ideas about what constituted housing values in the first place, but the government denied responsibility for these aspects of the housing market. In the agency's estimation, the FHA simply reflected the impartial logic of supply and demand. And its own position as a government agency required that it allowed such market mechanisms to operate freely.

CONTESTING THE FHA'S COLOR LINE

Over the next five years, the NAACP built a case that agency policy explicitly discriminated against blacks in the housing market. This culminated in a 1944 memorandum sent, once again, to FDR, which quoted each of the specific passages the organization had identified in the FHA *Underwriting Manual* that delimited blacks' access to housing on equal terms. One target was the *Manual*'s Risk Ratings section, in which the FHA required the valuator to ensure that a property had adequate "protection from adverse influences," defined as "prevention of the infiltration of business and industrial uses, lower class occupancy, and *inharmonious racial groups*" (NAACP's emphasis). Without adequate protection (which usually meant residential zoning and, in the case of "inharmonious racial groups," racial restrictive covenants), the *Manual* pointed out, the valuator "must not hesitate to make a reject rating of this feature." The NAACP also highlighted language in the *Manual* that explicitly linked neighborhood stability to racial homogeneity, as well as the FHA's particular interest in preserving racial homogeneity in new housing

---

[53] Franklin D. Roosevelt to Walter White, January 20, 1939, in NAACP II-L-17, Housing – Federal 1938–39.

[54] Ibid.

developments. The organization pointed to a passage in the manual declaring that the valuator should ensure that deed restrictions contain a "Prohibition of the occupancy of properties except by the race for which they are intended" and include a model covenant.[55]

The NAACP used these passages from the *Underwriting Manual* not only to rebut the FHA's position that its policy and regulations did not discriminate against blacks, but also to challenge the FHA's continued assertions that such provisions simply followed business practices to ensure a property's suitability within its local real estate market. Rather than challenging widespread beliefs among residents and the real estate industry that black occupancy led to neighborhood blight, the FHA "fosters the spread and acceptance of the fallacious conception that property values or deterioration is associated with race rather than economic factors," the NAACP wrote. "Instead of helping to reorient the thinking based on this outmoded concept, FHA has been guilty of allowing its operations to be charged with supporting the misconception by withdrawal or decrease of loans on property in areas newly occupied by Negroes."[56]

Finally, the NAACP argued to FDR, the FHA's racial positions put it at odds both with recent court decisions that had been chipping away at the legal enforceability of housing segregation, and with basic principles of democracy: "In the face of segregation and racial discrimination, the great hope of minority groups in a democracy is the fact that such segregation and discrimination are not Government policy."[57] In short, rather than accept distributional outcomes as driven by impersonal market forces, the NAACP and its allies recognized that access boundaries were backed by federal policy, and contested them on that basis.

The complaint was forwarded to the FHA, which responded with its own memo that outlined its record in promoting mixed-race housing. The agency maintained its stance that any racial inequalities arose not because of "discriminatory operations in the administration of the National Housing Act," but because of "market conditions and market attitudes rather than racial considerations." Since the problem was due to the "reticence of private capital to enter this field," the FHA suggested to the NAACP that it could play an important role in "encouraging the

[55] Letter from Walter White to Franklin D. Roosevelt, October 28, 1944, in RG 31, CCSF, Box 5, Racial Restrictive Covenants, 5–8.
[56] Ibid.   [57] Ibid.

cooperation of Negro financial institutions" to secure a greater amount of housing for African Americans.[58]

The FHA disagreed with the NAACP's indictment. While conceding that its public status generated certain obligations of conduct, the FHA disagreed that the agency had either a responsibility to ensure nondiscrimination among its constituent lenders or the authority to do so as a government agency. In fact, in response to the NAACP's charges, the FHA argued that, while not requiring racially restrictive practices, "it is difficult to see how it [the FHA] could fail to recognize the validity of such restriction and the right of private individuals to place them upon the property." Going further, the FHA reasoned that, if anything, the NAACP's arguments, and the court decisions it cited in support of them, actually justified the FHA's upholding of private practices. The agency's public obligation, the FHA explained, was to ensure the soundness of the loans it backed. Thus, if racial "infiltration will be unacceptable to the local real estate market and desirability of properties will be reduced in the market's mind, then this Administration has no alternative but to so recognize the conditions in its valuation of specific properties within that sphere of influence." As a public–private institution, the FHA viewed its main responsibility to the government and citizens as accurately reporting the market value of the houses it insured. The letter further argued that "contrary to allegations made [by the NAACP] the underwriting operation does not encourage or discourage segregation of races but records conditions as the market reflects them." While the FHA had already removed some specific racial references from the *Underwriting Manual*, it declared that the its "fundamental responsibility of recognizing market conditions will be fully retained."[59]

Notwithstanding its continued insistence that the market alone could explain the differential access of blacks and whites in the housing market, the FHA was forced to reckon with the fact that the specific regulatory language and procedures highlighted by the NAACP were, in the organization's terms, "unanswerable."[60] By 1947, the FHA had at least removed explicit racial references from its manual. The NAACP counted

[58] Letter to Walter White prepared by FHA, December 29, 1944, in RG 31 CCSF, Box 4A, Folder: Minority Group Housing, 1938–47.

[59] Ibid.

[60] Minutes of Conference on Strategy in Connection with Federal Housing Administration, New York, NY, August 5, 1948, in NAACP II-A-308, Folder: Housing – Federal Housing Administration 1940–45.

this action as a success of its memo and larger campaign.[61] But this victory was only partial, at best, as the organization soon recognized.

ARE PUBLIC AGENCIES RESPONSIBLE FOR PRIVATE PROVIDERS' ACTIVITIES? THE AFTERMATH OF *SHELLEY V. KRAEMER*

While the FHA had responded to advocates' demands to remove explicit racial criteria from its *Underwriting Manual,* getting the agency to accept a role in the conduct of its private collaborators was much more difficult. As the agency had maintained, it had an obligation to taxpayers not to insure in risky markets, including those in which racial diversity would erode neighborhood housing values. This was exacerbated by the FHA's replacement term for "inharmonious racial groups": though it removed the reference to "racial" groups from its 1947 *Underwriting Manual,* the agency maintained its preference for neighborhood homogeneity, using the race-neutral term "user groups" to suggest, without specifying race, that neighborhood diversity could be risky from an insurance standpoint. Elsewhere in the *Manual,* the FHA continued to rely on the idea of "continued market acceptance," which NAACP officials knew provided cover for discrimination.[62]

And then there was the issue of restrictive covenants, the legal provisions attached to deeds that forbade residents from selling their houses in the future to nonwhites. In its earlier days, the FHA had encouraged the use of covenants, even including a model one in its *Underwriting Manual,* but such explicit advocacy had been removed from the more the recent editions. This left the issue up to the buyer and seller, with a likely wink from FHA field officers. The FHA argued that it was absolved from any responsibility for the restrictive covenant issue, so long as it did not require restrictive covenants as a condition of eligibility. Officials also maintained that the FHA had no right to refuse insurance on otherwise sound loans that contained restrictive covenants.[63]

---

[61] Thurgood Marshall to Ray Guild (President Boston Branch NAACP), February 14, 1941, in NAACP II-B-130, Folder: Residential Segregation General, 1940–41; Memorandum on Racial Discrimination by the Federal Housing Administration [1948], in NAACP II-A-308, Folder: Housing – Federal Housing Administration 1940–45.

[62] Memorandum on Racial Discrimination by the Federal Housing Administration [1948].

[63] Letter to Robert Wagner from Franklin D. Richards (Commissioner, FHA) 10/3/47, in NAACP II-A-308, Folder: Housing – Federal Housing Administration 1940–45.

The FHA's culpability for insuring residences with private restrictive covenants in their deeds reemerged after the Supreme Court's *Shelley v. Kraemer* decision in 1948. *Shelley* was the culmination of a thirty-one-year effort by the NAACP involving hundreds of restrictive covenant cases, the vast majority unsuccessful.[64] Yet the organization held out hope that the enforceability of restrictive covenants was ultimately an issue it could win. Then it learned of, and took on, the case of J. D. Shelley.

Shelley moved with his family from Mississippi to St. Louis in 1939 as part of the Great Migration. In 1944, he purchased a house in a white neighborhood, using a common strategy that black home buyers had developed in order to circumvent discrimination by sellers: he arranged for a white real estate agent to purchase the house as an intermediary, who would then sell it to him. With Shelley unaware that the house's deed contained a restrictive covenant, the Marcus Avenue Homeowners' Association responded with a lawsuit seeking the family's eviction.[65] (The Marcus Avenue Homeowners' Association also financed the plaintiff's case, which was filed on behalf of the Kraemer family; black real estate brokers financed Shelley's defense.)

Shelley eventually made its way to the Supreme Court, where it was heard alongside two other restrictive covenant cases, *Hurd v. Hodge* and *Sipes v. McGhee* (*"Shelley"* became shorthand for all three). Shelley's lawyer, George L. Vaughn, himself the son of former slaves, presented the opening argument. Calling racial covenants "the Achilles' heel" of American democracy, he then declared that "the Negro knocks at America's door and cries, 'Let me come in and sit by the fire. I helped build the house.'"[66] "The justices never once interrupted him," wrote Clement E. Vose in his history of the case.[67] The Supreme Court ruled unanimously that restrictive covenants were unenforceable by the courts.

---

[64] See for example, letter from Frank Horne to Walter White, July 20, 1948, in NAACP II-A-308, Folder: Housing – Federal Housing Administration 1940–45; Minutes of Conference on Strategy in Connection with Federal Housing Administration, New York, NY, August 5, 1948; NAACP, "Leaders Hail Victory in Restrictive Covenant Cases," Press Release, May 6, 1948, in NAACP II-B-133, Folder: Restrictive Covenants, Shelley v. Kraemer, Sikes v. McGhee; Congratulations, 1948; Ware, "Invisible Walls," 738.

[65] Ibid., 752.

[66] Clement E. Vose, *Caucasians Only: The Supreme Court, the NAACP, and the Restrictive Covenant Cases* (Berkeley: University of California Press, 1959), 201.

[67] Ibid.

In spite of the ruling, the NAACP continued to field complaints from its members that private real estate agents, lenders, and sellers continued to honor racial covenants.[68] In Salinas, California, for example, at least fifteen real estate agents were implicated in a gentlemen's agreement to uphold existing covenants. NAACP branches also collected evidence from local chapters that documented further collusion between banks and realtors to uphold implicit covenants in Atlanta, Dearborn, Detroit, St. Louis, Washington, DC, and Chicago.[69] In a Levittown development on Long Island, developers flagrantly violated the court's ruling, continuing to require residents to sign a restrictive covenant. In response to continued evidence that racial covenants were being used and encouraged, civil rights groups (in particular the NAACP) targeted the FHA and its parent agency, the Housing and Home Finance Agency (HHFA), for their role in aiding and abetting the process.[70]

The NAACP did not have to make the FHA central to its strategy. After all, the Supreme Court had ruled on the issue of whether the courts could justifiably enforce a contract between a buyer and a seller. Unlike the years when its *Underwriting Manual* actively endorsed restrictive covenants, the FHA was not as clearly and directly implicated in this development. The FHA argued that it had accomplished all that was required of it by removing explicit racial references from the *Underwriting Manual* after earlier pressure and by not disseminating its own restrictive covenants with the underwriting guidelines.[71]

---

[68] For example, see Thurgood Marshall's letter on racially restrictive covenants in the Levittown subdivisions, complaining that the company continued to thwart new Supreme Court precedent by inserting the information into deeds and leases after the FHA already approved the mortgage. See letter from Thurgood Marshal to Franklin D. Richards, October 28, 1948, in RG 31, CCSF, Box 6, Folder: Racial Restrictive Covenants, 1938–48.

[69] "Bare Nationwide Plot to Restore Covenants," *Chicago Defender* (October 9, 1948), 1.

[70] Letter to Harry Truman, November 1, 1948, in RG 31 CCSF, Box 6, Folder: Racial Restrictive Covenants, 1938–48.

[71] To the extent the 1944 memo could be viewed as a success, it was due to the fact that there were concrete infractions that were "unanswerable" by the FHA. Proponents of drafting a similar memo in response to the FHA's refusal to enforce *Shelley v. Kraemer* four years later sensed that they faced a much more difficult battle, because there was no concrete policy that they could point to as evidence, and they worried that whatever anecdotal evidence they may have been able to provide would be explicable with respect to the details of each individual case of alleged FHA racial bias. Both the lack of overt racial criteria and the individualized and anecdotal nature of many of the claims of inability to access credit, they knew, would make it difficult to prove that discrimination – and not some other factor – caused someone to be denied access to FHA insurance. The "great deal of autonomy" retained by FHA underwriters, Horne warned, meant that "a

Yet the NAACP had good reason to target the agency. In the months following the Supreme Court's *Shelley* ruling, Loren Miller came into possession of a "very significant exchange of memoranda" between high-level government housing officials.[72] In the first of these exchanges, HHFA Administrator Raymond Foley had requested that top officials at the FHA, the Federal Home Loan Bank Board, and the Public Housing Administration make an "exhaustive analysis of all possible repercussions … including the legal implications" of the *Shelley* ruling for their agencies' programs.[73] "In response to your inquiry of May 18," assured FHA Commissioner Franklin Richards in his response to Foley, "I am informed that the Supreme Court decisions to which you refer will in no way affect the programs of this agency, particularly from the point of view of imposing any new restriction on the operation of these programs."[74] Richards then offered his assurance that "there has been no change either in our basic concepts or in any phase of underwriting processing or procedure as a result of the Court's decision."[75]

As before, Richards pointed to the FHA's position as an insurer of mortgages, rather than a seller or lender: "You are undoubtedly familiar with our longstanding policy not to suggest, require, or prohibit such restrictions but to leave such matters solely to the discretion of the property owner."[76] Furthermore, FHA officials claimed that they did not possess the legal authority to refuse to insure mortgages that had racial covenants.[77] The FHA's race relations advisor, Franke Horne, warned Richards and Foley that theirs was a naïve position to take,

---

statement of instances showing racial discrimination would not be effective as it would, in all probability, be answerable." In "Minutes of Conference on Strategy in Connection with Federal Housing Administration, New York, NY, August 5, 1948."

[72] Walter White to Thurgood Marshall, July 6, 1948, in NAACP II-A-308, Folder: Housing – Federal Housing Administration 1940–45.

[73] Raymond Foley to William Divers, Franklin Richards, and John Egan, May 18, 1948, in NAACP II-A-308, Folder: Housing – Federal Housing Administration 1940–45.

[74] Letter from Franklin Richards to Raymond Foley, May 21, 1948, in NAACP Group II-A-308, Folder: Housing – Federal Housing Administration 1940–45.

[75] Ibid.   [76] Ibid.

[77] Indeed, when pressed about its insuring Levittown communities that still used restrictive covenants, the FHA commissioner wrote to Marshall: "I find nothing in (the restrictive covenant) decisions to indicate that in the absence of statutory authority the government, or any agency thereof, is authorized to withdraw its normal protection and benefits from persons who have executed but do not seek judicial enforcement of such covenants." Letter to Thurgood Marshall, November 1, 1948, quoted in Memorandum on Racial Discrimination by the Federal Housing Administration [1948].

correctly predicting that the scores of activists who had pressed for years in order to win the *Shelley* ruling "will challenge any and every item of governmental policy and procedure which does not appear consonant with the several decisions on racial covenants recently handed down by the U.S. Supreme Court."[78]

After reading and discussing the memos with Miller and a "friendly representative of the FHA stationed on the west coast," Walter White suggested that the NAACP ask President Truman to convene a conference of the federal housing officials, NAACP representatives, and one representative each from the organizations that had filed amicus briefs in the restrictive covenants cases. The purpose of the conference, as White relayed to Thurgood Marshall for his consideration, "would of course be to smoke out FHA and other agencies to force them to operate in accordance with the Supreme Court decision instead of continuing to insist, especially FHA, on 'racial homogeneity.'"[79]

White reached out to Horne, the official in the government housing programs perhaps most friendly to the NAACP's case, for advice on how to proceed. "My own thinking at this point," Horne replied, "is that FHA will need to be *blasted* high, wide and handsome out of its barnacled position of hidebound medievalism."[80] Horne agreed that without Truman's buy-in, meeting with the housing agency heads would be futile. He also iterated his strategic concerns. Simply put, the NAACP and its allies would need to go in with a clear statement of their complaint and a comprehensive plan:

We must challenge, head on, the right of FHA to consider *in any matter* the factor of race in its entire risk rating structure; we must challenge their right to issue commitments on properties already covered with covenants – and we must offer, as we did in 1944, a specific set of recommendations that have to do with both agency policy *and* procedure. We've got to push FHA out of the position of "dragging its heels" to one of providing a species of leadership as it does in matters of housing, neighborhood design, improved mortgage structure, etc. That's a hell of a large order, but the same careful strategy that built up the covenant cases applied to the *administrative* side of the government can bring like results.[81]

---

[78] Frank Horne to Raymond Foley, n.d., in NAACP Group II-A-308, Folder: Housing – Federal Housing Administration 1940–45.

[79] Walter White to Thurgood Marshall, July 6, 1948.

[80] Frank Horne to Walter White, July 20, 1948, in NAACP II-A-308, Folder: Housing – Federal Housing Administration 1940–45.

[81] Ibid.

Horne's last sentence is important, because it suggested that the NAACP's challenge to the state action doctrine contained in its *Shelley v. Kraemer* arguments (and ultimately accepted by the Supreme Court), might also bear fruit at the agency level.

Horne also believed that no time should be wasted. "The iron is hot *now*," he argued. "We've cracked the draft open and applied a spark or two on the inside. If the NAACP pours on the *proper oil*, applied at the *proper points*, we set this whole business afire – right in August and September as the campaign begins to warm up."[82]

The NAACP convened several meetings in anticipation of its conference with housing agencies in order to strategize a new line of attack. To challenge both racial restrictive covenants and the FHA's continuing, albeit covert, refusal to insure open-occupancy developments, the NAACP decided to argue that far from simply recording or responding to market conditions, the FHA, by virtue of its position as a standards setter, exerted a major leadership role in nearly all facets of the housing and mortgage market.[83] In short, the FHA created the housing market conditions that everyone must abide by. As Frank Horne argued, the FHA "has affected the whole mortgage structure, influenced neighborhoods through its insistence on certain standards, and raised the level of standards in the building trades."[84] Such claims undercut the heart of the FHA's earlier assertions that its role in the housing market was confined to insuring private loans. On the contrary, NAACP officials argued in 1948, "FHA standards have in fact become 'the law of the marketplace.'"[85]

Next, advocates reasoned that if FHA standards had indeed become the law of the market, then it was not the impartial hand of the market that helped to produce racially discriminatory outcomes, but government power that contoured and shaped who could become homeowners, and on what terms. This not only was the case for market players who worked directly with the FHA, but extended to all facets of the housing market, since the federal government could shape marketwide standards. Finally, advocates argued that the government was using its position as a shaper of the housing market to provide benefits for some groups while

---

[82] Ibid.   [83] Ibid.

[84] "Minutes of Conference on Strategy in Connection with Federal Housing Administration, New York, NY, August 5, 1948."

[85] "Notes of discussion on Federal Housing Administration, Washington DC Conference, 9/17/1948," in NAACP II-A-308, Folder: Housing – Federal Housing Administration 1940–45.

arbitrarily withholding them from others, with the backing of US credit and taxpayers.[86]

From these premises, advocates argued that the FHA (as well as other federal regulatory and housing agencies) had an obligation not only to ensure that its own operation was nondiscriminatory, but also to withdraw its protections from private lenders and other market actors who discriminated against blacks, given the taxpayers' role in indirectly subsidizing private profits and its responsibility to, in Weaver's words, "furnish funds in case of failure. Therefore, the benefits of the original credit cannot be arbitrarily excluded to any citizen on the basis of race, creed, or color."[87] Some suggested rooting this claim within the Fifth Amendment, arguing that the FHA could not withdraw "its normal protection and benefits from Negroes who wish to live outside the ghetto, yet contend it is not authorized to withdraw such benefits from persons who contract with their neighbors who discriminate against Negroes."[88] Others wondered whether there might be a Fourteenth Amendment claim, arguing that the FHA, "being supported by funds of all citizens, should not use funds to discriminate against some citizens."[89]

An example of moving from strategy to action, and of the organization's reasoning, is the 1948 memo sent by the NAACP's Marshall to the FHA, modeled after its 1944 memo to FDR. In the memo, Marshall argued that *Shelley*'s ruling on the judicial enforcement of restrictive covenants extended to "all governmental action in support of racial restrictive covenants."[90] In the NAACP's definition, this extended to projects backed by the FHA, even if the FHA was not itself a lender or seller. For Marshall and the others who challenged the FHA's association with racial covenants, the federal government did not need to pass legislation to change the FHA's practices, since the Supreme Court had already made the "determination that government power may not be

---

[86] Memorandum to the Board of Directors from the Secretary, June 3, 1952, in NAACP II-A-309, Folder: Housing – Federal Housing Administration, 1952–55; Weaver, in "Minutes of Conference on Strategy in Connection with Federal Housing Administration, New York, NY, August 5, 1948."

[87] "Minutes of Conference on Strategy in Connection with Federal Housing Administration, New York, NY, August 5, 1948."

[88] "Memorandum on Racial Discrimination by the Federal Housing Administration [1948]"

[89] "Minutes of Conference on Strategy in Connection with Federal Housing Administration, New York, NY, August 5, 1948."

[90] Letter from Thurgood Marshall to Franklin Richards, October 28, 1948, in RG 31 CCSF, Box 6, Folder: Racial Restrictive Covenants, 1938–48.

exercised to aid private persons in accomplishing racial discrimination in housing."[91]

Although the FHA continued to resist this line of argument, it found itself again unable to defend its underwriting procedures, and finally agreed in December 1949 that it would no longer insure mortgages on properties that contained covenants after February 15, 1950, and would ignore existing covenants filed before that date.[92] The FHA also agreed that mortgages insured after February 15 would stipulate that the mortgagor would be unable to file for restrictive covenants so long as FHA insurance was in effect on the mortgage. Also in December 1949, the FHA added Section 242 to its *Underwriting Manual*, which stated: "Underwriting considerations shall recognize the right to equality of opportunity to receive the benefits of the mortgage insurance system in obtaining adequate housing accommodations irrespective of race, color, creed or national origin."[93]

In sum, in the fifteen years after the FHA's inception, the NAACP came to recognize black housing exclusion as something perpetuated by public policy, identified the specific policies that either discriminated against blacks or produced disparate effects on blacks and whites, and then contested what it saw as inequitable and government-backed boundaries to access. Far from occluding or obscuring paths to activism, the public-private structure of housing policy created political openings and opportunities: using that structure, civil rights groups argued that the government had not only the authority to overrule racially restrictive practices in the private housing sector, but also an obligation to do so.

CHALLENGING THE MARKET LOGIC OF EXCLUSION

Yet the episodes described above also reveal the limits of advocacy for the outcomes the NAACP sought. One important issue was the conceptual gulf between the FHA, on the one side, and the NAACP and its allies, on the other. Both the NAACP and the FHA acknowledged that the public-private structure of the government's homeownership programs

---

[91] Ibid.

[92] Raymond Foley, "An Integrated Approach to Community Housing Problems," Speech before the Annual Convention of the National Association of Real Estate Brokers, October 16, 1952, 2–4, in Records of the National Urban League, Library of Congress (hereafter NUL) I: C21, Folder: National Association of Home Builders.

[93] Richard C. Stearns, "Racial Content of FHA Underwriting Practices, 1934–1952," n.d., Baltimore, MD, 10–11.

conferred certain responsibilities on the FHA. But they fundamentally disagreed as to what those responsibilities were, and whether the FHA was acting in accordance with its public mandate.

The FHA perceived that its primary responsibility as a government agency was to accurately reflect market conditions. To the extent that the agency was willing to encourage black homeownership, its actions mostly involved suggestions to business leaders that they consider the "great opportunities" available to them by breaking into the minority housing market, and by encouraging local FHA field office directors to "use all available facilities at hand to stimulate the interest of builders and lenders in the planning and production of housing for sale and rent to minority groups," as the FHA commissioner explained to his field staff in 1948.[94] To the extent that the private housing industry was unable to recognize and exploit these "great opportunities," it was due to a deficiency of blacks in the housing market, not the FHA.

The NAACP and other civil rights advocates clearly disagreed with the FHA's reasoning and often challenged it, but they also recognized that the FHA was not entirely incorrect in pointing to the market to explain the difficulties blacks had in accessing housing. There was no denying that the FHA's justification for its own practices and explanation for disparate outcomes for blacks and whites had deep roots in the private housing market, among buyers of houses and sellers, among white households, and in the industry as a whole. Recall that, as Chapter 3 points out, the FHA's earliest appraisal materials were lifted almost verbatim from the private real estate sector literature, as the newly established profession it sought to standardize and homogenize its methods. Thus, even as they plotted their strategy to force the FHA to cease its discriminatory practices, advocates recognized that procedural and regulatory changes would be meaningless without also challenging the private beliefs (of both the real estate industry and citizens) that made African Americans seem less desirable in the housing market.[95]

In recognition of these challenges, advocates also pursued a parallel strategy to gather and disseminate new information to challenge market-based explanations for limited black homeownership opportunities.

[94] Letter from Franklin D. Richards (FHA Commissioner) to Directors of all FHA Field Offices, "Minority Group Housing," November 8, 1948, in RG 31 CCSF, Box 4A, Folder: Minority Group Housing 1948.
[95] See "Minutes of Conference on Strategy in Connection with Federal Housing Administration, New York, NY, August 5, 1948."

As Frank Horne stated, "We must be able to attack them through economics, money, and banking. They start out by saying that one of the first things they rate are adverse influences. Race is an influence. Our contention is that they must entirely eliminate the use of race as a factor in rating property."[96] The FHA's continued ability to portray itself as merely dispassionately recording and reflecting, but not creating, market conditions spurred many housing activists to regroup and work through the informational challenges. They called for an "objective and comprehensive factual study" of the experiences and opportunities of blacks in the housing market, of the effects of black occupancy on property values, and of the risks and profits of lending to black applicants. Then they wanted to disseminate this information to representatives of the private real estate industry, the financial sector, and the general public.[97] Activists, moreover, pushed local organizations to use the research findings to "develop and circulate an evaluation of the place, responsibility, and possibilities of private enterprise to meet the housing needs of Negroes."[98] It was suggested they reach out to local lending and real estate interests to educate them about market opportunities, but also to apply "continuous pressure" to private builders to increase the housing opportunities available to blacks.

Civil rights activists needed to challenge two assumptions that underlie private providers' claims for why blacks faced constrained housing options (and why, in turn, the FHA claimed itself to be only a mirror for these market realities). The first was the assumption that the racial homogeneity of neighborhoods did indeed correlate to neighborhood house values. As mentioned earlier, the belief in segregation as necessary to protect neighborhood house values had been articulated in real estate valuation manuals as early as the 1910s.[99] Related wisdom held that it was not the racial composition of the neighborhood so much as its stability or change over time that mattered for house price values. In his 1924 book, *The Appraisal of Real Estate*, Frederick Babcock indicated

---

[96] Ibid.

[97] "Blueprint of Action for the Negro Organization in the Field of Housing [draft]," attachment in letter from Robert Weaver to Lester Granger June 26, 1945, in NUL I: C2, Folder: Housing Activities Department, General Department File, American Council on Race Relations 1944–1947.

[98] Ibid., 6.

[99] McMichael and Bingham, *City Growth and Values*, quoted in Charles Abrams, "The New Gresham's Law of Neighborhoods – Fact or Fiction," *Appraisal Journal* 19, no. 3, (July 1951), 324–37. See also Freund, *Colored Property*, 15–16.

that *changing* racial characteristics (as well as changes in the religious makeup, income levels, or neighborhood social and civil institutions) instead might be indicative of a falling property value.[100] Both of these ideas, to recall, were codified into the FHA's original *Underwriting Manual*. Even as the FHA scrubbed racial language from the *Manual* in response to NAACP demands, it transliterated race into "user groups," which conveyed the same message about the relationship between neighborhood homogeneity and house values. Moreover, many textbooks in the 1950s continued to use racial language in connection with appraisal.

The second assumption was that the market for minority group housing was simply too unprofitable to draw the private sector in, due to the lower incomes and poorer credit histories of minorities. Indeed, this was the explanation given by the FHA Administrator Steward McDonald to FDR in 1936 when asked about the nonparticipation of blacks in Title II of the FHA:

It is difficult for the majority of Negroes to enjoy the benefits under Title II, as they are unable to furnish the necessary small, cash down-payment to build or buy a new home and, furthermore, as a rule their personal credit ratings are poor. And this, after all, is the crux of the matter as far as the banks, life insurance companies, and other lending institutions are concerned.[101]

An influential book on real estate valuation, published in 1942, articulated a similar assumption that native-born whites "dominate the situation; they are the typical purchasers of homes. The foreign-born and Negroes, because of their inability to pay the price that new housing commands, are usually found in the occupancy of older structures."[102] Even the documented rise in black household incomes over the following decades did little to erode this idea.

From the standpoint of civil rights groups, the problem with these assumptions was twofold. First, they reflected deeply held views that

[100] Frederick M. Babcock, *The Appraisal of Real Estate* (New York: Macmillan, 1924); Henderson's 1931 manual on real estate appraisal, moreover, suggested that the appraiser consider "the complexion of the community, the type of people living there, their habits, their movements socially, their racial characteristics and attitude toward property." Henderson, *Real Estate Appraising*, 139.

[101] Memo from Stewart McDonald to Franklin D. Roosevelt, July 7, 1936, in in FDR-L, PPOF, OF 1091, Folder: Federal Housing Administration June–Dec. 1936.

[102] Arthur May, *The Valuation of Residential Real Estate* (New York: Prentice-Hall, 1942), 74.

evolved over a long period of time, were codified, and were ingrained in real estate practices. These would be difficult to dislodge. Second, they were largely untested and unsupported. Conjecture abounded, but there was little empirical evidence to support the idea of a causal relationship between neighborhood diversity and house values. The same was true with regard to ideas about race posing some sort of repayment risk that warranted charging African Americans higher interest rates. The federal housing agencies certainly did not release this data, if they even collected it. And several advocates had concerns about how the data might be used against them. In 1948 meeting minutes, Robert C. Weaver conceded that "there are instances where the insuring of a loan for Negroes can, from an objective point of view, impair the value of property in certain areas, although we cannot afford to take that position."[103] Nevertheless, recognizing the information gap as a key issue in the fight for fair access to mortgage credit, civil rights advocates took various steps to challenge earlier understandings about race and the housing market.

First, they played a crucial informational role in researching and then challenging the validity of arguments that linked increasing racial heterogeneity in a neighborhood to declining house values. Advocates had many reasons to be skeptical about this claim, including their own observations that real estate agents had long profited from restrictive practices like blockbusting, which involved introducing a small number of black families to a white neighborhood, buying up the surrounding houses at reduced prices (after stoking white homeowners' fears), and then reselling or renting the houses to middle-class blacks at inflated prices.[104] Second, many had observed plenty of instances where the introduction of a middle-class black family into a white neighborhood had produced no ill social or economic effects. While these were anecdotal, they pointed to a lack of real evidence to back claims about homogeneity, as Frank Horne wrote to Walter White in 1943 (quoted at length):

---

[103] "Minutes of Conference on Strategy in Connection with Federal Housing Administration, New York, NY, August 5, 1948." For earlier instances where similar concerns were voiced, see, for example, Letter from Robert C. Weaver to Roger Baldwin, November 27, 1946, and Memorandum to Walter White from Marian Wynn Perry Re: Race Bias in Housing, by Charles Abrams, December 6, 1946, both In NAACP II-A-315, Folder: Housing: Pamphlets, 1945–54.

[104] Memo to Walter White from Frank Horne, Re: Influence of Negro Occupancy Upon Property Values, November 8, 1943, 1–2, in NAACP II-A-311, Folder: Housing: Influence of Negro Occupancy Upon Property Values, 1941–55.

What happens to the "values" of these respective properties? Who determines the "loss of value" of properties in neighborhoods recently opened to Negroes? Upon what basis are these determinations made? Who profits from these determinations?

These and associated questions have apparently never been thoroughly explored. The concepts and attitudes involved have not been seriously challenged. The time is ripe for a careful and comprehensive study of this problem. Such a study would involve investigations in a number of representative cities; shifts in property values in selected neighborhoods should be traced; the effect of occupancy by various economic and racial groups compared; the causes of value "losses" with indication of areas where such losses do not become evident; the Negro as tenant and property owner at various economic levels as compared to whites of similar income; the effect of restrictive covenants upon property values; evidence of manipulation of property values.[105]

By "reducing superstition and hearsay with facts in regard to the effect of Negro occupancy upon real property values," Horne reasoned in 1943, local and national agencies, as well as private agencies, would lose their main justification for covenants and other restrictive practices.[106] By the early 1950s, advocates could avail themselves of a growing body of research that cast doubt on the idea that neighborhood homogeneity (or changes therein) reduced home values. Some of this was conducted by researcher-activists in civil rights organizations, including the economist Charles Abrams, who used his 1951 *Appraisal Journal* article to blast early appraisal textbook authors for their almost circular logic regarding neighborhood racial homogeneity:

In determining what is the value of the lot at a certain time, the appraiser functions as an appraiser. But in setting down a rule of "behavioristics" he embraces not only dollar values but social values. In asserting that "it is people who make value" and then concluding that people like to live with their own precut prototypes, he is speaking in the multiple role of appraiser, economist, social psychologist, and expert in social discrimination, social organization, and the whole gamut of the social sciences.[107]

Abrams bolstered his case by outlining recent research that contradicted the previous findings. In the years that followed, others in the appraisal field came to similar findings, and at least a few of these publications were

---

[105] Ibid., 2.   [106] Ibid.

[107] Charles Abrams, "The New Gresham's Law of Neighborhoods' – Fact or Fiction," *Appraisal Journal* 19, no. 3 (1951), 324–37. NAACP reprint, in NAACP II-A-315, Folder: Housing: Pamphlets, 1945–54.

reprinted and disseminated by civil rights organizations.[108] By 1955, advocates had amassed statistical information that they could send to people curious about the relationship between race and neighborhood real estate values, and that they would provide upon request to realtors and others in the industry.[109]

Advocates also challenged, in a variety of ways, the conventional wisdom that there simply was not a profitable market for black housing. In 1953, the NAACP enlisted its local branches to form their own Housing Committees that would analyze the local housing market, highlighting the opportunities and constraints (land, stock, financing, and household financials) faced by blacks trying to become homeowners, with the purpose of disseminating this information to local private housing providers, the press, the public, other potential civic allies, government agencies, and elected officials. The NAACP urged branch Housing Committees to form good working relationships with each of these sectors. Committees were to cultivate relationships with private housing interests to educate them about opportunities in the black housing market, and to collaborate with and monitor government housing agencies and legislative allies. When necessary, the NAACP also counseled the Housing Committees to mobilize public support for improved access to housing, whether through protest, the courts, letter-writing campaigns, or media publicity.

THE NATIONAL URBAN LEAGUE TAKES ON THE INDUSTRY ASSOCIATIONS

Nationally, advocacy groups appealed to federal housing agencies and national organizations to stimulate business interest in black households. In 1945, the American Council on Race Relations drafted a "Blueprint of Action" that proposed to utilize the federal government to entice greater private sector involvement in the problems of housing black Americans. According to the blueprint, the FHA could expand its availability to blacks by a variety of changes, ranging from regulatory and

---

[108] See, for example, Luigi M. Laurenti, "Effects of Nonwhite Purchases on Market Prices of Residences," *Appraisal Journal* 20, no. 3 (1952), 314–29; Belden Morgan, "Values in Transition Areas: Some New Concepts," *The Review of the Society of Residential Appraisers* (1952), 5–10, both reprinted by National Committee Against Discrimination in Housing, in NAACP II-A-315, Folder: Housing: Pamphlets, 1945–54.

[109] Letter from Madison Jones (NAACP Field Secretary) to T.B. Hilton, February 18, 1955, and letter from T.B. Hilton to NAACP, February 2, 1955, both in NAACP II-A-311, Folder: Housing: Influence of Negro Occupancy Upon Property Values, 1941–55.

administrative changes to more thorough collection and dissemination of data on African American housing needs to lenders, real estate boards, and the general public. The agency was also in a position to advocate for longer-range studies on the repayment patterns of black mortgage holders, the blueprint argued.[110]

The blueprint called on civil rights groups to open negotiations with trade associations that represented builders, real estate agents, and lenders, to pressure them to develop plans for increasing the housing opportunities available to blacks. Through the 1940s, civil rights organizations made sporadic efforts to reach out to national professional associations, with mixed success. For example, the NAACP managed to convene a meeting in September 1948 with White House officials, federal agencies, and business interests. The discussion was collegial, but the organization was disappointed in the lack of business commitment for any change in practices.

This piecemeal approach began to change in the 1950s. On the urging of the FHA's race relations advisor, the National Urban League established its own Housing Committee in 1952 and appointed a twenty-two-year veteran of the league, Reginald Johnson, as its first national director of housing.[111] The Urban League's entry into the housing arena allowed for a two-pronged approach. The leadership resolved to let the NAACP handle most of the legislative and judicial issues, while the Urban League focused on implementation, working with "federal and private housing interests for the good of the Negro community."[112] The Urban League's Housing Committee accelerated its actions in the private sector, beginning by meeting with African American real estate agents, builders, lenders, and other housing industry representatives.[113]

Urban League members with ties to several of these associations reached out accordingly. The National Association of Real Estate Brokers (an association of African American real estate agents, not to be confused

[110] American Council on Race Relations, n.d., "Blueprint of Action," 3–5, in NUL I: C2, Folder: American Council on Race Relations.

[111] Letter from Floyd Covington (FHA Racial Relations Advisor) to Reginald Johnson (Director of Field Services, NUL), January 10, 1952, in NUL I: C9, Folder: Federal Housing Administration, Covington Floyd C.

[112] Letter from Lester Granger to Floyd Covington, April 3, 1951, in NUL I: C9, Folder: Federal Housing Administration, Covington Floyd C.

[113] Letter from W. H. Aiken (President, National Association of Real Estate Brokers) to Lester Granger, February 11, 1952, in NUL Part I: C21, Folder: National Association of Home Builders.

with the National Association of Real Estate Boards) lent its support early.[114] Robert Taylor, secretary of the Illinois Federal Savings and Loan Association and future Illinois housing commissioner, described his substantial experience lending to black homeowners in a speech at the United States Savings and Loan League's annual meeting in Chicago in 1952. Encouraging the attendees to pay more attention to the needs of minorities, Taylor reported that among the fifteen hundred black families his association had lent to during its seventeen-year lifespan, only one had fallen into foreclosure.[115]

The Urban League also forged connections between its own leadership and those of the largest organizations in the private real estate market, including the National Association of Home Builders, the Mortgage Bankers Association of America, and the National Association of Real Estate Boards. This included writing letters to the leaders of those organizations to set up meetings, asking for minority housing panels during national conferences, and, as the ultimate goal, getting each of the organizations to develop a standing committee on minority housing needs. While doing this, the Urban League paid careful attention to the turnover in leadership, using its local leadership to provide any pertinent information about how sympathetic an incoming president might be to the NUL's causes, and to suggest strategies to approach them.

The National Association of Home Builders was relatively receptive to the Urban League's requests. It agreed to hold a roundtable on minority housing at its annual conference in January 1953, and the following year the association invited Reginald Johnson back to address the conference. For the Urban League, this was a chance to acknowledge many builders' worries about the "headaches and difficulties they assume they will face in this area of operation," and to assuage many of their concerns, in particular that African Americans represented the low-income end of the market.[116] Johnson reassured them that "This market is *not different*

---

[114] This is not to say that black real estate professionals were necessarily in favor of desegregation; some may have had a financial interest in restricting the housing supply. However, the NUL considered professional associations representing blacks in different areas of real estate as potential allies.

[115] "S&Ls Urged to Expand Loans Among Negroes," *The American Banker* (November 17, 1952), in NUL I: C12, Folder: Housing and Home Finance Agency, Federal Home Loan Bank Board 1952.

[116] Reginald Johnson, "Working with the Minority Market," Speech delivered before the Annual Conference of the National Association of Home Builders, January 18, 1954, in NUL, I: C21, Folder: National Association of Home Builders 1953–55.

from usual operations. But it has been isolated and, to a large extent, ignored. This in itself has created problems that require special effort to overcome."[117] Johnson called on the builders, although not themselves lenders, to help deal with problems of financing black-owned homes.[118]

The next month, the NAHB devoted an entire section of its member magazine, *The Correlator*, to minority group housing. The Urban League was thrilled to see this attention given to minority housing problems, and mentioned in a memo with a known circulation of 26,000, the message was sure to reach every local home builder. For the local Urban Leagues, the wide circulation provided an "excellent opportunity to . . . confer with the local Home Builders Association and develop a working interest in behalf of more housing available to minority occupancy."[119]

The Urban League succeeded in getting the home builders to establish a Minority Housing Committee to focus exclusively on issues pertaining to the minority market.[120] By 1954, the Minority Housing Committee had collaborated with the FHA, the HHFA, and the Urban League to develop a plan for increasing minority housing. In a report of the committee's findings, it called on the NAHB's individual members to "do everything possible to induce private lending institutions to provide the necessary funds with which to do this job. . . . You, as individual builders, can help by insisting that your local lenders join in an aggressive campaign to improve the housing conditions of the minority groups, and to assist in arranging the necessary financing."[121] The committee also resolved to contact representatives from insurance companies and savings banks and other investors to help increase the availability of financing for minorities.

The Urban League ran a similar strategy to drum up support among the Mortgage Bankers Association of America. Like the FHA, the MBAA initially viewed the challenges of African American housing as driven primarily by income differences between blacks and whites.[122] Johnson countered this assertion by pointing to sixty Urban League branch offices

[117] Ibid., emphasis original.   [118] Ibid.

[119] National Urban League, Memorandum, March 19, 1954, in NUL, I: C21, Folder: National Association of Home Builders 1953–55.

[120] Report of the Joint Meeting of the Minority Group Housing and Rental Housing Committees, NAHB; Memorandum from Wallace Johnson (chairman, Minority Housing Group), to NAHB Board of Directors, May 15, 1954, in NUL I: C21, Folder: National Association of Home Builders 1953–55.

[121] Ibid.

[122] Letter from Whatley Brown (MBAA) to Reginald Johnson, March 10, 1953, in NUL I: C20, Folder: Mortgage Bankers Assn. of America.

that had indicated to him "unquestionably that mortgage funds are more limited for Negro occupied properties in all price categories. Our correspondence, requests for mortgage assistance, and personal contacts with many builders, real estate firms, financial institutions, and individual property owners fully substantiate the existence of this racial factor."[123]

Unable to make headway with the MBAA, Johnson successfully appealed to the FHA commissioner, asking him to reach out to the mortgage bankers.[124] Over the next few years, the MBAA and the Urban League were in regular communication about African American housing difficulties. Johnson wanted to impress upon the MBAA the need for the national leadership to help steer its local members toward solving problems of black housing availability. "It is in our interest to work with these organizations in behalf of meeting problems that limit the shelter supply available to nonwhite occupancy," he explained in a letter to the MBAA's incoming president in 1953.[125] Johnson argued that the MBAA was in a position to help, because it could "determine the problems involved that deflect mortgage finance from this market, and suggest ways and means by which these problems may be more satisfactorily met"; "develop a program to interest mortgage correspondents and prime lenders in the profitable possibilities of this market"; and undertake pilot programs in specific neighborhoods to begin with.[126] As with the home builders, Johnson also encouraged the MBAA to establish a standing committee to follow minority housing issues.[127] Several days later, the president of the MBAA responded, outlining his plans to reach out to the National Association of Home Builders to learn about what it had done in response to minority housing problems. The NAHB forwarded its materials to the MBAA to assist it in creating a housing committee.[128]

Through the Urban League's efforts, the MBAA's board of governors decided to establish a Committee on Financing for Racial Minorities in February 1954 "to study and review the obstacles in this area and to take constructive steps to overcome them." They devoted one of the five

[123] Letter from Reginald Johnson to Whatley Brown, March 27, 1953, in NUL I: C20, Folder: Mortgage Bankers Assn. of America.

[124] Letter from Reginald Johnson to Walter Greene, March 30, 1953, in NUL I: C20, Folder: Mortgage Bankers Assn. of America.

[125] Letter from Reginald Johnson to William Clarke (President, MBAA), October 28, 1953, in NUL I: C20, Folder: Mortgage Bankers Assn. of America.

[126] Ibid.   [127] Ibid.

[128] See letters dated April 1, 1954, June 21, 1954 (2), and June 23, 1954, in in NUL I: C20, Folder: Mortgage Bankers Assn. of America.

general sessions during the MBAA's annual meeting in October to minority housing and redevelopment, and invited the Urban League to participate.[129] Through the new committee, the MBAA conducted an eighteen-month study of minority mortgage issues, published in October 1955. The report made "plain that the lending industry cannot be said to be in the market on a wholehearted basis," and suggested that minority mortgage lending was possibly "the largest undeveloped opportunity for the expansion of mortgage activity."[130] Moreover, the report noted that between rising incomes, an increasing nonwhite population, and a persistent gap in homeownership between whites and blacks, expansion into the minority housing market posed "a prospect for additional business and additional service to the community that mortgage men cannot ignore."[131]

The NUL appears to have had the least success in reaching out to the National Association of Real Estate Boards (NAREB), whose local branches earlier had clashed publicly with the league.[132] Yet by the Urban League's own admission, "without the backing of representative and forward-looking real estate interests many aspects of the Urban League's programs cannot possibly be completed."[133] The problem with NAREB, an organization with a history of discriminating by race, excluding blacks from membership, and making its members take an oath to preserve neighborhood segregation, was a complex one by the 1950s. Some elements within the national leadership were sympathetic to problems in the minority market and to the Urban League's desire to reach out to the Realtors. The longtime executive director, Herbert Nelson, met with the Urban League leadership, as did several of NAREB's presidents, who, unlike Nelson, rotated through the office annually. In its dealings with the NAREB leadership, the Urban League managed to win a few very limited concessions.[134]

---

[129] National Urban League, Press Release, September 24, 1954, in NUL I: C20, Folder: Mortgage Bankers Assn. of America.

[130] MBAA, Committee on Financing Minority Housing, Report, October 29, 1955, 5, 10, in NUL I: C20, Folder: Mortgage Bankers Assn. of America.

[131] Ibid., 7.

[132] Letter from Alfred Kennedy to Lester Granger, September 17, 1951, in NUL I: C21, Folder: National Association of Home Builders 1951–1952.

[133] Letter from Lester Granger to Alfred Kennedy, September 24, 1951, in NUL I: C21, Folder: National Association of Home Builders 1951–1952.

[134] Ibid.; letter from Alfred Kennedy to Lester Granger, October 23, 1951, in NUL I: C21, Folder: National Association of Home Builders 1951–1952.

NAREB was long aware of the profits to be made from marketing to African Americans, as it had conducted its own research on the minority market through its Committee on Negro Housing. In November 1944, NAREB published a study of eighteen representative cities and of real estate boards in 147 member cities. The association found that real estate agents with experience lending to black applicants found them to be a good credit risk, often better at meeting their repayment obligations than other similarly situated groups.[135] The study quoted members of real estate boards in Savannah, Chicago, Kansas City, Denver, Erie, and Charlotte, who all weighed in on their positive experiences with the black housing market. The Detroit board even recommended that builders be required to designate a minimum percentage of their total construction for minority housing. At the time, NAREB had even begun to encourage its local member boards to find ways to expand access to blacks, although in its press release announcing the move, NAREB strongly emphasized that it "was developing its program as a business matter, based on an economic opportunity, and not from a reform standpoint."[136]

Although it recognized the promise of the African American housing market, NAREB was reluctant to form a minority housing committee on par with the Home Builders and Mortgage Bankers Associations, because the leadership recognized that such an action would be entirely unacceptable to its Southern boards. Wanting to avoid getting embroiled in internal conflicts, NAREB's leaders proposed a local alternative. They proposed that the Urban League team up with sympathetic local boards "wherever possible and that, if possible, the N.A.R.E.B. appoint a committee to serve jointly with the Urban League and to study the question of Negro housing in various parts of the country."[137] Some within the Urban League believed that the local strategy might also help burnish its conservative credentials with the notoriously reactionary real estate

---

[135] National Association of Real Estate Boards, Press Release No. 78, November 15, 1944, in NUL I: C21, Folder: National Association of Home Builders; see also Memorandum Prepared by the NAACP Concerning the Present Discriminatory Policies of the Federal Housing Administration (10/26/44), in NAACP II-A-308, Folder: Housing – Federal Housing Administration 1940–45.

[136] National Association of Real Estate Boards, Press Release No. 78, November 15, 1944; Memorandum Prepared by the NAACP Concerning the Present Discriminatory Policies of the Federal Housing Administration, October 26, 1944, in NAACP II-A-308, Folder: Housing – Federal Housing Administration 1940–45.

[137] Letter from Alfred Kennedy to Reginald Johnson, January 17, 1952, in NUL I: C21, Folder: National Association of Home Builders: 1951–1952.

lobby.[138] Writing to the president of NAREB in 1952, a real estate agent and Urban Leaguer said: "I find that generally the Negroes have a strong desire for home ownership and, when homeowners, maintain their property. They would become strong allies in the fight against socialized housing, if they could obtain decent homes in decent surroundings at a price with proper relationship to their earnings."[139] The Urban League managed to cooperate with a few of the more sympathetic boards, but as a national association, NAREB continued to have no policy on minority housing.[140]

Much like their efforts to move government policy, civil rights advocates' efforts to improve African Americans' housing market opportunities and counter earlier assumptions about the group's market desirability had mixed results. They did succeed in collecting information on the size and scope of the black housing market and constraints that blacks faced when trying to get housing. Advocates also conducted research that finally challenged and debunked assumptions underlying some of the most egregious practices, by both the government and the private sector. And they managed to convince others to conduct research on previously unstudied issues that nevertheless had a huge impact on minorities' capacity to buy houses. Perhaps most importantly, they were able to use this information to undermine the argument that had helped to justify racial covenants, as well as post-*Shelley* informal agreements to promote neighborhood racial stability. They also disseminated this information to the public, the media, the federal government, and businesses involved in the housing industry.

Essentially, then, civil rights advocates during this time helped to subsidize the cost of information gathering for market players, while accentuating opportunities for these market providers if only they would wholeheartedly embrace the business. This information might have been especially useful to businesses in the early 1950s, as the market for middle-class white homeowners had become saturated and builders, real estate agents, and lenders were looking for new opportunities. A *House & Home* article touted opportunities in the nonwhite housing market and

---

[138] Letter from Alfred Kennedy to Lester Granger June 13, 1952, in NUL I: C21, Folder: National Association of Home Builders: 1951–1952.

[139] Letter from Alfred Kennedy to Joseph Lund, February 23, 1952, in NUL I: C21, Folder: National Association of Home Builders.

[140] Letter from Henry Waltemade to Reginald Johnson, January 11, 1955, in NUL I: C21, Folder: National Association of Home Builders.

quoted Walter White's former executive assistant: "There is very little room here for sociological implications. The builder wants to make a buck and we have to help him."[141]

The FHA and other government agencies eventually did acquiesce to some of the civil rights groups' demands. For example, they began to disseminate their own information about the opportunities available to private lenders as African American household incomes rose, as well as the need for housing.[142] Government housing officials had also begun to show a willingness to coordinate with minority housing advocates. They reached out to business associations (including the National Association of Real Estate Boards, the National Association of Home Builders, and the Mortgage Bankers Association of America) that were initially cold to civil rights groups. Furthermore, several officials within various government housing agencies began to construe the 1949 Housing Act's mandate of a government responsibility to provide "a decent home and suitable living environment" for all Americans as a mandate to ensure that "American families of every race, creed, color, and national origin have the same opportunity to obtain decent housing."[143]

Rather than becoming invisible or submerged from view, the public–private structure of housing policy rendered the government's role in housing market segregation visible and legible, while the fact of the government's involvement opened up a new front of activism in the war against discrimination in homeownership. The public–private structure also helped advocates to pry open a second front, targeted not at the state, but at the market providers who benefited from the state's role in the housing market. In these ways the delegated state helped to generate new sites of political activism and change.

THE VOLUNTARY HOME MORTGAGE CREDIT PROGRAM

Dual – and mutually reinforcing – efforts on the government and business fronts culminated with the government's first legislative program to address minority housing exclusion, the Voluntary Home Mortgage

---

[141] "Non-White Housing," *House & Home* (April 1953), reprinted in NAACP II-A-315, Folder: Housing Pamphlets 1945–54.

[142] Message from FHA Commissioner to Be Read by Insuring Office Directors at NAHB Local Meetings Relating to Providing Homes Available to Minorities, July 16, 1954, in NAACP II-A-309, Folder: Housing: Federal Housing Administration General 1952–55.

[143] Ibid.

Credit Program (VHMCP), which was created as part of the Housing Act of 1954 and signed into law in August. Though the color line in home-ownership was by no means breached by 1954, this period reveals the crucial role of organized interests in making visible the previously invisible contribution of the government to discriminatory housing practices.

The VHMCP targeted minorities and residents of remote rural areas. Through its procedures, a prospective borrower could apply directly to the VHMCP for a loan after two unsuccessful attempts to secure a private loan. It included in its National Advisory Committee representatives from commercial banking, home building, life insurance, mortgage banking, mutual savings banks, real estate, and savings and loan associations. Though it fell far short of a decisive government repudiation of segregated housing, it tackled another problem that civil rights advocates had identified and toward which the private industry and the FHA were more sympathetic: the limited access to finance for African Americans.[144]

Within the subtext of the VHMCP was also a warning to businesses that they not shirk their responsibilities in the public–private housing market. In a speech to an association of savings bankers, HHFA Administrator Albert Cole pointed out that the program was ultimately a response to business calls for entering a market that the federal government otherwise would have to corner.[145] In a reversal from the FHA's earlier refusal to claim any obligation to compel the private sector to serve minorities' housing needs, Cole reminded banks that his position as housing administrator conferred on him "a good deal of authority that I haven't used. I haven't used it because I want private industry to do the job. I have leaned over backward, gentlemen, to see that private enterprise has – that you have – the opportunity."[146] Cole then outlined what he viewed as the responsibility of private industry to validate that his efforts at bringing them on board were not in vain:

You in the private industry of finance have a social, ethical, and, yes, a political, responsibility to consider and serve the requirements of minorities. This is just as much your responsibility as it is mine, and as it is that of the President of the United States. You cannot push the problem under the bed; you are the people who must solve the problem if you wish to see a republican form of government continued. Paternalism is achieved by shirking such responsibilities.

[144] Ibid. See also Letter to Homer Capehart from Albert Cole, April 6, 1954, in NAACP II-A-306, Folder: Housing: Bills, Federal – General, 1947–55.
[145] Albert Cole, Speech to Annual Conference of National Association of Mutual Savings Banks, May 12, 1955, in NUL I: C12, Folder: Housing and Home Finance Agency.
[146] Ibid., 8.

Your responsibility embraces not just part of the market, or the preferred market. It covers the total market, and you have a public obligation to service all those who can meet sound requirements for mortgage financing, including minority families. Yet the Negro has had, and still has difficulty, in obtaining funds to acquire a home on terms equal to those of other citizens. . . . The Negro's rights are equal to those of any other citizen, and his housing needs are greater. If private enterprise will not provide for them, then the Government proposes to assist him to get the home financing he needs on terms equal to those afforded others.[147]

Nor was Cole shy about explaining precisely how he intended to use the government to further this goal, should the private sector fail to meet its obligation: up to this point, he explained, he resisted using his authority over Fannie Mae to intervene more directly in the minority lending business. For now, he was "giving private enterprise, through the Voluntary Home Mortgage Credit Program, the opportunity to show what it can do – what it will do for these families. But I cannot wait indefinitely."[148]

The Voluntary Home Mortgage Credit Program was significant insofar as it was the first time a public law expressly attempted to address racial exclusion. Previously, the federal government dealt with racial exclusion in housing through either the Supreme Court, agency-level directives, or ad hoc advisory committees. The VHMCP, on the other hand, recognized explicitly that minorities had difficulties accessing credit and devised a procedure to help ease those problems. By April 1955, more than seventeen hundred lending institutions had agreed to cooperate with the program.[149] Within four years, the program had insured forty thousand loans.

A final positive sign could be seen in the evolving relationship between civil rights groups and the housing industry. A Conference on Housing Discrimination was convened in Washington by HHFA Administrator Albert Cole in December 1954 (a few months after the Housing Act was signed) at the behest of civil rights groups.[150] The conference included forty representatives from real estate, housing, finance, insurance, civil rights groups, religious groups, public interest groups, and federal

---

[147] Ibid., 9.   [148] Ibid.

[149] Albert Cole, quoted in "1700 Concerns Join Housing Loan Program," *Los Angeles Times* (April 10, 1955), 21.

[150] Draft memo from Lester Granger to Dorothy Roseman et al., July 25, 1954, in NUL I: C12, Folder: Housing and Home Finance Agency; Memo to NCDH and Board and Cooperating Organizations Re: Confidential Summary of Washington Conference on Discrimination in Housing, January 1955. In NAACP II-A-385, Folder: Leagues: National Committee Against Discrimination in Housing, 1952–54.

housing agencies to discuss ways to expand housing opportunities for blacks.[151]

Yet despite the seemingly forward progress with agencies, there were limits to what these changes really could accomplish when it came to expanding homeownership opportunities on the ground. The information strategy helped remedy the knowledge gap, but ongoing monitoring after these ostensible private and legislative successes revealed less progress. In 1954, the Urban League found that minority and mixed-occupancy housing continued to be held to higher standards for mortgage financing: "This market is not considered on merit alone as other markets are considered, but is frequently required to supply additional information and qualifications to meet the doubts and hesitations of the mortgagee."[152] The report further noted that much of the reason for this had to do with the persistence of "age-old stereotypes of the occupations, income, education, and living habits and interests of Negro families" within different communities, despite activists' efforts to debunk such assumptions.[153] And while commending the FHA for its efforts to convince private providers that the black housing market was promising territory, the report noted that the FHA tended to rely on its small Racial Relations Service on racial issues, rather than commit all branches of the agency to expanding the housing opportunities available to blacks.[154]

The VHMCP, meanwhile, never lived up to its promise to African Americans searching for better access to mortgage finance. The 1959 Commission on Civil Rights Report revealed that only eight thousand of the program's loans went to African Americans in metropolitan areas; the overwhelming majority of loans instead went to white World War II veterans, using their GI Bill benefits.[155] Reflecting Cole's desire to increase minority housing options without requiring desegregation, the program could not address the root problems, chief among them the restricted housing supply for blacks, and might have even exacerbated those problems by allowing speculators to profit from the artificially low housing

[151] "Memo to NCDH and Board and Cooperating Organizations Re: Confidential Summary of Washington Conference on Discrimination in Housing."

[152] National Urban League, "Mortgage Financing for Properties Available to Negro Occupancy" (1954), in NAACP II-A-309, Folder: Housing – Federal Housing and Home Finance Agency, General.

[153] Ibid., 13.   [154] Ibid.

[155] Arnold Hirsch, "'The Last and Most Difficult Barrier': Segregation and Federal Housing Policy in the Eisenhower Administration, 1953–1960," Report Submitted to the Poverty & Race Research Action Council (March 2005), 57.

supply.[156] For all of Cole's warnings, the fact that the program "relied totally on the good faith of private lenders to make available additional mortgage funding" precluded it from addressing the fundamental problems of black housing exclusion.[157] The limits of this "good faith" strategy help to explain its only partial success and the necessity for civil rights organizations to advocate for policies with stronger enforcement mechanisms. Thus, the failures of this era – despite the success in recognizing the precise ways that government involvement in housing provision had also shaped patterns of racial exclusion – helped to set the stage for the next wave of activism that culminated in the Fair Housing Act of 1968, the Home Mortgage Disclosure Act of 1975, and the Community Reinvestment Act of 1976.

THE GOVERNMENT IS ONE OF AT THE BULWARK OF THE BLOCKADE

Taking stock of the successes and failures of advocates' equal housing opportunity efforts to date, a 1955 report by the American Friends Service Committee described the vast gulf in experience between black and white homeowners. "Every day Negroes buy used homes, often at inflated prices, and the white sellers go off to modern suburbs. Every day FHA and VA make final commitments for all-white developments. Every day more vacant land is used up for all-white housing."[158] These varied experiences, the report continued, constituted a "blockade of custom and code" – a term that had recently been used by the HHFA administrator. The report was direct in its indictment: "the government is one of the bulwarks of the blockade."[159]

By the time the American Friends Service Committee issued its report, fair housing advocates had already been engaged in a two-decade deliberate effort to discover, articulate, and render legible the various ways that federal government power had been used to constrain African American opportunities in the housing market. They made a case that racial exclusion was not purely an artifact of private market factors, but also due to political decisions that reverberated back into market practices.

---

[156] See King, *Separate and Unequal*, 192.
[157] Robert Burk, *The Eisenhower Administration and Black Civil Rights* (Knoxville: University of Tennessee Press, 1984), 118.
[158] American Friends Service Committee, "Equal Opportunity in Housing," 15–16.
[159] Ibid.

Civil rights groups made limited headway in contesting their constituents' status in the public–private welfare state for homeownership. They convinced the FHA to remove language condoning (and previously requiring) restrictive covenants and racial redlining, pressured the government to fortify its enforcement of antiredlining court decisions, collected and disseminated information to challenge market-based justifications for blacks' limited housing opportunities, and worked with businesses to both convince them of the opportunities of black housing and highlight the risks of ignoring them.

Previously, neither the FHA nor the private housing providers it interacted with acknowledged that African Americans' housing difficulties were generated by anything other than market forces and dynamics. Builders and mortgage bankers had attributed the lower homeownership rate to African Americans' lower incomes, while real estate agents attributed it to neighborhood resident preferences and fears about property values. Through the activities of organizations such as the NAACP and the National Urban League, government agencies had to confront the possibility that their policies, rather than simply harnessing or reflecting the power of the market, actually helped to constitute the market. Advocates argued that this obligated the federal government to ensure that neither the procedures of federal agencies nor the practices of the private providers they underwrote were discriminatory. This also made private providers who benefited from these indirect social programs vulnerable. Civil rights groups explicitly recognized these vulnerabilities, with the NAACP pointing out, for example, that the vulnerability of those in the housing market to legal attack "varies in proportion to the involvement of governmental aid or action." They further argued that banks in particular "may be vulnerable because of their relations with certain federal institutions, such as the Federal Deposit Insurance Corporation and the Federal Home Loan Bank Board."[160]

Far from submerging the state from public view and depoliticizing issues of access and exclusion, the delegation of an important facet of housing provision from the state to private providers opened up new front lines. Civil rights organizations were crucial to this process of discovery, and of contestation.

[160] "Racial Discrimination in Housing," n.d., 5, in NAACP II-B-130, Folder: Residential Segregation General, 1942–53.

5

Bankers in the Bedroom

> Nationwide, men and women today don't have equal access to credit. Banks, savings and loan associations, credit-card companies, finance companies, insurance companies, retail stores and even the federal government discriminate against women in extending credit.
>
> – Representative Martha Griffiths, 1972[1]

"Discrimination is a necessary function in the extension of credit to determine whether a person has the ability and willingness to repay the debt," wrote Arvonne Fraser in a letter to senators as they prepared to vote on a bill that would have outlawed sex discrimination in lending.[2] Fraser was the president of the Women's Equity Action League, which belonged to a larger coalition of women's and civil rights groups that had helped to lift the issue of sex discrimination in lending to the public agenda beginning in 1972. Their aim was to convince the government to extend the existing ban on mortgage discrimination by race, national origin, and color to cover marital status and sex as well, and for legislation that dealt with sex discrimination in consumer lending

---

[1] Rep. Martha W. Griffiths, testimony before the National Commission on Consumer Finance, "Hearing on Availability of Credit to Women," 5/22/72, in Archives II, RG 220 Records of Temporary Commissions, Records of the National Commission on Consumer Finance (hereafter NCCF), Box 35, 9.

[2] Arvonne Fraser, form letter to senators re: Fair Credit Billing Act, July 12, 1973, in Schlesinger Library, Records of the Women's Equity Action League MC 311 (hereafter WEAL), Carton 2, Folder 93.

generally. Another year would pass before the 1974 Housing and Community Development and Equal Credit Opportunity acts would accomplish these goals.

Reformers faced several challenges in introducing nondiscrimination policies into an industry that, by its nature, discriminates. By the 1970s, racial discrimination in home lending was often concealed and typically not codified, but lenders were direct and blatant about their need to hold female applicants to different standards than male applicants. For decades, lenders had maintained that such differential treatment was necessary to protect banks' financial interests – that differences between the sexes created valid concerns about default risk. The federal government largely agreed, with several agencies explicitly requiring banks whose loans they underwrote to hold female applicants to a different standard than male ones, and others implicitly condoning sex discrimination by their failure to regulate it.

Credit discrimination against women emerged in the national political agenda in the early 1970s. In a multistage model of collective action common to boundary groups – and evident in civil rights groups described in the previous chapter – feminist credit advocates and their allies played four roles. First, they collected women's individual experiences of lending discrimination and aggregated those individual (and private) difficulties into collective grievances. Once aware of discrimination as a collective experience, groups then advocated for, and conducted, more, and more systematic, research into the scope and nature of lending discrimination. They used this information to shed light on widespread practices as well as to build a case against discrimination. This information also helped them identify concrete practices by businesses and the government. Third, they engaged in multiple forms of contestation, including especially the articulation of a legal justification for government involvement in private lending decisions. They argued that in backing private lenders through the federal regulatory system, the federal government had not only the authority to require private sector lending businesses not to discriminate, but also a responsibility to enforce nondiscrimination. Fourth, groups presided over the removal of barriers in law and on the ground and continued to monitor the implementation of new laws to ensure that they were followed. These four stages again illustrate how political pathways become visible, and collective action unfolds, precisely *when* and because a service is delegated to the private sector and through the public-private welfare state.

WOMEN AND CREDIT IN THE CONSUMER REPUBLIC

By the 1970s, lenders viewed women as a particular credit risk for several reasons. They assumed that a woman's income was temporary and supplemental, liable to be interrupted by children and family obligations. This made lenders uneasy about counting the wife's income when calculating a household's loan eligibility, as least as long as she was of childbearing age. Often lenders would require assurance that there was minimal risk of pregnancy. This sometimes took the form of a "baby letter" (a term used within the banking industry), usually signed by the woman's doctor, attesting that she had either undergone a hysterectomy or was using an approved form of birth control.[3] In addition, lenders were often confused about what state laws allowed in terms of married women's property. The laws could be ambiguous about who was responsible for individual debts accumulated over the course of a marriage if the marriage were to dissolve. Consequently, some banks justified issuing credit in the husband's name only to secure their legal right to repayment. Moreover, bureaus often issued just one single credit report on married couples, with the wife's prior credit history subsumed into the husband's. If the couple divorced, the husband usually could still benefit from the credit history, while the wife would be left with none.[4,5] Many divorced women found that lacking a credit history made it impossible to qualify for any type of credit.

Finally, some lenders expressed concern about the fitness of a single (i.e., unmarried) woman to carry out the everyday maintenance tasks of homeownership necessary to preserve the house's value, and thus the bank's security if the loan should fail. A 1973 article in *Banking* explained:

[R]eal estate lending presents a special problem for women. Bankers, appraisers and others who deal with real estate know that from a practical viewpoint, "It's nice to have a man around the house."

The reason for this is that there is often a lot of heavy labor around a house – labor that a male head-of-family frequently does. If there is no male, the work

---

[3] The incidence of banks requiring baby letters is unknown, though the prevalence was well documented in congressional hearings, at National Commission on Consumer Finance hearings on women's credit availability, in complaints lodged with national women's organizations, and in surveys of lending institutions.

[4] See, for example, Margaret Gates, "Credit Discrimination against Women," 413–15.

[5] See, for example, Hyman, *Debtor's Nation*, 192–4; Emily Card, *Staying Solvent: A Comprehensive Guide to Equal Credit for Women* (New York: Holt, Rinehart and Winston, 1985), chap. 2.

must either be left undone or be done by professionals who charge for their services. In the first case, the property itself declines in value. In the second case, the owner's cash assets will be reduced. In either case, the woman involved finds her creditworthiness reduced.[6]

A decades-long history of mortgage underwriting codified similar biases against single men, who were viewed as less likely to maintain their obligations than married men. But when it came to other issues pertaining to repayment, single men did not receive the same scrutiny.[7] For instance, creditors did not require men to reapply for credit cards after they married, nor did credit bureaus erase a husband's prior credit history. While a husband generally would be expected to cosign on his wife's mortgage, the reverse was not always the case, nor was the wife's signature always required when jointly held property was disposed.[8] If a couple divorced, only the woman's credit standing was erased (this is even though a debt collector might pursue her to repay any outstanding debts, including those actually accumulated by her husband). While women might have their private lives scrutinized, a man with children was not automatically considered a credit risk, nor did lenders question his ability to "budget his income to pay the loan" on the chance he might have children in the future. And while women past childbearing age may have been required to document their infertility, "men of the same age who are higher health risks," according to a study on lending discrimination commissioned by the State of New York, were seldom asked to produce certification that they did not have any medical conditions that might impair their future ability to repay the debt.[9] Even proof of a husband's sterilization was often not considered sufficient assurance. One woman, upon asking whether her husband's vasectomy would qualify as proof of the couple's intention to remain childless, was told by her loan officer that such documentation would be insufficient, as "you could still get pregnant."[10]

---

[6] Richard M. M. McConnell, "Take a New Look at Women Borrowers," *Banking* (August 1973), 26–30, 72; 28.

[7] Hyman, *Debtor's Nation*, 195–6.

[8] Sharyn Campbell, Statement at CACSW October 1972 Meeting, Reel 6, Frame 145, CACSW.

[9] Nancy Russo, "Lessons in Applied Mythology: The Case of Women and Credit," October 1973, Report, 21, in Schlesinger Library, MC 477 Catherine East Papers (hereafter CE), Box 10, Folder 11.

[10] Letter to Carole De Saram, October 29, 1972, in Schlesinger Library Records of the National Organization for Women (hereafter NOW), Box 44, Folder 36.

This was not always the prevailing view. It is true that a number of factors constraining women's participation in the workforce and married women's ownership of property have long circumscribed equal access to housing and, relatedly, mortgage credit, but women's formal exclusion from credit markets is in some respects recent. After the first building and loan society decided to allow women members in 1840, women participated widely in this early and important lending institution. A federal survey conducted in 1893 found that out of 4,260 thrifts, only 27 had no female members. Industrywide, more than one-quarter of thrift members were female.[11] As David Mason describes, low monthly share payments enabled many to join to ensure their personal or family's financial security.[12] Women's participation was also critical to growing the movement, through both word of mouth and the promotion of thrift and personal morals in their children.[13] Even beyond the building and loans, there is little indication that a borrower's sex was a key consideration in loan eligibility.

Sex was less relevant in the early twentieth century, in part because of the shorter time horizon for loans and the high down payment requirements. In the mortgage lending environment of the early twentieth century, personal characteristics of an applicant were often secondary to his or her ability to amass a large down payment. With 50–60 percent equity in the house, the lender was already well protected from losses, since he or she could foreclose on the house and resell it if the borrower defaulted. (Obviously this did not function quite as anticipated during the Great Depression.) The federal mortgage programs that came out of the Great Depression required participants to offer much longer loan terms in comparison, with much lower down payments. Suddenly, these conditions made the riskiness of the borrower herself seem much more relevant to the safety of the loan.

These unprecedented changes in the contract structure were a challenge for FHA officials tasked to design evaluative criteria for the suitability of

---

[11] Mason, *From Building and Loans to Bail-Outs*, 29.

[12] As David Mason describes, "[i]n Massachusetts, where thrift share payments averaged just $1.25 per month, more than 12,000 women owned shares valued at $11.5 million. Most single female workers used their memberships to save for their well-being, while married women joined to have a financial cushion should their husbands lose their jobs, become disabled, or die. . . . Several states recognized these motives and allowed married women to hold accounts as individuals with ownership rights separate from their husbands." Mason, *From Building and Loan to Bail-Outs*, 32.

[13] Ibid., 30–1.

the borrower. For guidance, officials looked to the nascent consumer credit industry, which had already developed criteria to help determine which types of borrowers would be likely to repay or default. The FHA contracted with one of the major consumer finance associations to help develop its own borrower criteria. The resulting Factual Data Report advised lenders to hold women and single applicants to a stricter standard; for example, prompting lenders to inquire after a female applicant's husband or father to ascertain her credit risk.[14]

Through the 1950s, little had changed in how federal housing agencies treated female credit applicants. The FHA's 1955 *Underwriting Manual* advised underwriters to consider a working wife's "age, size of family, length of time employed, length of time employed since marriage, nature of the employment, training for the work, and whether her employment is definitely needed or required to meet the minimum living necessities of the family" to determine whether to count her income in the application.[15] In practice this tended to mean that women younger than thirty-two could expect their income to be fully ignored.[16] While the FHA left some discretion to the lender, the VA continued to categorically refuse to count any of a wife's income toward loan amounts – even for the few female veterans eligible for GI Bill benefits.[17]

Officials began to relax requirements on a wife's income in the mid-1960s. In 1968, the FHA revised its underwriting criteria, allowing lenders to count 100 percent of a wife's income if she worked, provided that she had a long enough work history and that her "income and motivating interest may normally be expected to continue throughout the early period of mortgage risk."[18] The FHA justified its shift in policy by explaining that so long as a couple could demonstrate the ability to repay their loan during the early years (considered the riskiest for lenders), the risk of their defaulting because the wife decided to have

---

[14] Stuart, *Discriminating Risk*, chap. 2.

[15] FHA, *Underwriting Manual* (1955), Sec. 1616.

[16] Testimony of Quinton Wells (Director of Office of Technical and Credit Standards, HUD), in National Commission of Consumer Finance, "Hearing on the Availability of Credit to Women," May 23, 1972, 89, in NARA, RG 220, Records of Temporary Commissions, Records of the National Commission on Consumer Finance (hereafter RG 220 NCCF), Box 35.

[17] See Lizabeth Cohen, *A Consumer's Republic: The Politics of Mass Consumption in Postwar America* (New York: Vintage Books, 2003), loc. 2597–2612, Kindle.

[18] FHA, *Underwriting Manual*, cited in US Commission on Civil Rights, "Mortgage Money: Who Gets It?" US Commission on Civil Rights Clearinghouse Publication No. 48, June 1974, 48.

children was minute enough to make discounting her income unneces-
sary.[19] That same year, the Veterans Administration circulated a directive
to its field offices to announce that it would begin to allow loan officers to
consider part of the wife's income when they determined a married
couple's eligibility.[20]

The agencies' shift in underwriting standards for women by the 1960s
was not unidirectional, and produced mixed results. In 1969, the FHA
fully counted a working wife's income in about 90 percent of the cases
where the wife worked – but its success on that dimension was marred by
the fact that it kept no data on approved loans, to say nothing of women's
accounts of being denied FHA loans from local lenders.[21] Positive trends
were also undercut by the vague and contradictory nature of the changes,
which confused both field office personnel and local lenders. For example,
a 1974 study by the US Commission on Civil Rights interviewed
mortgage brokers who still believed that the FHA required them to
discount 100 percent of the wife's income in their calculation of loan
eligibility. The study's authors noted that the brokers' belief "is not
groundless because the mortgage table on which many local brokers
and lenders rely states, incorrectly, that FHA will not count the income
of a wife under 32 years of age."[22]

Similarly, some speculated that the 1968 VA directive that allowed a
wife's income to be counted did more to exacerbate agency discrimination
by codifying it; in particular, by encouraging loan officers to require
couples to submit baby letters and refusing to count more than 50 percent
of a wife's income toward loan limits.[23] New bulletins circulated by the

---

[19] Recounting the change in policy, an FHA official stated: "The possibility of pregnancy is
no longer a concern of the FHA. There is a – obviously an element of risk involved; it's an
acceptable risk in our opinion, and the potential of pregnancy is something that the offices
are not to concern themselves with in any respect." Wells, testimony in NCCF, "Hearing
on the Availability of Credit to Women," May 23, 1972, 107.

[20] See Cohen, *A Consumer's Republic*, 2597–2612.

[21] Quoted in US Congress, House, Committee on the Judiciary, *Federal Government's Role
in the Achievement of Equal Opportunity in Housing: Hearings before the Civil Rights
Subcommittee of the Committee on the Judiciary*, 1971–2, 153; US Commission on Civil
Rights, "Mortgage Money," 48.

[22] US Commission on Civil Rights, "Mortgage Money," 48.

[23] The VA program did not have an underwriting manual to guide the lenders (as the FHA
program did). Instead, the national office would occasionally issue directives to local field
offices mentioning changes in broad policy, such as the change making it possible to
count a wife's income. This left local field offices with a great deal of discretion in deciding
whether to back a loan, and how large a loan they would be willing to back. It also meant
that mortgage brokers would make recommendations to couples to provide

agency did little to clarify the VA's position. A February 1973 VA bulletin advised loan officers to consider a wife's age, employment type, and family composition in order to decide how much (if any) of her income to count toward the loan, cryptically suggesting that baby letters, if "voluntarily submitted by the veteran to the lender ... cannot very well be refused upon receipt in the VA."[24] The CNPR argued that such language was so vague as to be "read as making VA policy even more stringent than before." The phrasing made it seem that the VA required assurances that the wife would work for the full term of the loan.[25]

Progress in women's access to mortgages was also undermined by the fact that most of the government agencies with some relationship to the mortgage market had issued no guidelines regarding sex discrimination by lenders. This included the Federal Deposit Insurance Corporation (FDIC), the Comptroller of Currency, the FHLBB, and Fannie Mae, which by 1968 was in the process of being privatized into a government-sponsored enterprise. In short, there was little indication of an inexorable shift toward greater lending openness for women, in part owing to the nature of the public–private system that channeled mortgages to citizens. For women's groups that were beginning to take notice of a sexual double standard in lending, the lack of any uniform progress across government agencies suggested that waiting for the problem to correct itself was not a viable option.

THE "GOLDEN AGE" OF FEMINIST ORGANIZING

Despite decades of open discrimination against women in lending, there had been no wide-scale effort to change this until the early 1970s. The timing was clearly tied to the rise of the second-wave feminist movement, which grew out of the rapid change in female labor force participation (doubling from about 20 percent in 1950 to 40 percent by the late 1960s), which was coupled with persistent workplace inequality, as well as changes in patterns of marriage, divorce, and family formation. Finally, both the success of the civil rights movement and the exclusion of women from leadership roles within it, despite the rhetoric of formal equality,

documentation based on what they thought would be necessary to get loans approved by their local VA branch, even in the absence of explicit directives.

[24] Veterans Administration, quoted in Card, *Staying Solvent*, 36.

[25] CNPR, "VA's Restrictive Credit Practices – Comparative Analysis with Policies of Other Federal Agencies" April 1973, in NCNW Series 34, Box 2, Folder 14.

combined with these factors to provide a "favorable context for the resurgence of feminism."[26]

Several national organizations developed units to focus specifically on women's credit discrimination issues. The most active was NOW (founded in 1966), which had grown to over eight hundred chapters across all fifty states by 1974. Through its National Task Force on Credit (which was led by Sharyn Campbell, whose own experience with credit denial opened this book), NOW raised awareness of women's credit exclusion at the federal level, called for hearings and regulatory changes, and later championed legislation to outlaw sex discrimination in lending. The National Task Force on Credit partnered with other women's and civil rights groups with an interest in credit discrimination, and also worked with independent local groups to convince state and local governments to pass their own laws against lending discrimination. By 1974, they had succeeded in about half the states. Also relatively new to the scene and active on women's credit issues was the Women's Equity Action League (WEAL), which was founded in 1968 as a less radical counterpart to NOW. Like NOW, WEAL also used its local branches to monitor lending discrimination, raise consciousness about the difficulties women faced in obtaining loans, and pressure state and local governments to legislate against credit discrimination.[27]

In addition to NOW and WEAL, the Women's Rights Project, established by the American Civil Liberties Union (ACLU) in 1972 and run by Ruth Bader Ginsburg (then a law professor at Rutgers), selected credit discrimination as one of its core issues.[28] The Center for Women's Policy Studies (CWPS), founded in March 1972 by a lawyer-and-economist duo, also worked on the issue. The center decided to focus on providing "the

---

[26] Joyce Gelb and Marian Lief Palley, *Women and Public Policies: Revised and Expanded Edition* (Princeton, NJ: Princeton University Press, 1987), 16.

[27] WEAL Credit Resolution, December 1972, 29, in MC 500 WEAL 21. Arvonne S. Fraser, "Insiders and Outsiders: Women in the Political Arena," in Irene Tinker (ed.), *Women in Washington: Advocates for Public Policy* (Beverly Hills, CA: Sage Publications, 1983), chap. 6, 123.

[28] Despite the Women's Rights Project's having only two paid staffers, its reach was to be amplified by the ACLU's national structure, allowing Ginsburg to reach out to liaisons virtually anywhere in the country to help "coordinate the nation-wide effort." As part of the nationwide effort, the project envisioned providing direct counsel and assistance to litigants, publishing informational pamphlets on women's rights, holding conferences and trainings, and keeping a catalog of laws pertaining to discrimination. See American Civil Liberties Union, "Prospectus for the Women's Rights Project," draft, October 1972, 2–4, in Library of Congress Manuscripts Division, Ruth Bader Ginsburg Papers, Box 11, Folder: ACLU File on Women's Rights Project, Prospectus.

instruments least available at that time to most women's organizations – namely, carefully prepared, technically sound, and sex-equitable program and policy proposals."[29] Reinforcing these advocacy groups' efforts was a network of federal commissions and committees, including the National Commission on Consumer Finance, the Citizens' Advisory Council on the Status of Women, and the US Commission on Civil Rights, as well as state commissions on civil and women's rights.

Clearly, by the early 1970s there had been marked growth in the advocacy environment, which encompassed new nongovernmental organizations and committees and commissions sponsored by federal, state, and local governments. Often in coordination, they were able to conduct research on the problem, apply public pressure on banks and regulators, raise public awareness of lending discrimination against women, and work through the legal process by petitioning regulators, filing suits, pushing for new laws, and promoting new ways to interpret existing laws to cover sex discrimination. Next, they had to make the issue more visible.

RAISING PUBLIC AWARENESS: THE NATIONAL COMMISSION ON CONSUMER FINANCE

The National Commission on Consumer Finance was an appealing stage to launch a public awareness campaign.[30] The bipartisan commission had been established as part of a law passed by Congress in 1968, and was tasked with investigating the rapidly changing field of consumer credit. From 1970 to 1972, the commission ran studies and held hearings on various topics, including interest rate ceilings and state usury laws, low-income access to credit, defaults, credit scoring, and revolving credit.

Women's access to credit was not initially on the agenda. In fact, the chapter devoted to women's credit discrimination looked out of place in the commission's final report, which dealt mostly with technical issues such as credit scoring and interest rate limits. But women's groups seized on the commission as an opening – albeit imperfect – to bring national attention to their grievances. The commission's executive director, Robert Meade, wrote to a fellow member that the "militant feminist wing has

---

[29] Chapman, "Policy Centers," 178.

[30] See also Hyman, *Debtor's Nation*; Hyman, "Ending Discrimination"; Lawrence Bowdish, *Invidious Distinctions: Credit Discrimination Against Women, 1960s-Present*, PhD Diss., The Ohio State University, 2016. Gunnar Trumbull, *Consumer Lending in France and America: Credit and Welfare* (New York: Cambridge University Press, 2014). chap. 8, for additional discussions of the National Committee on Consumer Finance hearings.

persuaded me that we might want to do more" and that the issue was likely to draw media attention.[31] One member of this "militant feminist wing," NOW, had helped introduce women's credit exclusion to the commission's agenda by directing its members to forward their complaints about unfair lending treatment to members of the commission.[32]

The commission agreed to hold two days of hearings to discuss women's credit discrimination in May 1972. It invited women, representatives of women's groups, and related civic groups to testify.[33] It also invited representatives from the credit industry to "give their side of the picture."[34] With little time to spare, NOW and WEAL mailed a joint letter to members asking for volunteers – separated, widowed, or divorced women – to help them conduct an audit of credit-granting institutions.[35] By this time, NOW had already begun collecting letters from women who had experienced credit discrimination, and planned to share them at the hearings.[36]

During two days of testimony, members of the NCCF listened as witnesses detailed their experiences with being refused credit (whether for a mortgage, car, or credit card), or asked to provide doctors' notes to certify that they were sterile, or ignored in a bank's assessment of household income because of their age. One witness shared a story from a woman in her thirties who, despite stable income, was unable to get a loan to buy a vacation house. Her fiancé easily obtained a loan for the same property, despite the fact that he had previously filed for bankruptcy.[37] Another witness recounted a letter from a working woman in her forties who was forced to ask her seventy-year-old pensioner father to cosign on a mortgage loan. For an issue that primarily affected the middle class and above, it surprisingly cut across many other dimensions: young

---

[31] Letter from Robert Meade, Executive Director, NCCF, to Hon. Lenor K. Sullivan, April 12, 1972, in NCCF, Records of the Executive Director, Box 8, Folder: Sullivan, Lenor K.

[32] Ira Milstein, testimony in NCCF, "Hearing on the Availability of Credit to Women," May 22, 1972.

[33] See also Hyman, *Debtor's Nation* Trumbull, *Consumer Credit*; Bowdish, *Invidious Distinctions*.

[34] Letter from Robert Meade to Timothy Colcord (National BankAmericard, Inc.) May 5, 1972, in NCCF, Box 12, Folder: Miscellaneous Correspondence – Hearing: Availability of Credit to Women – 5/22–23/72.

[35] Letter from Pat Massey and Barbara Key to NOW/WEAL Members, April 26, 1972, in NCCF, Box 12, Folder: Miscellaneous Correspondence – Hearing: Availability of Credit to Women – 5/22–23/72.

[36] Bowdish, Invidious Distinctions, 89–90.

[37] Betty Howard, in NCCF, "Hearing on the Availability of Credit to Women," May 22, 1972, 74.

newlyweds, middle-aged divorcees, high-income professionals, and even a committee member's own congressional staffer all complained of unfair treatment by lenders.[38]

NCCF witnesses also presented what limited statistical evidence they had to indicate discrimination and suggest that lenders were acting against their own economic interests by holding women to different standards. One study surveyed member banks of the Federal Home Loan Bank Board.[39] A witness representing savings associations described the results of a survey her organization had conducted of forty lenders, which found variation in the treatment of a wife's income.[40] These survey findings were debatable, but an audit of twenty-three lenders in St. Paul, Minnesota, that used equally qualified male and female applicants for a car loan showed irrefutably that lenders discriminated against women.[41]

For women's credit advocates, the National Commission on Consumer Finance hearings accomplished two goals. First, they brought public attention to issues that were previously individual and often deeply private.[42] Second, they convinced legislators that women faced real problems in credit markets that deserved further research. In the final report, the commission identified five problem areas pertaining to women and credit:

---

[38] One witness testified that during a break she stepped into a congressman's office. The front desk staffer, upon learning that she was testifying at the hearings, regaled her with her own experiences of lending discrimination when she needed to move to Washington, DC, for the job! Statement of Faith Seidenberg, in NCCF, "Hearing on the Availability of Credit to Women," May 22, 1972, 115.

[39] Howard, in NCCF, "Hearing on the Availability of Credit to Women," May 22, 1972, 74. Griffiths, in ibid.,16. For further discussion, see also Hyman, *Debtor's Nation*, 195–6.

[40] Jane Sullivan, in NCCF, "Hearing on the Availability of Credit to Women," May 23, 1972.

[41] Howard, in NCCF, "Hearing on the Availability of Credit to Women," May 22, 1972, 74. Griffiths, in ibid., 16. See also Hyman, *Debtor's Nation*, 195–6; Richard M. M. McConnell, "Take a New Look at Women Borrowers," 26–30, 72; 28.

[42] See Elizabeth Fowler, "'Personal Finance' Some Women Find Discrimination When Trying to Establish Credit," *The New York Times* (May 15, 1972), 53; Carole Shifrin, "Women Allege Credit Bias," *The Washington Post* (May 23, 1972), D7; Edward Rohrbach, "Women's Credit Woes Heard," *Chicago Tribune* (May 24, 1972), D4; Carole Shifrin, "Credit Institutions' Bias against Women Outlined," *The Washington Post* (June 4, 1972), E1; Edward Rohrbach, "Wife Tells Fight over Her Credit," *Chicago Tribune* (May 23, 1972), 19; James Hyatt, "No Account Females: Women Complain They Often Can't Get Credit Because of Their Sex," *The Wall Street Journal* (July 18, 1972), 1.

1. Single women have more trouble obtaining credit than single men. (This appeared to be more characteristic of mortgage credit than of consumer credit.)
2. Creditors generally require a woman upon marriage to reapply for credit, usually in her husband's name. Similar reapplication is not asked of men when they marry.
3. Creditors are often unwilling to extend credit to a married woman in her own name.
4. Creditors are often unwilling to count the wife's income when a married couple applies for credit.
5. Women who are divorced or widowed have trouble re-establishing credit. Women who are separated have a particularly difficult time, since the accounts may still be in the husband's name.[43]

The commission's conclusions conveyed factors that had affected women for years (in some cases decades), yet had not been articulated so clearly and publicly. These findings showed that the issues had been recognized by a government committee, and they became talking points over the next few years. Major newspapers publicized them, congressional hearings cited them, and women's groups used them in their pamphlets and literature.

The final report stopped short of recommending federal legislation, one of the objectives of the women's groups, as this was beyond the tasks and purview of the deliberative commission.[44] Nevertheless, lenders' testimonies on the second day, and several questions asked by commission members, highlighted the potential complexities of legislating away the problem. The biggest concern was that legislation might not give banks the flexibility they needed to make sound lending decisions.

Testifying on behalf of the American Security and Trust Company, Joseph Barr argued that banks would not discriminate against good credit risks, as "profit is still a more powerful motive than discrimination, especially in public institutions" – a common refrain in the banking industry.[45] Banks, it stood to reason, were only doing what was necessary to ensure that their loans were repaid. Others agreed. The president of the

---

[43] Report of the National Commission on Consumer Finance, quoted in Margaret Gates, "Credit Discrimination against Women," 411.

[44] US National Commission on Consumer Finance, *Consumer Credit in the United States* (Washington, DC: Government Printing Office, 1972), 152–3.

[45] Joseph Barr, testimony in NCCF, "Hearing on the Availability of Credit to Women, May 23, 1972," 61.

National League of Insured Savings Associations, Jane Sullivan, testified that some practices might appear discriminatory but reflect sound business practices, given that "it's necessary for a savings and loan association to come out in the black at the end of the year or it wouldn't be in existence."[46] Savings and loans could not afford to take bad risks and were operating accordingly, Sullivan explained:

If we have a young couple and they have been married perhaps a year or two, have saved up enough money for a down payment on a house, we ask them very pointedly, do you expect to have children, do you expect to stay home and take care of them? If she expects to stay home and take care of them, obviously, the money is not going to be there to make the mortgage payments and pay the taxes. If she intends to continue working, we might give her income a 100 percent credit. It's so personal in those instances as to the situation of each of those couples that it's very, very difficult to lay them down in a across the board rule.[47]

In sum, while it was clear that lenders regularly treated women differently in matters of lending, many within the industry believed that they were acting according to a sound economic rationale.[48] To be sure, there were also members of the industry, including the president of the United State Buildings and Loans League, who believed that lenders' practices reflected outdated thinking that was unlikely to be dislodged without new regulations.[49] But if experts in the industry were not uniformly convinced that they were undermining their economic self-interest by applying a double standard, then it would be difficult to make a case that the government should outlaw behavior intended to protect lenders from risk. At the close of the hearings, one of the commission members remarked, "I hope that the industry listens to those hearings and listens to the women and responds. I think the response is also better if it comes from the industry, in response to needs, than if it comes as a result of some legislation."[50]

Chief among their main achievements, the National Commission on Consumer Finance's hearings exposed problems that theretofore had been experienced privately. Lenders at the time were not required to disclose their reasons for refusing a loan. If a married couple's loan was approved, they often had no way of discovering just how much of the wife's income

[46] Jane Sullivan, testimony in NCCF, "Hearing on the Availability of Credit to Women," May 23, 1972, 163.

[47] Ibid., 164.   [48] See also Bowdish, *Invidious Distinctions*, 10.

[49] John Farry, testimony in NCCF, "Hearing on the Availability of Credit to Women," May 23, 1972, 77.

[50] Johnson, in NCCF, "Hearing on the Availability of Credit to Women," May 23, 1972, 168.

was counted toward the loan. Moreover, the sensitivity of the request that women provide documentation of their fertility may have deterred banks from publicizing the requirement.[51] Finally, as the testimony of banking representatives at the NCCF hearings revealed, there was no clear consensus as to whether holding women to a different standard constituted unfair discrimination, or a sound risk assessment.

Although interpretations of the practice varied, the differential treatment between men's and women's income was now out in the open. That this took so long is partly explained by the difficulty of transforming individual instances of credit exclusion, whether warranted or not, into collective problems that require political solutions. In its final report, the NCCF noted that the extensive publicity around the hearings had itself prompted many lenders to reexamine their policies toward women, and had also awakened them to the possibility that competitor firms that responded more effectively to women's credit complaints might draw business away from them.[52]

OUTREACH THROUGH WOMEN'S MAGAZINES

"One person cannot do it alone – I am confident that your organization will help the less powerful independent gripers unite into a strong lobby,"[53] a woman who had experienced credit difficulties wrote to NOW. After the National Commission on Consumer Finance hearings, NOW reached out to more of these "independent gripers," within and beyond their own membership, to collect individual experiences of credit market exclusion and aggregate them into broader collective patterns. NOW collaborated with women's interest magazines to publish articles about lending discrimination against women. Between 1972 and 1975, at least a half-dozen magazines, including *McCall's, Ladies Home Journal,*

---

[51] In fact, one woman enclosed in her letter to NOW her correspondence with her lender. She had agreed to provide a baby letter with her mortgage application, but after including it wrote to her loan officer to express how uncomfortable and humiliating she had found this requirement. The loan officer responded with an apology and offered to remove the letter from her file.

[52] National Commission on Consumer Finance, *Report of the Commission, Consumer Credit in the United States* (Washington, DC: Government Printing Office, 1972), 153.

[53] Letter to Carole De Saram (NOW), October 26, 1972, in NOW, Box 45, Folder 12.

Family Circle, House Beautiful, Woman's Day, and *Ms.,* had published articles on the topic. The articles suggested that women write to the director of NOW's Task Force on Credit about their own experiences.

Nearly three thousand letters poured in to the Credit Task Force. They documented experiences of unfair credit discrimination, and many letter-writers mentioned that they were inspired to write to NOW after reading one of the magazine articles.[54] Though outnumbered by complaints about credit cards and retail credit, mortgage lending drew a sizeable share of criticism. One woman wrote that she had supplied the majority of the down payment for her and her fiancé's house, but found that the deed listed only him as the owner.[55] A young married woman from New Jersey described applying for a home loan as "the most frustrating and unfair experience of my life." She was "laughed at for thinking I could include my income as surety for a loan" and "told I would have to show written proof from a doctor that I was on birth control pills and written proof from my employer that I would be hired if I became pregnant to the REAL ESTATE AGENT before he would show us any homes!"[56] Many others described that banks required similar letters, or even a or surgeon's letter to certify that an applicant had undergone a hysterectomy, before they could get a loan.[57]

Several women who wrote to NOW about mortgage difficulties specifically targeted the FHA and the VA. The most vivid complaint came from a magazine editor working in Washington, DC, named Carole Lewicke.[58] Lewicke earned twice as much as her husband, Martin, and was furious that after four months of pursuing a loan through the VA, the loan officer only agreed to the loan after she and her husband produced signed affidavits that she would have an immediate abortion if she were to become pregnant, and that her husband would undergo a vasectomy if she ever quit using birth control.[59] "The whole thing was just unreal," she

[54] The figure of three thousand comes from Bowdish, *Invidious Distinctions,* 89.

[55] Letter to Carole De Saram, November 16, 1972, in NOW, Box 44, Folder 39.

[56] Letter to Carole De Saram, November 13, 1972, in NOW, Box 45, Folder 6. See also Trumbull, *Consumer Credit,* chap. 8, which also the contents of several of these letters.

[57] For example, Letters to Carole De Saram (October 21, 1972), in NOW, Box 45, Folder 16, and NOW Box 45, Folder 17.

[58] See also Trumbull, *Consumer Credit,* chap. 8 for a discussion of this case.

[59] According to Sharyn Campbell's account of the Lewicke's story, the husband called the regional VA to confirm that they needed to produce these documents, and the regional office advised him to do whatever the mortgage broker asked. Campbell, "CACSW October 1972 Meeting," 155.

said. "I didn't believe that something like this could happen in this country."[60] After the loan was approved, she went public with this information. She forwarded the documentation to her congressional representatives, had her friends and family members do the same, and took her case to *The Washington Post* and women's groups, including NOW and the Women's Legal Defense Fund.

When asked about the case, the couple's VA loan officer admitted that he had received the letters, but contended that he had requested only a doctor's certification that she was using birth control and had fertility problems. He claimed that Lewicke herself had suggested the additional documents. ("I've just about had it with Mrs. Lewicke and her emotional problems," he said to *The Washington Post*.[61]) The loan officer explained that his only concern was that her income would be a "normal and continuing part of the family income." In the same conversation, the lender maintained, "We are in the business to lend money at a profit," and said that if the couple ever had children, "the husband does not go home and take care of the children ... if her income stopped, they would not be able to make payments."[62] NOW and other supporters of nondiscrimination laws often pointed to this case as an extreme example of lending double standards.[63]

Women's credit advocates also used Lewicke's case to call out the government's role in the perpetuation of discrimination. Sharyn Campbell, at the time the head of the Women's Legal Defense Fund's Credit Counseling Project, called this

one of the few cases that I have ever come across where we have had direct government complicity with the request of a private lender for what – if there were a right for privacy then this is clearly an invasion of it, but unfortunately we are left with a situation where there is not a thing that we can do at the moment. There is no cause of redress, no litigation, we have no established right of privacy for most intent and purpose.[64]

Several of the women who wrote in to document their difficulties getting FHA and VA loans emphasized the role of the state, and not just private lenders, in their frustration and exclusion. One woman from Delaware

---

[60] Jay Mathews, "Wife Says Loan Tied to No-Child Vow," *The Washington Post* (February 24, 1973), A1. Letter to Amy Scupi, August 1, 1972, in NOW, Box 45, Folder 19.

[61] Mathews, "Wife Says Loan Tied to No-Child Vow." However, Campbell, in her statement to the CACSW in October 1972, did mention that she had received a copy of the request from the mortgage company representative asking for those items. Campbell, "CACSW October 1972 Meeting," 154.

[62] Matthews, "Wife Says Loan Tied to No-Child Vow."

[63] Campbell, "CACSW October 1972 Meeting," 154.   [64] Ibid., 155.

disapproved that "the State of Delaware or the Government of the United States would be a party to such an oppression; that the prospects of homeownership for us rest on my sterilization."[65]

Some women gave up on federally insured loans altogether after deciding that the requirements were too onerous or realizing that an undercount of their income would result in a loan that was too low to make homeownership realistic.[66] Those who looked toward conventional (not FHA- or VA-backed) lenders often did so at higher cost. For some, the experience of being denied an affordable, federally backed loan warmed them to the women's movement. After learning that her age would disqualify her salary from counting toward an FHA loan, a young woman from Ohio wrote, "This seems unfair to me. I don't agree with everything Women's Lib dictates but I'm beginning to see the light."[67]

In addition to encouraging women to contribute to an ever-growing archive of anecdotal evidence that could be used in future hearings and court cases, articles in women's magazines also explained how to identify whether they, too, might have been discriminated against, and provided advice on how to proceed. An editorial published in the November 1972 issue of *Glamour*, entitled "You Won't Get CREDIT for Being a Woman," is a typical example. The editorial outlined the problems that women faced in getting credit, and lenders' typical response of blaming these problems on the different earning profiles of women and men. A bank executive explained, "It is impossible ... to put a man and a woman on the same level completely as far as extending credit is concerned."[68] Yet, as the editorial pointed out, lenders had no statistical evidence to back their claims. NOW recommended that women who believed they had been unfairly discriminated against send complaints to their banks and request a reversal in the decision, and also consider discussing possible legal actions with NOW representatives. "If you threaten a bank with publicity," a NOW representative said, "it'll often come across. ... Banks respond to pressure."[69]

National organizations hoped to find instances that could be used as court challenges, and instructed local leaders to refer those cases to the

[65] Letter to Carole De Saram, October 29, 1972, in NOW, Box 44, Folder 36.
[66] For example, Letter to NOW, February 1, 1973, in NOW, Box 45, Folder 5; letter to NOW, May 20, 1972, in NOW, Box 45, Folder 12; and letter to NOW, October 19, 1972, in NOW, Box 45, Folder 19.
[67] Letter to NOW, October 24, 1972, in NOW Box 45, Folder 12.
[68] "You Won't Get Credit for Being a Woman," *Glamour* (November 1972), 64.
[69] Carole De Saram, in ibid., 64.

ACLU or the Women's Legal Defense Fund. Although NOW and WEAL disseminated information about the types of action to take, including boycotts, pickets, and divestment from discriminatory lenders, it is unclear whether local branches followed this guidance. More often, local groups played an advisory role for women who had been victims of lending discrimination, helping them navigate with their banks and providing customizable form letters. Some of the work provided valuable, hands-on experience and information: WEAL officials wrote to their local branches, "The only way we can learn how to deal with credit discrimination is by trial and error and profiting from each other's experiences."[70]

BRIDGING THE CREDIBILITY GAP

Vivid illustrations of discrimination in letters to NOW, *Ms.*, and other venues could help mobilize support in congressional hearings and public relations campaigns. However, without better and less anecdotal evidence, it would be difficult to make a case that these practices were widespread, and that lenders actually were discriminating on the basis of sex. Advocacy groups desperately wanted this more reliable data, as did state-level human rights commissions and the dozen or so state legislators who wrote to NOW and WEAL officials to get more information.

In the 1970s, a hybrid network developed of government committees and agencies, nongovernmental organizations, and individual researchers who shared information and collaborated on surveys and strategies.[71] These groups, once they became expert on the issues, also consulted with government agencies about potential solutions, including new regulations.[72] CWPS became a particularly important resource for the movement, as did the Center for National Policy Review (CNPR), which was founded in 1970 by a former NAACP Legal Defense Fund lawyer and civil rights activist, Bill Taylor. Their operating budgets came largely from foundations and nonprofits, both receiving grants from the Ford Foundation, CWPS also receiving seed money from Ralph Nader's Public Citizen,

---

[70] Memo from Paula Latimer and Pat Massey to WEAL Presidents and Conveners, Members and Other Interested Women, June 1973, in MC 500 WEAL, Box 77, Folder 52.

[71] Center for Women Policy Studies, n.d., "Sex Discrimination in Credit Practices," MC 311 WEAL, Carton 3, Folder 178.

[72] Letter from Margaret Gates and Jane Roberts, February 1975, in CE, Box 10, Folder 41.

and CNPR receiving support from the Catholic University of America Law School.[73]

Together, the two centers played an auxiliary role for the more activist organizations by conducting research into existing laws and their implementation. They would then provide that information to women's organizations, state and local policy-makers, and federal policy-makers, in addition to reaching out to government agencies directly. In 1972, CNPR produced a detailed memo that delved into the minutiae of existing housing and bank agency policies, identifying language that explicitly prevented women from accessing credit and implicitly constrained them.

While the precise methods were different, this network of organizations came to fill a similar set of roles as the civil rights organizations did to root out anti-black housing market discrimination, identifying specific forms of housing discrimination and explicitly linking them to the public-private structure of housing provision, which in turn implicated the government. In addition to collaborating, these organizations kept in close contact to avoid duplicating their efforts and shared best practices on things such as surveys and letter templates. Finally, the network made it possible to share information across agencies with different areas of specialization; for example, forwarding the legal defense groups individual complaints that might make for good court cases.

By 1974, advocates had coalesced around several basic findings. First, they had found substantial evidence of lender discrimination. Unlike in the case of African Americans, where discrimination was subtle and often concealed, lenders openly conceded that they used separate procedures to evaluate the creditworthiness of men and women. A 1972 NOW audit of New York area lending institutions found that, of 180 applications from women across three lending institutions, only five of their mortgages were approved.[74] One woman who was turned down was a widower with children and a guaranteed income. She reported that the loan officer had said to her, "What does a woman need a house for?"[75]

Lender surveys revealed the same pattern. One study, conducted by the Federal Home Loan Bank Board, found that only 22 percent of savings and loan institutions surveyed would count 100 percent of the income of a hypothetical wife with two school-age children and a stable, full-time job as a secretary. Twenty-six percent of savings and loans responded that they would count up to half of her income, and 25 percent stated that they

---

[73] Chapman, "Policy Centers," 178–9.
[74] NOW New York Credit Survey 1972, in NOW, Box 45, Folder 31.   [75] Ibid.

would count none.[76] In another survey, conducted by the United States Savings and Loans League of 421 members (together making up 25 percent of the combined assets of all savings and loans), nearly 72 percent reported that they would ignore all or part of the wife's income, and 61 percent reported that they took marital status into account when making their decisions.[77] The survey also showed that 73 percent of lenders believed that lending policies toward women had liberalized in recent years, and 62 percent did not "foresee any [further] liberalization of loan standards for women" in the future.[78]

Second, advocates underscored that there was very little evidence at all that women were a worse credit risk than men. Instead, the limited evidence available suggested that women posed a similar, or in some cases lower, risk than men. For example, a 1964 study found that women were more likely than men with the same marital status to keep their credit accounts in good standing.[79] An even earlier study, from 1941, looked specifically at mortgages and found that women were a better risk than men, and that two-earner families defaulted at lower rates than families with only one breadwinner.[80] Sensitive to the problem that earlier studies only examined the outcomes of borrowers who made it through the application process (and not those filtered out along the way), activists also pointed to two studies that could apply to women more broadly. The first was conducted by an organization that provided home improvement loans to elderly and low-income households, many of which were headed by single women. A study of the program found that female-headed households had a delinquency rate of 2 percent, while the overall delinquency rate was 4 percent. Another study, conducted by two researchers

---

[76] The remaining one-fourth did not provide an answer. Russo, "Lessons in Applied Mythology," 5–6.

[77] Perhaps tellingly, the nonresponse rate was 21 percent for the question on counting a wife's income, compared to 1 percent for the other questions. Given the wording of the question, Russo interpreted it to mean that a large proportion of the respondents did not consider it applicable to themselves, since they categorically excluded a wife's income. United States Savings and Loan League, "Survey on Credit to Women," May 1972, Reel 12 beginning at Frame 38, in CACSW. For further discussion, see statement of John P. Farry (President, US Savings and Loan League), in NCCF, "Hearing on the Availability of Credit to Women," May 23, 1972, 73–4; Russo, "Lessons in Applied Mythology," 6.

[78] United States Savings and Loan League, "Survey on Credit to Women."

[79] Paul Smith, "Measuring Risk on Installment Credit," *Management Science* 2 (1964), 327–40; David Durand, *Risk Elements in Consumer Installment Financing* (New York: National Bureau of Economic Research, 1941).

[80] Center for Women Policy Studies, "Sex Discrimination in Credit Practices."

from CWPS, examined only banks that had a history of lending to women and men on similar terms, and found no evidence that women were a worse credit risk than men. Instead, the evidence pointed to key explanatory variables for risk that had to do with the "characteristics of the loan itself (i.e., the terms of the financing, particularly the loan to value ratio, the presence of junior financing and loan purpose), rather than the characteristics of the borrower."[81]

In making the case that there was no economic justification for holding women to separate standards, advocates also produced evidence that cast doubt on past assumptions about women's marriage, family, and career trajectories. They refuted the axiom that marriage increased credit risk. If a woman married, that potentially increased the total income to support any outstanding debts, especially if her spouse earned more than she did. Advocates also pointed to a 1964 study conducted by the US Savings and Loan League for evidence that two-income families were less likely to be delinquent than single-income ones.[82] Women's advocates also challenged the assumption that women would leave the workforce after having children, pointing to the eightfold increase in working mothers since 1940. Reflecting on these findings and related ones, the NOW manual stated:

The morbid preoccupation of creditors with pregnancy is certainly outmoded. . . . In the cases where both incomes are necessary to maintain mortgage payments, if the couple still decides that the wife should terminate her income-producing employment, it is more likely that the couple would sell their home than leave themselves in a position of having insufficient funds to make the mortgage payments. We have yet to hear of a foreclosure caused by a pregnancy.[83]

Finally, casting doubt on the assertion that women were more prone to quitting their jobs than men, advocates presented evidence from the Department of Labor that labor turnover was influenced less by sex and more by characteristics of the job itself, the age of the worker, and the worker's length of service.[84]

---

[81] Russo, "Lessons in Applied Mythology," 3–5.

[82] Statement of William L. Taylor before the Federal Deposit Insurance Corporation, December 1972, in the Matter of Fair Housing Lending practices, Notice of Proposed Rule Making, 37 Federal Register 19385, 4, in Library of Congress, Records of the Center for National Policy Review (hereafter CNPR), Box 59, Folder: Fair Housing – Lending Practices, Federal Deposit Insurance Corp. 1972–6.

[83] NOW, "Women and Credit," 3. This "morbid preoccupation" comment is also discussed in Trumbull, *Consumer Credit*, 88.

[84] Russo, "Lessons in Applied Mythology," 17–20.

These activities were significant because they cut to the quick of lenders' justifications for holding female credit applicants to separate standards. So long as lenders could assert that female lending was inherently risky to the banks' business model, it would be difficult for women to argue not only that banks should go against their own interests, but also that the government should play a role in ensuring that banks did not discriminate against female applicants. Yet, as women's credit movement advocates showed, this argument was based on a number of unfounded assumptions about the risk of family formation to a woman's future income, as well as a presumed but untested relationship between gender and repayment prospects. These assumptions underlay decades of practice, professional training, and government policy. The end result was to show that lending discrimination was widespread, while simultaneously casting doubt on economic rationales for its continuation. All of this helped to address the "credibility gap" that women's credit advocates had worried about, and left lenders vulnerable to the charge that their policy toward women was "an erratic science, but often irrational."[85]

CONTESTING MARKET-BASED EXPLANATIONS

The information gathered by women's credit advocates was an important tool to contest business practices on multiple fronts. National organizations disseminated their findings to local women's groups along with instructions for what to do if a woman believed a lender was discriminating. Both NOW and the Women's Equity Action League developed credit kits for their local branches, with advice on how to identify potential discriminatory practices and distinguish lending discrimination on the basis of sex from lending discrimination based on a reasonable assessment of risk (for example, if the applicant's income was unstable). They also contained examples of studies that other branches and groups had conducted in their own areas, on which branches could model their own larger-scale studies of local lending practices.[86]

Credit kits contained materials to help women who were victims of lending discrimination, including form letters they could use to file

---

[85] Lenor Sullivan, testimony in NCCF, "Hearing on the Availability of Credit to Women," May 23, 1972, 4. On the credibility gap, see Campbell, testimony in "October 1972 Meeting," CACSW.

[86] Memo from Paula Latimer and Pat Massey to WEAL Presidents and Conveners, Members and Other Interested Women, June 1973.

complaints with creditors and credit bureaus. For example, the NOW Credit Manual included fictional correspondence between a female loan applicant and her creditor (a man by the name of "A. Jirk") that women could adapt to their own circumstances.[87] Lastly, NOW provided instructions through its credit kits for local leaders on how to "keep the issue in the public eye."[88] The organization recommended that local task forces team up with other local women's groups to threaten discriminatory banks with bad publicity; wage local publicity campaigns in newspapers and magazines and on radio; collect, organize, and document lending problems in their communities, including loan applications, newspaper articles, written complaints, and so on; and research the existing city, state, and federal laws to more effectively target their actions and advice.[89]

When those tactics were too blunt, activists went through other channels to contest boundaries to women's access. Where regulators failed to act or were proposing new potentially discriminatory rules, groups under the leadership of the CNPR banded together to petition agencies for rule changes, deploying data they had collected to challenge earlier assumptions and arguments. They also brought in outside reinforcement. In 1972, CNPR presented the Federal Home Loan Bank Board with a statement signed by 180 economists across the political spectrum as well as five previous chairmen of the Council of Economic Advisers.[90] The letter echoed the movement's claim that sex (and indeed all "nonfinancial") discrimination was based on faulty assumptions and economically unsound, and, as such, the FHLBB must prohibit the practice among its member banks

in order to fulfill the mandate of your agency to prevent member institutions from carrying out a home finance policy that is inconsistent with "sound and economical home financing." Arbitrary exclusion of persons who have the economic

---

[87] National Organization for Women, "Women and Credit," January 1973, 4–10, in NOW, Box 209, Folder 40.

[88] Memo from Paula Latimer and Pat Massey to WEAL Presidents and Conveners, Members and Other Interested Women, June 1973.

[89] "Now Task Force on Credit," November 1973, in NOW, Box 30, Folder 59.

[90] Form Letter from Samuel Gubins (Director of Research, CNPR), March 10, 1972, in CNPR, Box 59, Folder: Fair Housing – Lending Practices, FHLBB 1972.; American Friends Service Committee et al., Petition before the FDIC in the Matter of Fair Housing Lending Practices, 37 Federal Register No. 183, 19385, November 1, 1972, 7, in CNPR, Box 59, Folder: Fair Housing-Lending Practices, Federal Deposit Insurance Corp. 1972–76.

capacity to participate in the market place [*sic*] is a distortion of our economic system and can not be considered "sound and economical home financing."[91]

The signatories further argued that the costs of discrimination fell not only to prospective borrowers, but also to businesses that missed out on potential profits. The economists excoriated the use of any underwriting criteria "which are not justifiable by business considerations ... and which have a discriminatory impact on various segments of the population."[92] In short, they argued that regulators must act, because otherwise they would be allowing their members to engage in unsound practices, in defiance of their public mandates.

Advocates extended this reasoning to argue that *banks* (not just regulators) also had an obligation not to discriminate against women, lest they, too, violate their regulatory obligations. Advocates echoed the "financial soundness" arguments made about regulators, but extended them to the lender level: "It cannot be considered sound business for a bank to arbitrarily limit its market and deny itself potentially profitable loans," remarked one of the CNPR directors during FDIC hearings in late 1972.[93] In this and other instances, advocates cited social and community obligations imposed on banks by regulators.[94] Beyond the language of the Housing Act of 1949 and the Fair Housing Act of 1968, advocates scrutinized banking industry regulations and argued, for example, that Section 6 of the FDIC Act required the agency to consider the "convenience and needs of the community to be served by the bank." A "bank which thwarts national housing goals by discriminating against women clearly can not rank high on its servicing of the 'needs of the community.'"[95]

A final set of justifications enlisted banks' social obligations, whether to serve their own communities or the general public fairly. For instance, advocates highlighted that women were excluded from benefits that had no equivalent in the private lending sector. As Sharyn Campbell noted:

If you are entitled to a VA mortgage, it is a better mortgage than a conventional mortgage. The buyer is protected, you get a lower interest rate and there is no

---

[91] Statement of Economists, n.d. (but appended as part of March 10, 1972, letter from Samuel Gubins), in CNPR, Box 59, Folder: Fair Housing – Lending Practices, FHLBB 1972.

[92] Ibid.

[93] Statement of William L. Taylor before the Federal Deposit Insurance Corporation, December 1972, 13.

[94] Ibid.   [95] Ibid.

reason not to take advantage of every benefit that the government offers you if you have served in the Armed forces. But yet there are people who will not bother, now, to apply for a VA mortgage because they don't want to be subjected to this sort of humiliation and I know that I regret having done it.[96]

In short, the objection to private discrimination drew explicitly on the indirect nature of the federal government's support for banks. This avenue of political opportunity was created by the hybrid welfare state for housing that had been set into motion in the 1930s. Contra the submerged state scholarship, women's groups both identified the role of the state in shaping national housing opportunities and argued that this role had also obligated private banks not to discriminate.[97]

Federal housing and banking agencies defended themselves by saying that they had no legal authority to sanction private lenders for their behavior in the absence of positive discrimination to outlaw sex discrimination. Advocates disagreed. In response to the agencies, feminist credit advocates drew on the language of the Housing Act of 1949 and the Fair Housing Act of 1968. They argued that these existing laws and related regulations already authorized the federal government to ensure that private banks did not discriminate. Moreover, they interpreted the laws as also requiring that the federal government not be a party to sex discrimination – even when such discrimination was carried out by private providers and not directly by federal agencies. During NCCF hearings in 1972, Representative Martha Griffiths, a Democrat from Michigan, argued:

Federal agencies having duties with respect to housing are required by law to act so as to further this goal. Mortgage lenders who unfairly discount the income of a working wife are wrongly denying that wife and her family a home. Yet federal agencies have not tried to prevent this kind of discrimination. The Federal Government backs every mortgage, and the Federal Government should not back mortgages where the lender discriminates on the basis of sex.[98]

Invoking the language of the Housing Act, Griffiths argued that the FHA "not only could correct it, they have been obligated to correct it since 1949."[99] The Fair Housing Act outlawed private discrimination in "federally related" mortgage lending on the basis of race, ethnicity, and

---

[96] Campbell, "October 1972 Meeting," 174.
[97] Statement of William L. Taylor before the Federal Deposit Insurance Corporation, December 1972, 14.
[98] Griffiths, testimony in "Hearing on Availability of Credit to Women," May 22, 1972.
[99] Ibid., 28–9.

national origin to establish that Congress did have the authority to legislate on private sector discrimination.[100]

In sum, proponents of a federal solution took as a starting point the notion that the government conferred benefits on private financial institutions through the FHLBB, the FDIC, the Federal Reserve Board, and the Comptroller of Currency. Consequently, the federal government had not only the authority to direct lenders whom they indirectly supported not to discriminate, but also the responsibility to enforce compliance, and the ability to do so by the removal of benefits.[101] The chairman of the US Commission on Civil Rights, Arthur Fleming, testified in a hearing on credit discrimination that the commission

> has concluded that Federal regulatory agencies are under a constitutional obligation to assure nondiscrimination by those they regulate even where there is no statutory requirement. ... We believe, based on our analysis, that the regulatory agencies are so intimately involved in the practices of the private entities within their jurisdiction that their supervisory, regulatory responsibilities bring such practices within the scope of the fifth amendment.[102]

The argument that the government had an obligation to ensure nondiscrimination only had teeth insofar as there was some corresponding

[100] Statement of William L. Taylor before the Federal Deposit Insurance Corporation, December 1972, 14. In making this argument, women's credit advocates also tried to argue that the designation of women as a protected class by the 1964 Civil Rights Act should have also carried over to the 1968 act. Some tried to link credit to employment as part of the justification, arguing that the denial of credit also made it impossible for women to open businesses or buy franchises, "or do any of the things men freely do." See Litwiller, testimony in NCCF, "Hearing on Availability of Credit to Women," May 22, 1972, 63. Finally, others pointed to the recent Supreme Court decision in *Reed v. Reed*, which interpreted the Fourteenth Amendment as also applicable to sex discrimination. American Friends Service Committee et al., "Petition before the FDIC in the Matter of Fair Housing Lending Practices," 37 Federal Register No. 183, 19385, November 1, 1972, 7, in CNPR, Box 59, Folder: Fair Housing-Lending Practices, Federal Deposit Insurance Corp. 1972–76.

[101] Testifying on behalf of CNPR, Steven Rohde said: "Finally, there already exists a federal regulatory structure with the potential for effectively eliminating the problem. However, these agencies, the Federal Home Loan Bank Board, the Federal Deposit Insurance Corporation, the Comptroller of the Currency, and the Federal Reserve have thus far been unwilling to exercise the authority they have to deal with the problem; despite the weight of opinion from public interest groups and the economics profession." Steven Rohde, testimony in NCCF, "Hearing on Availability of Credit to Women," May 22, 1972, 161–2.

[102] Statement of Arthur Fleming, in US Congress, House, Committee on Banking and Currency, *Credit Discrimination Part I: Hearings before the Subcommittee on Consumer Affairs of the Committee on Banking and Currency*, 93rd Cong., 2nd sess., 1974, 135.

enforcement mechanism. Continuing, Fleming argued that regulatory agencies had a constitutional obligation to withdraw the benefits they conferred on private providers, for example federal insurance of deposits, if those providers engaged in discrimination on the basis of "race, color, national origin, religion, sex or marital status. If it does not then the regulatory agency may be participating in and perpetuating discrimination."[103]

ADMINISTRATIVE LOBBYING: THE CNPR CHALLENGES FANNIE MAE

Women's groups drew from all of these arguments to appeal to businesses, state and local governments, and the federal government to change professional norms, business practices, and the laws that governed women's access to credit. Even before the National Commission on Consumer Finance hearings raised the issue in the public consciousness, they saw some important victories. Since 1970, the Center for National Policy Review (CNPR) had been working behind the scenes to challenge "agencies responsible for federal housing credit policy," including the Federal Reserve, the FDIC, the Comptroller of Currency, the FHLBB, the VA, and Fannie Mae, to issue fair lending criteria (on behalf of women and minorities).[104] The CNPR had a multipronged strategy with agencies to focus on enforcing – and extending the interpretation of – existing laws, rather than pushing for new legislation. To do this, it would litigate, apply pressure from other groups and the public, and lodge formal petitions.[105]

---

[103] Ibid., 136.

[104] Memo from Sam Gubins to Bill Taylor, Glenda Sloane, Steve Rohde, and Edgar Feingold, Re: Equal Opportunity for Home Ownership and Federal Credit Policies, a proposed report from the center, May 15, 1972, in CNPR Box 59, Folder: Fair Housing-Lending Practices Reports of Banking Agencies, 1972, 1.

[105] At the time, and especially before the equal credit for women movement took off following the NCCF hearings, the CNPR was virtually the only organization to advocate on behalf of citizens for fair bank regulations. In a letter between two CNPR officials, one remarked that "with the exception of Nader's organization, we seem to be the only public interest organization that has been making a concerted effort with the banking agencies. (The lack of public interest involvement in the home finance area was typified by the hearings last fall on the FHLBB's major new reform proposal, the 'Housing Institutions Modernization Act.' The hearings were dominated entirely by government officials and industry representatives, with no public interest representation.)" Letter from Steve Rohde to Bill Taylor, May 10, 1972, 1, and memo from Sam Gubins to Bill Taylor, Glenda Sloane, Steve Rohde, and Edgar Feingold, Re: Equal Opportunity for

In 1970, Fannie Mae proposed new rules that would have (among other things) not counted income from paid overtime, bonuses, or part-time work, and counted only up to 50 percent of the wife's income. Adding to the complexity of the situation, since 1968, Fannie Mae was no longer a fully public agency, but had been transferred to private ownership and existed in the regulatory netherworld of the "government-sponsored enterprise." Moreover, Fannie Mae was proposing to purchase mortgages from private banks that specifically were not insured by the government, non-FHA and non-VA loans.[106] Testifying on behalf of the Center for National Policy Research, Steven Rohde noted that its members were "horrified" upon reading the new guidelines at the government legitimation of the practice and expressed concern "about the psychological impact on lending institutions of a quasi-government agency putting its stamp of approval on such a discriminatory policy."[107]

In response, the CNPR organized thirty organizations representing racial minorities, labor, consumers, senior citizens, and women to mobilize against the provisions. In a petition drafted by the center, the signatories complained that Fannie Mae's proposed guidelines "flagrantly discriminate against members of minority groups, blue collar workers, families with working women, and senior citizens. If allowed to go into go into effect in their present form ... the guidelines threaten to make it difficult or impossible for many of the people in these groups to obtain conventional mortgages."[108]

Home Ownership and Federal Credit Policies, a proposed report from the center, May 15, 1972, both in CNPR Box 59, Folder: Fair Housing-Lending Practices Reports of Banking Agencies, 1972.

[106] Rohde, NCCF "Hearing on Availability of Credit to Women," May 22, 1972, 171–2.

[107] Ibid.

[108] "Organizations Issuing Joint Statement in Opposition to FNMA's Guidelines Restricting Mortgage Credit" (October 4, 1971), reprinted in US Congress, House, Committee on the Judiciary, *Federal Government's Role in the Achievement of Equal Opportunity in Housing: Hearings before the Civil Rights Oversight Subcommittee of the Committee on the Judiciary*, 1974, 152. The signatories included Ralph Nader's Public Interest Research Group, the AFL-CIO, the United Auto Workers, the NAACP, the Southern Christian Leadership Council, NOW, the National Council of Senior Citizens, the National Retired Teachers Association, the American Association of Retired Persons, the National Council on the Aging, the League of Women Voters, the National Urban Coalition, the Congress of Italian American Organizations, the New York Project, the National Center for Urban Ethnic Affairs, the Center for National Policy Review, the National Council of Churches, the Housing Opportunities Council of Metropolitan Washington, the NAACP Legal Defense and Education Fund, the Mexican American Legal Defense and Education Fund, the Puerto Rican Legal Defense Fund, the Suburban Action Institute, the Center for Community Change, the Nonprofit Housing Center,

In the letter, the organizations demanded that Fannie Mae recall and redraft the guidelines so "that they are fair to all citizens."[109] In making its case, the coalition appealed to the idea that government agencies should not be allowed to encourage or legitimize private sector discrimination. "FNMA's status as a quasi-public agency," the coalition argued, "cannot be used to shield it from its public responsibility. It is answerable for what it does, and we mean to hold FNMA accountable for its lack of concern for the public interest."[110]

The coalition also sent its complaint to HUD Secretary George Romney, requesting that the agency withhold Fannie Mae's permission "to enter the secondary market until the guidelines are purged of their discriminatory provisions." It asked the agency to use "the one effective sanction it possesses – the authority under title VI of the Civil Rights Act – to terminate Federal assistance to members who discriminate."[111]

The strategy worked, for the most part. Not only did Fannie Mae remove the language that restricted the wife's income, to allow full consideration of both incomes, it went further by prohibiting sex discrimination.[112] To address any troubling gap between policy and implementation, Fannie Mae cooperated with public interest groups to explain the new guidelines during twenty-four public meetings nationwide.[113] The Federal Home Loan Mortgage Corporation (created in 1970 to expand the secondary market), in the midst of issuing new underwriting criteria, took note of the developments at Fannie Mae and decided preemptively to bring CNPR and its coalition partners on board. It invited them to a series of meetings and included them as they designed new underwriting criteria.[114]

Although they counted Fannie Mae and Freddie Mac (as the Federal Home Loan Mortgage Corporation became known) as successes, activists also came up against the limits of the agency's strategy several times,

Westchester Residential Opportunities, Inc., the Potomac Institute, the National Association of Real Estate Brokers (an organization of African American real estate agents, not to be confused with the National Association of Real Estate Boards), the National Tenants Organization, the National Committee Against Discrimination in Housing, and the Citizen's Advocate Center.

[109] Rohde, in NCCF, "Hearing on Availability of Credit to Women," May 22, 1972, 152
[110] Ibid., 154   [111] Ibid., 155
[112] Statement of William L. Taylor before the Federal Deposit Insurance Corporation, December 1972.
[113] Rohde, in NCCF, "Hearing on Availability of Credit to Women," May 22, 1972, 174–5.
[114] Ibid., 173–4.

because other regulators, including the Federal Reserve Board, the FDIC, and the FHLBB, resisted their efforts. Typically, these resistant agencies retorted that in the absence of clear congressional legislation, they did not need to (and were unable to) adopt the groups' nondiscrimination policies.

CONGRESSIONAL ACTION FOR WOMEN'S CREDIT EQUALITY

Just as the National Commission for Consumer Finance hearings were under way in May 1972, New York Representative Bella Abzug introduced legislation to outlaw sex discrimination in lending, with more than a hundred cosponsors.[115] Nothing came of Abzug's bills that year, but in the wake of the hearings, momentum for sex discrimination legislation rapidly picked up. In 1973 and 1974, Congress introduced and debated dozens of bills relating to women and credit. "In the 22 years I have served in the Congress, I have seldom seen an issue take fire as quickly as this issue of discrimination in extensions of credit by reason of sex or marital status," remarked Representative Lenor Sullivan during a hearing in 1974.[116]

Several factors explain why the issue was able to take off so quickly. Feminist efforts on the Equal Rights Amendment (ERA) had helped to propel the movement's legitimacy in Washington. Members of Congress were beginning to see the potential electoral benefits of taking on a "women's issue," particularly one less divisive than abortion and less controversial than the ERA.[117] Members of Congress wanted to be able to sign on to an issue that furthered women's equality – this particular issue resonated with wide swaths of the public and did not overly challenge women's social standing. Credit in particular was a politically advantageous issue, since it required no outlay of public funds: it was easy for legislators to support, particularly in the run-up to midterm elections.[118]

In 1974, spurred by the failure to get any legislation through Congress the previous year, groups including NOW, WEAL, the General Federation of Women's Clubs, and the National Council of Jewish Women recruited women from their member lists to flood their representatives' offices with letters and telegrams in support of the legislation.[119]

---

[115] Gelb and Palley, *Women and Public Policies*, 70.
[116] Lenor Sullivan, testimony in US Congress, House, Committee on Banking and Currency, *Credit Discrimination Part 1*, 16.
[117] Marilyn Bender, "Women Equality Groups Fighting Credit Barriers," *The New York Times* (May 25, 1973), 1.
[118] Gelb and Palley, *Women and Public Policies*, 69.
[119] Chapman, "Policy Centers," 181; Gelb and Palley, *Women and Public Policies*, 69–73.

Related to this, the issue also had widespread appeal and strong bipartisan support. Tennessee Republican William Brock became an early supporter of equal credit legislation, after having been a member of the NCCF. Brock used his position on the Senate Banking Committee to champion the issue. (Brock's legislative assistant, Emily Card, had been informed that Abzug's efforts in 1972 had largely failed because she was not a member of the relevant committee. Speaking to a bureaucrat from the FDIC about the possibility of sex discrimination legislation in 1973, the bureaucrat suggested to Card, "You, on the other hand, are in the right kind of office."[120])

In 1974, women's credit advocates secured two important policy victories. First, the Housing and Community Development Act of 1974 contained an amendment to the Fair Housing Act of 1968, prohibiting discrimination on the basis of sex from any housing "program or activity funded in whole or in part with Federal financial assistance."[121] Sponsored by Senator Brock, the amendment contained language that targeted members of the private housing industry (including bankers and builders) that received government support in the form of loan insurance or preferential interest rates. Second, women's groups secured the passage of the Equal Credit Opportunity Act (ECOA), which outlawed lending discrimination across all types of consumer credit. Though the ECOA was targeted primarily at lending institutions that fell outside the purview of the Fair Housing Act (in particular, those concerned with credit cards), it also charged federal regulators who oversaw housing finance institutions with the responsibility of enforcing banks' compliance with the new laws. This included the Federal Reserve Board, the Federal Home Loan Bank Board, the FDIC, and the Federal Savings and Loan Insurance Corporation, in addition to eight other regulators. This was useful for the feminist credit movement, since the Fair Housing Act alone had weak enforcement provisions. The ECOA, on the other hand, contained language to enforce provisions through individual legal action.[122]

Together, the two laws meant that lenders were no longer allowed to discount any of a woman's income, request credit information from a

---

[120] Card, *Staying Solvent*, 30.
[121] "Housing and Community Development Act of 1974," 24 CFR 6, Title I Section 109, online at http://portal.hud.gov/hudportal/HUD?src=/program_offices/fair_housing_equal_opp/FHLaws/109.
[122] Chapman, "Policy Centers," 182.

spouse as part of an application unless he was specifically liable for the credit, or discourage qualified borrowers from applying on the basis of sex.[123]

MOBILIZATION AFTER THE EQUAL CREDIT OPPORTUNITY ACT

One of the most important changes in the political climate from 1973 to 1974 seems to have been the relative complacency of private lenders and banking regulators. While neither had exactly warmed to the issue, both began to fear the public backlash of going on the record as being against women's credit equality.[124] Some lenders also began to suspect that in the long term it might be profitable to expand their markets to the women left out.[125] "No one said outright, 'We don't want women to have equal credit,'" explained Card, the legislative aide behind Brock's ECOA, "but they mustered seemingly logical, rational, and legalistic arguments to resist change."[126] By 1974, then, bankers seemed resigned to the fact that some legislation on the issue would eventually pass Congress and withdrew their earlier resistance. Beyond the apparent inevitability of sex discrimination legislation (after all, nearly two dozen bills had been introduced over this two-year period), members of the lending industry might have calculated that they were more likely to be successful at the rulemaking stage. There, they would be able to draw from their strong ties to the Federal Reserve (the agency tasked to write the regulations needed to implement the ECOA) to try to influence implementation of the policy.

They might have also expected the women's credit movement to have waned by that point, satisfied that it had secured a policy victory. Social movement scholarship has suggested the social movements are more influential at earlier stages in the policy-making process – say, agenda-setting – than later on, when the institutional constraints increase along with the number of interested parties. Administrative venues are considered to be particularly challenging for advocacy organizations, historically viewed as being biased toward business interests with greater technical expertise, money, and organizational capacity.[127] Moreover, theories of protest cycles posit that social movements will be unable to maintain their momentum for a sustained period of time. Eventually, participants lose interest or turn toward new and pressing issues.

[123] Jay Lamont, "Dwellings: The Landlady," *Philadelphia* 69 (May 1978), 213–14, 213.
[124] Gelb and Palley, *Women and Public Policies*, 69.   [125] Ibid., 70.
[126] Card, *Staying Solvent*, 43.   [127] Gelb and Palley, *Women and Public Policies*, 77–8.

And the movement did lose some of the support structure that had helped to bolster the legislative momentum in 1973 and 1974. "Some of the women's groups just dropped off the vine after the law passed," explained Jane Chapman, a cofounder of the CWPS.[128] But not all did.

Contrary to industry expectations, the rulemaking featured a back-and-forth between the Fed's traditional banking constituency and the newly empowered voice of feminist and consumer advocates, most centrally NOW and CWPS, the latter of which the Fed also invited to help draft regulations. If lenders expected to throw their muscle during the rulemaking process, they may have been surprised by NOW's and CWPS's decisions to linger awhile, and their growing strength to counterbalance them during negotiations. The CWPS and NOW had a surprising amount of technical expertise for nonindustry actors trained in law and economics, and many with experience in government. Possessing this technical expertise meant that in the context of rulemaking, they were able to offer the Fed detailed and specific comments "couched in the appropriate professional jargon."[129] The remaining feminist advocates also, by this time, had developed countless "contacts with government due to their experiences with the passage of ERA and other legislation."[130] Finally, CWPS in particular benefited from the move from legislation to administration. The organization's 501(c)(3) status had prevented it from taking an active role in legislative lobbying, due to IRS restrictions. But those restrictions did not apply to administrative lobbying. CWPS took advantage of this.[131]

Thus, even while some advocates exited after legislation was passed, enough advocates remained and devoted considerable time to the rulemaking process, issuing point-by-point memos about the Federal Reserve's proposed rules, identifying where they thought the rules succeeded and where they thought the Fed needed to adopt stronger or more specific language.

By and large, NOW and CWPS were satisfied with the general direction of the Fed's first draft of the ECOA regulations, issued in April 1975, though they highlighted specific problems that they thought ought to be addressed. Responding to the Fed's preliminary provision to require lenders to maintain two years of records, CWPS noted that this would

---

[128] Flora Davis, *Moving the Mountain: The Women's Movement in America since 1960* (New York: Simon & Schuster, 1991), 150.
[129] Gelb and Palley, *Women and Public Policies*, 78.   [130] Ibid.
[131] Davis, *Moving the Mountain*, 150; Chapman, "Policy Centers," 182–3.

create problems in monitoring lenders' compliance with the new rules. CWPS also pointed out the general lack of monitoring mechanisms across the agencies charged with enforcing the new law.[132]

CWPS and others noted proposed rules that seemed to promote gender discrimination, albeit sometimes unintentionally. For example, while approving the Fed's draft requirement that no numerical value be assigned to sex or marital status in credit scoring plans, it critiqued the regulations for being silent on other indicators that often had a tacit discriminatory impact. For instance, some credit scoring plans assigned points to applicants who had telephone service in their own name. This could put married women at a disadvantage, because the phone would likely be in their husband's name. A practice of assigning points to specific job titles, regardless of income, also seemed problematic: "The concentration of women in certain occupations is a function of employment discrimination, past and present, and of society's expectations of women," argued a memo dissecting the rule. "It is not a reflection of the dependability or financial responsibility of women credit applicants."[133] Yet many of these issues were considered minor oversights to be corrected.

Women's groups and the banking industry experienced the most conflict over Regulation B, a provision pertaining to disclosure of the reasons for credit denial. The ECOA required some sort of written disclosure, but banks claimed that the high cost of complying with written disclosure would simply be passed on to consumers. Banks instead preferred rules stipulating that applicants must first request disclosure. Women's organizations countered that it was crucial that applicants *automatically* receive a written explanation as to why their application had been rejected; otherwise, they maintained, it would be difficult for many applicants to know whether their rejection was legitimate or potentially discriminatory. The first draft of regulations released by the Fed came down on the banks' side. The CWPS and NOW argued that this was inadequate and pushed for automatic disclosure in the revised rules.

With the organizations seemingly satisfied with their participation in the early rounds of rulemaking and related hearings, "additional hurdles"

---

[132] Center for Women Policy Studies, "Comments on Proposed Regulations for the Equal Credit Opportunity Act" n.d., in Northwestern University Specially Collections, Papers of Karen DeCrow (hereafter KDC), Folder: Equal Credit Opportunity Act, 1975–2008, 3.

[133] Ibid., 4.

appeared when a new round of revised rules were issued in September 1975. Rather than revise the rules closer to what women's organizations wanted, banks apparently worked behind the scenes to weaken the regulation further, fully removing any reference to disclosure in the new rules. These revisions also quietly lifted the prohibition against lenders asking applicants about their childbearing intentions.[134]

"In retrospect," wrote CWPS's Chapman, "it seems that the first regulation may have influenced the activist groups, including CWPS, to neglect the second round."[135] These moves by the Fed – and the stealth tactics by which they transpired – spurred NOW, CWPS, and other allies to swift action. In a complaint to the Federal Reserve's Board of Governors dated September 11, Margaret Gates of the CWPS wrote:

We feel you have responded to the complaints of financial institutions and businesses which were made known to you by many highly paid, experienced lobbyists and other representatives of the industry whose daily presence at Reserve Board headquarters is a known fact. Many of their complaints essentially protest the very existence of the act. Turning from Congress to the Federal Reserve Board, the industry has tried to weaken and erode the fundamental protections legislated by Congress in the ECOA, a process which you have abetted. ... Admittedly, women's organizations and public interest groups are not the traditional constituency of the Federal Reserve Board, but we represent the people whose interests Congress determined to protect when it passed ECOA. We are outraged at the ease with which you have ignored our rights and our numbers. In our attempts to represent the interests of millions of American women, we cannot boast of unlimited resources. But we will make it clear that these women are a new constituency for which you have accepted responsibility before Congress and whom you have then, in our opinion, betrayed.[136]

The head of NOW's National Credit Task Force, Linda Cohen, responded to the proposed revisions by contacting female members of Congress the day after the regulations were issued. If left unchanged, NOW contended, the regulations "would destroy the opportunity of equal access to credit for millions of women for whom you guaranteed this equal opportunity." NOW compelled a dozen female members of Congress to meet with Federal Reserve Chairman Arthur Burns.[137] To Burns, Cohen also sent her own telegram, castigating him for his "sell-out to the banking hierarchy" and notifying him and the rest of the governors

---

[134] Chapman, "Policy Centers," 183.   [135] Ibid., 183–4.
[136] Reprinted in Chapman, "Policy Centers," 184.
[137] Karen DeCrow, Letter to Female Congress Members, September 9, 1975, in Schlesinger Library, Cynthia Harrison Papers (hereafter CH), Box 1, Folder 13.

that "the feminist movement will not permit the rich and powerful institutions of our society to dominate the regulatory process."[138] Meanwhile, advocacy groups also reached out to their members to flood the Federal Reserve with written complaints, and to inspire sympathetic coverage. After this effort, women's groups managed to win back some of the provisions they had lost in the September regulations. A new Regulation B was formally issued on October 16, 1975, though the issue of automatic written disclosure was not resolved in the advocates' favor until 1977.[139]

Advocates' activities with the Fed were particularly noteworthy, because they helped in several ways to redefine the relationship of the Fed to consumer groups more broadly. In their dealings, advocates came to understand the Fed's disappointing response to their demands in the rulemaking phase as a function of the new expectations ECOA had placed on the agency. Historically, the Fed's responsibilities were confined to understanding the effects of various policy actions on banking, finance, and the economy. Yet ECOA added a new mandate to that list, essentially making the Fed responsible for consumer protection. In several regards, the Fed was genuinely caught off-guard by being required, almost overnight and with no prior experience, to consider consumer interests. To be sure, women's credit advocates found allies within the Fed who both desired "to change the board's image with regard to emerging issues, such as consumer rights," and understood that advancing consumer and women's rights would pose basic challenges to the way that the Fed had fundamentally operated in the past. The fact that the Fed formally contracted with the CWPS (an unusual move at the time) spoke to the sympathy at least some in the agency had toward the feminist credit movement.[140] Yet, the challenges of this dual mandate still became evident during the rulemaking process, when the Fed was faced with competing demands from banking and women's advocates and competing justifications based on incommensurable metrics for why each group should prevail. The more precise budgetary analyses provided by banks was, some reasoned, more persuasive to the Fed than the more amorphous social benefits described by the ECOA advocate.[141]

In these issues, NOW and CWPS decided to intervene by filling in informational gaps, persuading the Fed to think differently about

[138] Karen DeCrow, telegram to Chairman Arthur Burns, September 8, 1975, in CH, Box 1, Folder 13.
[139] Chapman, "Policy Centers," 184.
[140] Chapman, "Policy Centers," 182–3; Gelb and Palley, *Women and Public Policies*, 80–1.
[141] Testimony of NOW before Senate Committee on Banking, Housing, and Urban Affairs, July 28, 1976, in CH, Box 1, Folder 13.

consumer issues, helping to counter what they viewed as a clear resource imbalance between creditor and consumer in their respective capacities to affect government policy and implementation.

In the ensuing years, CWPS, NOW, and CNPR (the organization that had helped to intervene with Fannie Mae in the early 1970s) all played a role in monitoring how the ECOA was enforced (or not) across regulatory agencies and lending institutions. They also worked with government agencies to publicize new credit rights to consumers, a task that broadened after their success with the ECOA became the model used by senior citizens, civil rights groups, and (unsuccessfully) welfare recipients, to extend the act's original reach beyond sex discrimination.[142] With HUD sponsorship, the National Council of Negro Women also took the National Commission on Consumer Finance model national, holding fact-finding hearings in six cities. Altogether, more than a hundred national women's organizations joined in the project.[143] And the CNPR continued its own pattern of filing suit against administrative agencies to get them to enforce the new laws, securing agreements among three federal banking agencies for "the collection and analysis of race and sex data on mortgage applications, enhancing examiner training and improving examination methods, refining complaint handling procedures, and appointing policy and supervisory level civil rights personnel."[144]

Finally, the movement for access to credit permeated popular culture. NOW President Karen DeCrow's correspondence with a writer for *All in the Family* were incorporated into an episode of the show, "Edith Versus the Bank," in which Archie refuses to loan Edith $500 and she confronts him. "I think this is one of the funniest we've done this [sic] far," noted the writer in a letter to DeCrow.[145] Emily Card, a legislative aide to

---

[142] See, for example, letter from Linda Cohen (NOW Credit Committee) to John Heimann (Comptroller of Currency), January 20, 1978, in CH, Box 1, Folder 13.

[143] "Hearing Book, Women and Housing, Atlanta Georgia," November 8, 1974, in National Archives for Black Women's History, Papers of the National Council of Negro Women (hereafter NCNW), Series 34, Box 1, Folder 1.

[144] Center for National Policy Review, "Proposal for Monitoring Federal Civil Rights Enforcement [draft]," Attachment to letter from William L. Taylor to Harry Dodds, September 21, 1978, 18, in CNPR, Box 30, Folder: 1978 – Ford: Monitor/Civil Rights/Funding-Projects.

[145] David Latt to Karen DeCrow, October 26, 1978; in KDC, Folder: Correspondence from David Latt Re: All in the Family (1978). In an earlier letter, Latt writes: "Thanks for your help. I think the best story materials are in areas we don't want to go into – simply because we don't want Archie and Edith to get divorced. I'm still hoping that we get one out of consumer credit." (Latt to DeCrow, September 28, 1978, in ibid.).

Senator William Brock, who had written much of the ECOA, went on to work for HUD and produced a comprehensive review of ECOA and Fair Housing Act compliance and shortcomings across the many agencies involved in administration of the laws. Eventually she left to found the Women's Credit Project at the University of Southern California and the Women's Credit and Finance Project at Harvard. She would go on to host a television program in the 1980s and write a regular column in *Ms.* magazine, both aimed at improving women's access to credit.[146]

MAKING SEX DISCRIMINATION LEGIBLE

"Before the campaign began," Flora Davis writes, "most Americans weren't even aware that women had difficulty getting credit. Those who were turned down often assumed it was their own personal problem."[147] This sentiment changed quickly after the NCCF hearings were held in May 1972. In 1974, the Virginia Slims American Women's Survey added a question about women's credit discrimination that it continued to ask periodically (in the first survey, 56 percent of women believed that sex discrimination in credit and mortgage lending was a problem).[148]

The success in issue definition cannot be understood apart from the efforts NOW, WEAL, CWPS, and their government and grassroots allies expended to bring the issue onto the political agenda and to tear through the economic and political arguments that had previously allowed sex discrimination to occur unnoticed and unchallenged. This newfound concern over an issue that had previously gone unnoticed is a testament to the success of the women's credit movement in using the media and grassroots organizations to publicize the issue, using the different levers of government available to them to move the issue further through the policy process, and monitoring it. "Without the input of women activists

---

[146] Emily Card, "Women and Mortgage Credit: An Annotated Bibliography," US Department of Housing and Urban Development Office of Policy Development and Research, March 1979; Emily Card, "Women and Mortgage Credit Project Agency Enforcement and Impact Evaluation," US Department of Housing and Urban Development, Office of Policy Development and Research Report No. HUD-001715, January 1979. Janice Mall, "Emily Card Continues Credit Crusade," *Los Angeles Times* (May 19, 1985).

[147] Davis, *Moving the Mountain*, 148.

[148] In Gelb and Palley, *Women and Public Policies*, 64.

pushing for credit reform," remarked a member of Congress, "there would be no Equal Credit Opportunity Act."[149]

The feminist credit movement was not just about collectivizing the problem and raising it onto the agenda. Fundamentally, it also consisted of a process of actively making sex discrimination in mortgage lending – and credit more broadly – into an issue that was caused and shaped by the state, and therefore remediable by the state. Memos detailing precisely how government housing agencies both explicitly required and implicitly condoned discrimination helped to accomplish this, as did the rhetorical strategies employed by women's groups and their allies. Through their actions, sex discrimination was moved from the realm of private and individual to collective and state-sponsored.

Other factors also shaped the success of the feminist credit movement. Drawing from the lessons of the Civil Rights Movement, women's credit advocates pursued their goals through a coalition of organizations, each focused on different a part of the policy process. There were NOW and WEAL, which worked to publicize issues and lobby member of Congress; CWPS and CNPR, which performed research functions; and the traditional grassroots women's organizations, whose presence was not as constant, but whose members could be called upon to pressure their congressional representatives at opportune times.[150]

Feminist credit advocates also kept the scope of the issue narrow, framing it as "a role equity issue" that "threatened no fundamental values."[151] Though advocates were concerned about discrimination on the basis of sex *and* marital status, they were willing to compromise if it would help them achieve their goals. Feminist credit advocates accepted the amendment of the Fair Housing Act to include only a ban on sex discrimination (and not on marital status) out of this spirit of compromise. Sex discrimination already fit the logic of how the Fair Housing Act was structured. Marital status discrimination did not, so out it went (it would be included in the ECOA). During the rulemaking process for the ECOA, feminist credit advocates were relatively receptive to the concerns of industry and were willing to compromise – in fact, this created some internal tension in the movement. NOW President Karen DeCrow and NOW Credit Task Force President Susan Onaitis became embroiled in a heated battle over DeCrow's dissatisfaction with what she felt was an overconciliatory view of the industry's demands without enough input from the rest

---

[149] Ibid., 63.   [150] Ibid., 61–2.   [151] Ibid.

of the group. But for the most part, the narrow targeting of the issue and their willingness to compromise likely allowed it to take off quickly.

This narrow strategy also prompted a range of responses, from silence to defensiveness, when issues of race or class were broached. For the most part, feminist credit advocates made their claims on the back of a model upper-middle-class professional woman who should have been qualified on the basis of income alone, and who was clearly disqualified on the basis of her sex. (The question of whether women's unpaid labor should still qualify them for credit was noted, and deliberately set aside.) This upper-middle-class professional woman was also assumed to be white. When asked whether they wanted to join forces with a broader coalition interested in legislation to prohibit racial discrimination in mortgages and consumer credit, members of the feminist credit movement declined, preferring to keep the ECOA focused narrowly on sex discrimination. They cited the fact that the NCCF, which had spurred interest in sex discrimination, had not been able to "find clear-cut proof of racial discrimination other than for mortgage credit," and worried that adding a racial discrimination provision to the bill would divert attention to "discussing race discrimination in mortgage credit, which was already covered in the Fair Housing Act."[152]

Feminist credit advocates were particularly uneasy where race met class. Testifying at the National Commission on Consumer Finance's 1972 hearings on credit, Representative Martha Griffiths of Michigan complained that the "right of a woman on welfare with illegitimate children to buy housing under Section 235 of the Housing Act makes a mockery of the same Housing Act to guarantee a middle class woman the same right to buy a house."[153] She was referring to a program that had been introduced as part of the 1968 Housing Act. That program explicitly targeted very-low-income households in urban areas historically cut off from FHA housing support. Within two years, Section 235 had been mired in scandal and was considered a failure. Clearly the movement preferred to keep its distance from controversial issues such as Section 235.

Yet these class and race differences also predicted access to credit, and these often intersected with gender, creating particularly thorny challenges for activists pushing for more inclusive homeownership policies. The next chapter details these challenges, and the development of a set of strategies to address the housing problems of households that, beyond being largely black and often female-headed, were also poor.

---

[152] Card, *Staying Solvent*, 41.
[153] Martha Griffiths, in NCCF, "Hearing on Availability of Credit to Women," May 22, 1972, 19.

6

From Public Housing to Homeownership

Unita Blackwell first became involved in politics in June 1964, after some organizers from the Student Nonviolent Coordinating Committee (SNCC) came into town looking for black volunteers to register to vote. "I was thirty-one years old, stuck in poverty, and trapped by the color of my skin on a rough road to nowhere, doing what Mississippi black people had been doing for generations – working in the cotton fields." About a week later, Blackwell found herself standing by the side door of the Issaquena County Courthouse with her husband and six other African Americans, waiting to register.[1] After some back-and-forth, the clerk allowed two of them into the courthouse, leaving Blackwell and the others still outside. A bevy of pickup trucks with long hunting guns hanging in the back windows appeared, and the group soon found themselves surrounded by a bunch of armed white men, "their faces ... bright red."[2] That was the moment, she would later write in her memoir, when she decided the right to vote was risking her life for. Blackwell would go on to spend her career working on civil rights, and on political and social issues in her home state of Mississippi, initially as an organizer for SNCC, and eventually as mayor of her town. Yet she also later noted her disillusionment with voter registration drives like the one that had sparked her political interest. While perhaps well-intentioned, voter registration efforts seemed to have made little impact on the daily experiences of

[1] Unita Blackwell, *Barefootin': Life Lessons from the Road to Freedom* (New York: Crown, 2006), 3.
[2] Ibid., 7.

living in rural Mississippi: "Now people is *still* hungry, people *still* didn't have no housing, no clothes, no jobs."[3]

Blackwell found an opportunity to address these persistent challenges in 1967, the year that Dorothy Height, then the president of the National Council of Negro Women (NCNW), approached her about joining the organization's effort to address the housing needs of Mississippi communities.[4] From 1967 to 1975, Blackwell worked alongside Height and Dorothy Duke (NCNW's housing specialist) to tackle the housing problem. Duke and Blackwell made "a great team," Blackwell wrote in her memoir:

[Duke] understood the white power structure, and I understood people. So when we came up with projects, we could hash them out and figure out what would work or not work and how to handle them. We were both on new ground because we were creating a program from scratch and we were women. Any two women would have had a hard enough time, but a black woman and a white woman running around the country together coming up with ideas that folks were always telling us we couldn't do – people didn't know what to make of us.[5]

Beyond the novelty of this black-and-white female duo traversing the country in pursuit of better housing was the novelty of what they were proposing: a project called Turnkey III that would enable households poor enough to qualify for public housing to become homeowners.

INCOME AND ITS INTERSECTIONS

Income – or, more accurately, lack thereof – was central to the politics of Turnkey III in a way that was distinct from the other two cases in this book. In pressing for more equitable terms of access to homeownership for their constituents, neither the civil rights nor women's groups made much of a case for extending homeownership opportunities to their poorer constituents. On the contrary; at least in the time frames examined in the earlier chapters, organizations focused deliberately on those constituents whose income and wealth should have qualified them for homeownership, yet who still were deemed ineligible for reasons of race and

---

[3] Unita Blackwell, "Views from the Field," Speech prepared for National Conference on Homeownership through Public Housing, July 10–12, 1970, Washington, DC, in NCNW, Series 20, Box 1, Folder 19, 1.

[4] Debbie Harwell, *Wednesdays in Mississippi: Proper Ladies Working for Radical Change, Freedom Summer 1964* (Oxford: University Press of Mississippi, 2014), 176; Blackwell, *Barefootin'*, 177–8.

[5] Blackwell, *Barefootin'*, 186.

sex. The focus on the Sharyn Campbells and the Frank Summerses – upstanding citizens who had reached the conventional heights of success but faced challenges in attaining one of its basic markers, homeownership – helped to illuminate boundary groups' central claim that it was noneconomic considerations that kept their constituents from homeownership. On the aggregate level, these cases also helped to challenge conventional wisdom that said observed differences in homeownership rates and access by African Americans and women were due simply to individual economic differences (whether in the creditworthiness of the applicant or the home values of the neighborhood). This strategy of revealing and then contesting the *non*economic logic of their constituents' exclusion all but required them to set aside the ones for whom the economic case was harder to make.

Their strategy of setting income off to the side speaks to the work of the political scientist Dara Strolovitch, who has found that advocacy groups often fail to represent the interests of their most disadvantaged constituents.[6] Indeed, the first "target group" of Blackwell and Duke's efforts consisted of poor black households in rural Mississippi, usually with large families, and many headed by women. Such a collection of characteristics certainly would qualify them as a disadvantaged subgroup insofar as they were marginalized by not one, but multiple overlapping social characteristics and factors. It should be unsurprising, then, that their interests would be ignored by those groups pushing for revised terms of access to homeownership. Of course, that makes it all the more surprising that a movement did emerge to advocate for this marginalized subgroup, that this movement successfully pushed for homeownership opportunities, and that the model for pursuing homeownership for the poor then traveled to other communities.

THE NCNW AND BOUNDARY GROUP MOBILIZATION

In the late 1960s, the NCNW challenged long-held assumptions that confined government housing subsidies to poor people on rental assistance. The organization asked whether homeownership might also be a viable option. Working with the Department of Housing and Urban Development and the Office of Economic Opportunity, NCNW developed a pilot program that would test this logic, and initiated it in

[6] Dara Strolovitch, *Affirmative Advocacy: Race, Class, and Gender in Interest Group Politics* (Chicago: University of Chicago Press, 2007).

rural Mississippi and then across the country. The program was called Turnkey III. The idea was to use federal public housing funds to help members of qualified households become homeowners instead of renting. Leveraging their relationship with the federal government and forging new relationships with businesses and local communities, NCNW worked in 1967 and 1968 on the blueprints for the program, in which private developers would use public funds to construct or rehabilitate housing. Developers would turn the housing stock over to local housing authorities and residents, and residents would perform basic maintenance tasks that allowed them to build up "sweat equity." Once they accumulated enough sweat equity or had otherwise become able to qualify for FHA financing (for example, if their incomes or savings rose), they would be able to own their home. By the early 1970s, the idea of homeownership through public housing had reached the national stage, with national conferences, task forces, and congressional legislation all dedicated to this objective.

NCNW engaged in similar activities as the organizations described in previous chapters. Through an NCNW-sponsored program called Workshops in Mississippi, poor women throughout the state began to share and learn about each other's concerns and realize that their individual challenges of "deplorable" housing were in fact something they had in common. As they moved from community to community, the aggregation and information-gathering activities continued; for example, NCNW organized local housing surveys, conducted by locally trained residents, in order to get better data on the scope of housing conditions faced in a particular area, challenging earlier beliefs held by both businesses and public housing authorities about the low-income housing market. Representatives of NCNW then researched the scope and causes of the housing problem, as well as possible remedies, before working with HUD to convince the agency to creatively push the boundaries of existing public housing programs. As in the other cases in this book, NCNW representatives had to convince both business and government officials of the viability of their approach, which entailed challenging an earlier logic that explained why poor people should be ill-suited for homeownership.

Yet, unlike with the other cases, it was impossible to argue that these constituents were marginal cases, just barely eligible to become homeowners. These were households with such low incomes that qualifying for a mainstream mortgage at this time was out of the question – a very different position from the middle- and upper-middle-class African American and female homebuyers who found themselves denied access despite their incomes. This reality influenced NCNW's contestation and expansion strategies in important ways. Absent was the rhetoric about the use of government authority to deny otherwise qualified applicants equal access to homeownership. Also absent was an argument seen in the other two cases, that the government had an obligation to ensure that government housing policies not deny a group of constituents (this time low-income households) the opportunity to become homeowners. NCNW took a different approach, emphasizing instead the advantages of channeling public housing subsidies to homeownership programs: "We knew that there's a lot of dignity connected to a family buying and owning a place they can call their very own," wrote Blackwell. "We wanted to find a way for poor people, who couldn't qualify for bank mortgages, to put their money toward a house they could eventually own and never have to move out of as long as they fulfilled their obligations. We believed that home ownership would actually decrease the need for federal subsidies over time."[7] The organization also argued that such programs could be profitable to businesses, and should be preferable to public housing programs that home builders and real estate agents had long organized against. Finally, the nature of the program itself did not put its occupants on even ground with other homeowners; instead, NCNW proposed a program of delayed ownership; whereas even those taking on large amounts of mortgage debt to buy their houses nonetheless received the titles to their houses upon purchase, Turnkey III residents did not become officially the owners until they had invested a substantial amount of time and sweat equity into their dwelling.

HOUSING IN THE DIVIDED WELFARE STATE

The shift toward homeownership through public housing reflected the melding of two policy areas that had developed along parallel tracks, with their own constituencies, agencies, and logics. To recall from Chapter 2, a two-tiered system, characterized by competing visions for the nation's housing program, had emerged in US housing policy during the 1930s and 1940s.[8] Private industry groups backed a plan organized around homeownership for the middle class through private enterprise – subsidized, of course, by the FHA, the VA (after 1944), and, somewhat less directly, through an alphabet soup of other housing-related agencies.

---

[7] Blackwell, *Barefootin'*, 180.   [8] See also Radford, *Modern Housing for America*.

Meanwhile, a public housing lobby comprising urban mayors, redevelopment officials, and organized labor groups advocated for more direct government sponsorship of housing, and ultimately for a broad-based program of public housing, as well as for cooperative and limited dividend housing that would make housing affordable to workers, partly by deterring profit-seeking speculators.

Ostensibly, this would mean a program of homeownership for the working class and public housing for the poor, but the reality was more complicated. Neither program was able to fully satisfy the housing needs of its target constituency. Public housing struggled for public funding and political support, nationally and locally; consequently, there was never enough public housing to accommodate all who qualified. Private housing had income cutoffs, too, albeit less explicit than the public housing ones. Informal rules about the percentage of a borrower's monthly income that could be devoted to housing costs, as well as underwriting guidelines about the source and stability of income, meant that not everyone who desired homeownership would be able to qualify for an FHA-insured house, or homeownership through any other means. A 1959 study of mortgage credit, for example, found that a huge swath of Americans – even middle-income households – were "presently outside the market for new housing."[9] Housing experts and the federal government usually referred to this area between public and private housing as the "no-man's land."

These challenges were exacerbated in rural areas. The public housing program created by the 1937 Housing Act was designed with cities in mind, not the housing challenges faced by residents in low-density rural areas. The 1949 Housing Act tried to address this gap by providing funds for rural areas, but those funds were originally intended either for the purchase or construction of housing, both still out of reach for the rural poor. Nor was the rural counterpart to the FHA, the Farmers Housing Administration (FaHA, established in 1946), of much use to the poor, who lacked the up-front capital and whose incomes were too low and

---

[9] The median income of purchasers of FHA-insured houses was $6,600. Less than 6 percent of FHA-insured houses were purchased by households making less than $4,200, which was just under the median household income of $4,350 in 1957. In Charles Abrams and Morton Schussheim, "Credit Terms and Effective Demand for New Housing," Appendix to US Congress, Senate, Committee on Banking and Currency, *Study of Mortgage Credit: Hearings before the Subcommittee on Housing, of the Committee on Banking and Currency*, 86th Cong., 1st sess., 1959, 81.

unstable to qualify.[10] Housing standards – including FaHA's requirement that houses be within a certain distance of public sewers, pipes, and paved roads – also made housing costs through this program prohibitive for the poor. In general, FaHA could benefit farm owners, but was of little help to farm laborers with "low income, unsteady employment and, hence … regarded as poor risks by commercial lending institutions and the federal government as well."[11]

Thus, even when many around the country began to see their housing situations improve, residents of rural areas found their housing in a persistent state of dilapidation. By 1960, 42 percent of rural housing was considered substandard (either deteriorating or dilapidated), compared to 14 percent nationwide and 9 percent in rural areas. Only one-third of the nation's population resided in rural areas, yet rural households accounted for more than half of the country's 8.6 million substandard housing units. There were also stark racial disparities in rural housing quality. Ninety-two percent of all rural housing units (farm and non-farm, owner-occupied and rental) with a nonwhite head of household were considered substandard. Among rental housing, 22 percent of renter-occupied units with a white head of household had central heating, in comparison to less than 3 percent of units with a nonwhite head of household. These were national figures, but there were sharp regional variations, with the lowest quality of rural housing "by all measures" located in the South.[12]

---

[10] It is worth noting that like the FHA, FaHA had its own history of sex and race discrimination in lending. Blackwell experienced this firsthand when she tried to get a loan to build a new house on some land she (by this point working for the Ford Foundation) and her husband, Jeremiah (who worked for the Army Corps of Engineers), owned. Having a decent understanding of how the program worked, Blackwell was sure that they were technically eligible for a construction loan from FaHA, whose reason for being was "[p]roviding low-interest loans to rural people who can't get a bank loan." At the loan office, Blackwell was informed that, as a woman, she would not be considered for a loan without her husband also being present to sign the application. After Jeremiah signed the application, they qualified but continued to get the runaround from the FaHA office. Blackwell suspected that the agency did not want to give them a loan for a brick house because it was too great a status symbol for a black family to have. The couple finally got their FHA loan after filing a lawsuit for discriminatory practices. (Blackwell, *Barefootin'*, 180.)

[11] Clifton Jones, "Rural Housing," 1960, in Lyndon B. Johnson Presidential Library (hereafter LBJ-L), Papers of the National Advisory Commission on Rural Poverty, Box 12, Folder; Reports & Recommendations, Washington, DC, June 24–25, 1967, 3–4.

[12] Ibid., 1–2.

Problems of poor people's housing, whether in cities or rural areas, received more attention in the late 1950s and early 1960s, especially as the line between public and private housing began to blur. New FHA policies encouraged the agency to serve households down the income scale, and new public housing programs began to incorporate more private sector participation. The Housing Act of 1959, for example, added Section 202 to provide below market interest rate loans to non-profit organizations, which in turn would build and sponsor rental housing for elderly and disabled residents. Two years later, Congress expanded this approach to provide private, for-profit builders with interest rate subsidies in exchange for sponsoring low-income housing. Like Section 202, the 1961 Housing Act's Section 221(d)(3) was targeted to those above the local public housing cutoff – households earning between $4,000 and $6,000 per year for a family of four, for example. By reducing the sponsor's effective interest rate to 1 percent, the builder could then pass on the savings to tenants in the form of reduced monthly rents. A Brookings Institution economist estimated in 1973 that the subsidy might have reduced rents by as much as 27 percent.[13] Around the same time, the Public Housing Administration (by this time under the jurisdiction of the HHFA) began to experiment with using private providers to build and manage public housing, initially through the Bureau of Indian Affairs, to create low-rent housing for Native Americans on tribal lands. This paved the way for a new legal framework, administratively developed, for a publicly financed program of homeownership for low-income residents of tribal lands.[14]

The harnessing of public–private partnerships to expand the income reach of government housing programs departed from the usual practices of both public and private housing agencies, the former of which tended to act as their "own general contractor," with local housing authorities responsible for locating, designing, constructing, and managing housing, and the latter of which tended to stay away from low-income rental housing altogether.[15] Yet neither had ever challenged

[13] Aaron, *Shelter and Subsidies*, 132.
[14] Mark K. Ulmer, "The Legal Origin and Nature of Indian Housing Authorities and the HUD Indian Housing Programs," *American Indian Law Review* 2, no. 2 (1987/88), 109–74.
[15] Joseph Burstein, "Outline of Remarks by Joseph Burstein, General Counsel, Housing Assistance Administration, Department of Housing and Urban Development, On The New Assistance Methods of the Housing Act of 1937, NAHRO National Housing Policy

the basic idea, reinforced since the 1930s, that rental housing would comprise the lion's share of low-income housing options.

To be sure, at least one prominent housing specialist had been questioning the conventional wisdom keeping the poor ineligible for government homeownership programs since the 1940s. Charles Abrams was a housing economist, the first general counsel of the New York Housing Authority, and, from 1951 to 1959, president of the National Committee Against Discrimination in Housing. Abrams spent much of his career railing against the "contemporary rhetoric" charging that poor people were incapable of meeting the obligations of homeownership. He pointed out that many poor tenants had actually owned their homes before slum clearance programs pushed them out of their neighborhoods.[16] He also complained of a double standard in federal housing policy. The federal government had long been using its powers to remake the mortgage market for the middle class, farmers, and even colleges and universities. To Abrams, this history suggested that the decision of who would have access to credit and on what terms was essentially "a political question"[17]: "I think it is a reflection of Government policy to find that Government insurance of mortgages is directed toward the higher income and middle-income groups and not toward the needs of the lower income family. It smacks of a philosophy of socialism for the rich and private enterprise for the poor."[18] Abrams was particularly disappointed with the federal government's reliance on a "business welfare state" to channel homeownership to those who he felt needed assistance the least, and on numerous occasions argued that such programs would be easier to justify if they at least included lower income groups among their beneficiaries.[19] But while he was a formidable figure on the housing scene, Abrams's views on homeownership for the poor were largely on the fringe until the mid-1960s.

Forum, Shoreham Hotel, Washington, DC, February 13, 1967, p. 5. In NCNW Series 20, Box 3, Folder 61.

[16] A. Scott Henderson, *Housing & the Democratic Ideal: The Life and Thought of Charles Abrams* (New York: Columbia University Press, 2000), 203.

[17] Abrams and Schussheim, "Study of Mortgage Credit," 84.

[18] Testimony of Charles Abrams, in US Congress, Senate, Committee on Banking and Currency, *Study of Mortgage Credit*, 32.

[19] Abrams and Schussheim, "Study of Mortgage Credit," 86; Henderson, *Housing & the Democratic Ideal*, 203.

FROM DIVIDED WELFARE STATE TO HOMEOWNERSHIP
FOR THE POOR

Several factors in the 1960s helped to move Abrams's views on home-ownership for the poor from the fringe to the mainstream of thinking. One was the persistence of substandard housing faced by the poor. Even as housing conditions vastly improved for the middle class in the midst of government housing policies and rising postwar incomes, it was becoming increasingly clear that poorer families were failing to make the same gains – and this was even more pronounced in rural areas. This was a rebuke of both public housing programs. Some supporters of public housing were beginning to view the program as a failure (at least in terms of its inability to live up to its initial promise); meanwhile private housing supporters were also increasingly forced to reckon with the fact that the hoped-for "filter process" had failed to increase housing standards for those with low income.[20]

Homeownership was not necessarily an obvious solution to the lack of decent housing for the poor, but it was a solution that linked up well to another problem at the time, the falloff in home construction. The home-building industry had come of age during the postwar housing shortage, when the biggest challenge builders faced was keeping pace with the demand, which itself was shaped by the new middle-class mortgage credit infrastructure. As the demand started to wane by the late 1950s, builders attempted to adjust their business models to deal with it. Some found salvation in the multifamily housing sector, but found that by the mid-1960s demand there was also either stabilizing or falling off (to about five hundred thousand units per year), despite overall economic growth in

---

[20] Between 1950 and 1960, the number of substandard owner-occupied units fell by 16 percent. Owner-occupied substandard housing also fell over this time, from 23 percent to 11 percent of all owner-occupied units (this was while the number of owner-occupied units had increased by 73 percent). However, the overall increase in housing standards coincided with poor people occupying a higher proportion of substandard units than they had in the past. In 1950, households in poverty accounted for 51 percent of substandard owner-occupied housing stock; in 1960, that number was 60 percent. A similar trend could be seen in rental housing, where families in poverty accounted for about one-third of total rental housing in 1950 and 1960, but whose share of substandard rental housing rose from 58 percent in 1950 to 64 percent in 1964. See "Restrictive Housing: An American Anachronism," Remarks by Samuel C. Jackson (Asst. Sec. for Metropolitan Planning, HUD) before the Mid-Winter Conference of the National Association of Real Estate Brokers, Washington, DC, February 18, 1971, in NCNW Series 20, Box 21, Folder 13, 7.

those years.[21] An open letter to the president in *House + Home* in 1964 castigated the administration for its failure to do so little for an industry that was "limping along at about 60% of its true potential."[22] While HUD's Robert Weaver doubted the industry's appraisal, he and others in the administration, including the Council of Economic Advisors, were concerned about the jobs at stake.[23] A memo to one of LBJ's aides in September 1966 laid out the president's basic thinking: "The President is committed to two objectives: (a) economic relief for homebuilding and (b) housing for poor people, and all the tools given to us ought to be used at least in some small measure."[24]

A final factor in shifting attention toward low-income homeownership was the crisis in American cities. Beginning in 1964, each summer witnessed an escalation of riots and unrest in US cities. The rioting reached a peak in the summer of 1967, with reports of unrest in over 150 cities and two major disorders in Newark and Detroit. In Newark, the catalyst was the arrest and beating of a cabdriver, whose main crime had been to drive around a double-parked police car. As the violence escalated, the National Guard was brought in. The six days of rioting left twenty-six people dead and over seven-hundred injured, and led to nearly fifteen-hundred arrests.[25] In Detroit, the riot occurred after the police decided to bust an illegal after-hours saloon; over five days of violence, it drew in a force of 17,000 law enforcement officers. The riots resulted in forty-three dead (thirty at the hands of law enforcement), over 7,200 arrests, $36 million in insured property damage, and over 2,500 buildings burned.[26]

---

[21] Letter to Joe Califano from Bernard Boutin, October 21, 1965, in LBJ-L White House Central File (hereafter WHCF) Confidential File Box 55 HS Housing.

[22] Letter from Gurney Breckenfeld to Lyndon B. Johnson, December 27, 1963, in LBJ-L, Papers of Lyndon B. Johnson, GEN FA 4, Housing 11/22/63–11/1/65, Box 16.

[23] See, for example, Robert Weaver to Lyndon B. Johnson, January 24, 1964, LBJ-L, Papers, GEN FA 4 Housing 11/22/63–11/1/65, Box 16; Memo from Gardner Ackley to Lyndon Johnson, March 29, 1966, in LBJ-L, WHCF, HS Box 1, EX HS 12/22/65–8/31/66.

[24] Jake Jacobsen and Milton P. Semer to Joe Califano, September 30, 1966, Box 256, FG170–6 Federal National Mortgage Association. Also, Memo from Gardner Ackley to Lyndon Johnson, March 29, 1966.

[25] Jessica Mazzola and Karen Yi, "50 Years Ago Newark Burned" NJ.com, July 12, 2017, at www.nj.com/essex/index.ssf/2017/07/what_you_need_to_know_about_the_1967_newark_riots.html. See also von Hoffman, "Calling upon the Genius," which also describes the Newark and Detroit unrest in setting the context for the government's shift toward bringing in private industry to help solve the problems of urban housing.

[26] See Thomas Sugrue, *The Origins of the Urban Crisis: Race and Inequality in Postwar Detroit* (Princeton, NJ: Princeton University Press), 1997.

Early on, there was some recognition that both poor-quality housing and isolation from mainstream credit were major factors shaping urban unrest.[27] Further study of the roots of the crisis corroborated the role of inadequate housing and credit. In its final report, the National Advisory Commission on Civil Disorders listed segregated substandard housing and limited housing opportunities among the most pressing grievances of urban residents and causes of the unrest.[28] The commission made several recommendations for increasing access to housing, the most controversial of which was to renew support for a law to end discrimination in sales and rental housing. Included in the final report was also a recommendation for government measures to "make home ownership possible for low-income families."[29] The Kerner Commission's report and recommendations were not directly targeted at the areas where NCNW initially set out to create homeownership opportunities – and in response to these competing pressures, policy-makers

[27] Writing to LBJ in the wake of the Watts and Compton riots, a member of the Los Angeles County Commission on Human Relations said, "I and my fellow commissioners have surveyed the area. We have come to several conclusions. There is not proper housing both for the minorities or other poor people that live there as it is in other large cities in the United States. I therefore recommend that, if a human being is to live with dignity in this great country of ours, then under your great society program the government should come up with a plan for low priced homes federally financed with a small down payment and low interest rates, and the government should build cities of them under this federal plan all over the United States where there are crowded conditions. We do not mean any federal housing projects as we have built in the last 25 years – these must be individual homes, because we have found out that, where a person in the low income [sic] bracket, whether he is in the minority groups [sic] regardless of color or race, he should be able to buy a federal [sic] financed home right there in the districts where they now live or would like to live in." Philip Froomer to LBJ, 11/23/65, in LBJ-L – Papers of Lyndon B. Johnson, GEN FA 3 8/1/64, Box 14, Folder: FA4 11/2/65.

[28] The Kerner Commission listed housing problems as among the most severe grievances of urban residents. See National Advisory Commission on Civil Disorders, *Report of the National Advisory Commission on Civil Disorders* (Washington, DC: Government Printing Office, 1968), 13. Louis Hyman describes how rioters typically targeted property over people, and that one of their grievances in doing so had to do with the unavailability of credit networks like the ones in the suburbs. In the case of housing, this often meant that urban residents were unable to obtain financing from a bank and had to receive private financing from the sellers or other sources. This type of financing was abused in the 1950s and 1960s, with speculators purchasing slum housing, making a few cosmetic repairs, flipping the house at a higher price, offering to finance the buyer, and then purchasing the house back from the buyer (or foreclosing) when the cost of new repairs became too high. See Hyman, "Ending Discrimination, Legitimating Debt," 200–32, esp. 203–13.

[29] National Advisory Commission on Civil Disorders, *Report*, 13.

set out to create a homeownership program (Section 235 of the 1968 Housing and Urban Development Act) for low-income residents primarily in cities that had previously been cut off from finance. Yet several of Turnkey III's supporters explicitly linked the conditions in the cities to those in rural areas, arguing that by providing better housing opportunities in the countryside, fewer people would be induced to migrate. After Turnkey III was first developed for rural areas, the concept was then exported to cities as well.

Thus from two parallel, very distinct housing policy tracks in the 1930s and 1940s, the policy arena of public and private housing gradually began to commingle and see their lines blurred in the 1950s and 1960s. Public housing agencies adopted new techniques first used in the Bureau of Indian Affairs' housing programs to encourage private industry and eventually private nonprofits to play a greater role in the production, provision, and management of public housing, while private housing agencies began to experiment with new incentives, including rent subsidies and demonstrations to reduce construction costs, to channel rental housing to lower-income tenants. As those changes occurred, some advocates began to question whether the line that kept poor people in rental housing needed to be tread on so sacredly. Finally, the increased attention given to the rural poor by books like Michael Harrington's *The Other America* and to the living conditions in cities, as outlined by the Kerner Commission report, helped draw more attention to the idea of low-income homeownership.[30]

THE NCNW AND WORKSHOPS IN MISSISSIPPI

NCNW was founded in 1935 by Mary McLeod Bethune to serve as an umbrella organization representing the concerns of black women, and housing was not what initially brought the organization to Mississippi in the mid-1960s. Rather, NCNW's venture to the state began with its sponsorship of a program during the Freedom Summer of 1964 called Women in Mississippi (WIMs). Women in Mississippi brought about fifty Northern and Midwestern women – black, white, Christian, Jewish – to the state. The women would fly into Jackson on a Tuesday, spend Wednesday travelling in small teams to areas of racial tension, talk to local women about their concerns, and fly back home on Thursday.

[30] Michael Harrington, *The Other America: Poverty in the United States* (New York: Macmillan Publishing Co., 1962).

A major goal of the project was to "build a bridge between the Negro and white women of the south."[31] The program was an alternative to student organizations that were also active in the state that summer. Where the Congress of Racial Equality, SNCC, and SNCC's umbrella, the Council of Federated Organizations, overtly challenged racial norms, WIMs attempted to fly beneath the radar.[32] Dressed as "proper" ladies in dresses, white gloves, and handbags, WIMs volunteers saw themselves not "as activists, but as listeners and interpreters of the struggle."[33] At the same time, they hoped that by opening a dialogue with Southern women, they would be able to dispel fears about the students coming into the state as part of Freedom Summer. The women also hoped to learn more about the daily lives and struggles of blacks in Mississippi and to communicate that to their Southern white counterparts.[34] WIMs involved itself in the Mississippi civil rights struggle in other ways, too. Unita Blackwell first became aware of WIMs when, in June 1965, she was among the over 1,100 demonstrators arrested for protesting legislation at the Mississippi State House intended to defang some of the new federal Voting Rights Act. WIMs posted the $50,000 bail to free those who remained in jail. "I'll be forever grateful for their aid," Blackwell later wrote.[35]

Following Freedom Summer, the organization repurposed itself as Workshops in Mississippi (still using the acronym WIMs, and still

---

[31] Polly Cowan, "Wednesdays in Mississippi," n.d., in NCNW Series 19, Folder 221, 2.

[32] As one of the organizers, Polly Cowan, recalled: "Every effort has been made to keep the 'Wednesday' visits out of the press. Indirect mention of women going from cities has slipped through but, as of the moment, the weekly project and the goal of reaching southern contacts has not been mentioned. The news medium has given complete co-operation by its understanding that, if the project were given publicity, the Mississippi staff would be discovered and their ability to broaden southern contacts would be curtailed. It would also compound the risks taken by the many southern women of both races who have talked to us frankly but off-the-record. We believe that many of the doors which have been opened with such effort would slam shut immediately if the southern press drew attention to the concept and organization of the project." Ibid., 3.

[33] "We have made contact with southern women of every faith: women who ranged in political opinion from those few who already believed in our purpose and our goals, to those who opposed our being in Mississippi on any basis whatsoever. But even the most hostile southern woman has been impressed by the honesty and sincerity of team members, and the presence of northern women of such 'respectability' plus a quiet and dedicated approach did modify many of the most antagonistic attitudes." Ibid., 4; Harwell, *Wednesdays in Mississippi*, 47.

[34] Harwell, *Wednesdays in Mississippi*, 68.

[35] Blackwell, *Barefootin'*, 128. Harwell, *Wednesdays in Mississippi*, 128.

sponsored by the NCNW) and shifted its focus to improving some of the community and social problems that had come up in conversations with women across the state. President Height described their goal as "to reach and assist more and more groups of hard core poor women."[36] As it turns out, there *was* demand from those groups. WIMs invited twenty-five women to its first workshop in Jackson in November 1966; the organizers were stunned when sixty showed up. Those who came "were animated about their need for housing, community centers, and school breakfast and lunch programs," wrote Blackwell. "They talked of finding more women for volunteer service, of their desire to bridge the gap between those who had received the benefits of education and those who had not. They spoke of the responsibility of women who had a better education and a good job to work for the general good, because they had access to information and knew how to use it."[37] The new WIMs followed its old blueprint of meeting with and learning from local residents, this time holding small group meetings and training sessions in which local residents would identify pressing social issues, learn how to use existing levers of the federal government, and apply for grants to solve urgent issues ranging from employment to education to hunger. WIMs also drew from a model of organizing that the federal government had begun to advance when President Johnson created the Office of Economic Opportunity in 1964 as part of his War on Poverty. Though OEO concerned itself with a wide range of policy areas, again and again it returned to the idea of identifying problems and delivering solutions through community participation. WIMs worked from a similar premise upholding the importance of community participation at multiple points in the process. This was a central principle throughout WIMs's programs: communities would identify critical problems to address, WIMs would then hold workshops to empower community members to devise their own solutions and assist them in enlisting support from government agencies and foundations. Following that, WIMs would be there to oversee the implementation and evolution of programs once enacted. This workshop and support model would also extend outside of the specific programs developed by WIMs; NCNW also created opportunities for tenants' voices to be represented across HUD committees and task forces.

---

[36] Dorothy Height, *Open Wide the Freedom Gates: A Memoir* (New York: Public Affairs, 2005), 189.

[37] Ibid., 189.

DISCOVERING THE HOUSING PROBLEM IN OXFORD, MISSISSIPPI

In January 1967, WIMs held a workshop in Oxford, Mississippi, with the purpose of training participants in program and grant writing for areas identified as a high priority in their communities. Women in Oxford and elsewhere consistently singled out and described in detail the poor housing conditions their families faced.[38] At both this meeting and an earlier planning meeting in November, the conversation returned "again and again to [participants'] lack of humanly decent housing – lack of plumbing, sewage, roofing, space, crowded like cattle."[39] One woman at the meeting lived in such poor-quality housing that she needed to wear a raincoat, hat, and boots when cooking in bad weather: "If anyone comes to see me, they think I'm on my way out, but I'm just trying to stay dry and get supper for the kids."[40]

WIMs heard many stories like this. Blackwell recalled talking to "a man in the Mississippi Delta. [H]e said, 'All my life I've wanted something nice. I was very proud of my wife. I got 10 children. Every year we would have a child. I kept thinking for each child, that when this one gets big enough he would pick and hoe and we was going to save up something and get us a decent place to live.' Here come the mechanical pickers. He was throwed off the plantation. He moved into town. He paid $40.00 a month rent plus his utilities. Stayed in a two room shack with all them people."[41]

However dire the problem, workshop participants initially decided not to focus on housing; in fact, it was not even an option on the list of priorities that participants were asked to rank, nor did any attendees write in the issue. Participants instead selected to focus on four ostensibly more tractable target areas.[42]

NCNW's housing specialist, Dorothy Duke, who was at the Oxford meeting, later recalled the significance of this decision not to focus on

---

[38] See, for example, Polly Cowan's undated notes on her experiences as part of the Wednesdays in Mississippi and Workshops in Mississippi programs from 1964 through 1966. In NABWH, Polly Cowan Papers, Series 1, Folder 7 (see esp. 6, 10, 13); Meeting notes, n.d., in NCNW Series 19, Folder 80, 3, 24, 27.

[39] Nancy Spraker, "Untitled," n.d., in NCNW Series 20, Box 16, Folder 23, 2.

[40] Height, *Open Wide the Freedom Gates*, 194.

[41] Blackwell, "Views from the Field," 7.

[42] "Mississippi Women's Workshop Materials," January 1967, in NCNW Series 19, Folder 195.

women's housing conditions: "Housing for the poor person in the rural South is deplorable. The possibility of effecting any change in this situation seemed so insurmountable and beyond reach that the women chose other areas of need where they felt they might make something happen."[43] Yet as Duke continued to listen "to the women speaking of their housing problems, of the kind of conditions children were being brought up in, of the regulations in public housing units," she began to question her and NCNW's initial unease about the issue.[44] Duke suspected that one of the reasons for such poor-quality housing was not a lack of federal interest or public policies to support it, but rather residents' lack of information about the programs that could potentially help them. "I spoke with them about new legislation that had been enacted for housing low-income families and they knew nothing or had very limited knowledge of these programs," Duke recalled. "It all seemed most complicated and most remote. They only knew that they had bad housing."[45]

After the Oxford meeting, Duke resolved to use WIMs and NCNW to "act as a 'bridge of communications' for the poor person needing decent housing to the people and agencies that could make housing possible."[46] This was not a task to be accomplished by Duke alone; Height hired Blackwell to assist Duke as a local organizer for the housing programs.

RESEARCHING THE SCOPE OF THE PROBLEM

Duke spent the following month poring through Census data to understand the scale of the housing problem in the state.[47] She also looked into the different federal programs that might potentially be useful for the people of Mississippi, in particular "large families, with no steady income, with women, in many cases, the head of households. ... The desire for home ownership had been expressed so strongly that this too became one

---

[43] Duke, "How It Began: Training in Grant-Writing," August 15, 1967, in NCNW, Series 20, Box 4, Folder 94, 1.

[44] It was likely that Duke's own background helped her to recognize this problem. By the time she became engaged in WIMs, Duke had nearly a dozen years of experience bringing public agencies and groups together with private business interests for social aims. She had also worked in the low-income housing field, having worked in her own community to improve the seemingly intractable housing conditions of another population, senior citizens. Dorothy Duke, Resume 1/30/69, and Letter of Recommendation from Senator Tower to Richard Nixon, n.d., in NCNW Series 20, Box 3, Folder 8.

[45] Duke, "How It Began," 1.   [46] Ibid.

[47] Dorothy Height, "Preliminary Report: Project Homes," OEO Contract #4226, May 1968, in NCNW Series 20, Box 4, Folder 10, 4.

of our objectives."[48] She quickly ruled out the Farmer's Home Administration, deciding that the unstable incomes of the target households presented too much of a barrier for them to ever qualify for the program. After ruling out the Federal Rent Supplement Program because of its limited applicability to the rural South, she looked toward public housing programs, which admittedly presented their own challenges. In 1962, the Mississippi State Legislature had passed a law that required voters to pass a local referendum before they could construct new public housing in their community. This was a formidable barrier to using any public housing to address the problems identified in the Oxford meeting, yet there was also a reason to be hopeful.

Over the course of her public housing research, Duke learned that communities typically requested more public housing than they intended to build initially, with some leeway to build the remainder in the future. Duke was "amazed" to discover nearly six thousand units across thirty communities that had been approved *prior* to the 1962 legislation but had not yet been built.[49] (Further research put that number closer to eleven thousand in seventy-five communities across the state.[50]) The existence of these untapped housing approvals suggested that, at least in theory, NCNW could circumvent the 1962 legislation by tapping into localities' committed but unbuilt public housing. This possibility inspired Duke and NCNW to push on, working with the federal, state, and local governments, private providers, and voluntary associations to design a program that might take advantage of this potential loophole.[51] After months of rapid work, NCNW laid the groundwork for a plan that would bring homeownership to poor residents of rural Mississippi. HUD announced the plan on September 16, 1967, calling it "precedent shattering."[52]

The program, Turnkey III, encapsulated many different ideas about private sector participation and homeownership. As one of its architects emphasized, it "call[ed] for a complete change in the thinking and operating relationships of many in both the public and private sector." It brought together businesses, all levels of government, and voluntary organizations in a partnership to create homeownership opportunities

---

[48] Duke, "How It Began," 1–2.
[49] NCNW, n.d. "How It Began: Training in Grant-Writing," in NCNW Series 20, Folder 187, 2.
[50] Height, "Preliminary Report: Project Homes," 4.   [51] Ibid., 5.
[52] Letter from Helen Rickler to Sid Goldberg, October 4, 1967, in NCNW Series 20, Box 21, Folder 1.

for citizens whose incomes were low enough to qualify them for public housing.[53] With the backing of the federal government, a private developer would choose sites, secure private financing, and construct housing for public housing-eligible tenants, which, upon completion, would be purchased by a local housing authority with a federal mortgage. Private corporations and civic organizations would then work together to identify and select "homeownership suitable" applicants as tenants for the Turnkey III projects. The tenants would pay roughly 20 percent of their monthly income as rent, and gradually build up sweat equity in the property by performing basic maintenance tasks. The money paid in rent would go toward paying down the debt incurred by the local housing authority in financing the construction of the house, while the money saved by performing basic maintenance would be credited to a homebuyer's ownership reserve, meaning that the debt on the property would decrease as the tenant's equity increased. Once either the amount in the reserve exceeded what was owed on the place or the tenant's income increased to the point of eligibility for FHA or VA financing, the tenant could take ownership of the house and receive the title. It was estimated that this could take about twenty to twenty-five years.[54]

After HUD announced the program, Height referred to it as "the most constructive, far reaching role NCNW has ever undertaken in its concern for family life."[55]

BARRIERS TO HOMEOWNERSHIP FOR THE POOR IN RURAL MISSISSIPPI

Moving from recognizing an untapped public housing supply to proposing and then implementing a project such as Turnkey III was a massive undertaking. The NCNW program ran contrary to the notion that private providers and the government could – and should – support low-income homeownership, a source of many of the program's challenges. On the one hand, the rural poor indisputably faced dire housing conditions. Such conditions not only came up during the workshops, but had been searingly documented by Michael Harrington in *The Other America*, the book credited for drawing the attention of Americans

[53] NCNW, "Turnkey III Project Homes: Interim Report to the Ford Foundation," January 6, 1970, in NCNW, Series 20, Box 4, Folder 95, 5.

[54] HUD Circular 12–17–68, in NCNW Series 20, Box 21, Folder 4.

[55] Letter from Helen Rickler to Sid Goldberg, October 4, 1967.

(especially liberal white Americans) to the challenges of the poor and spurring the War on Poverty.

On the other hand, the reasons for poor-quality housing among the poor were economically straightforward, it seemed. As an OEO memo explained, "the cost of producing decent housing, whether new or rehabilitated, and the incomes of poor people just do not match. It simply costs more to produce good housing than poor people can afford to pay. The inescapable conclusion is the necessity of expanded subsidies to make decent housing available to poor people."[56] The idea that poor people desired, and were capable of, homeownership had not received wide acceptance at this time. There were few, if any, studies on the demand for homeownership among very-low-income citizens.[57]

Beyond problems of ability to pay, the contemporary rhetoric charged that the poor were incapable of meeting the responsibilities of home-ownership.[58] NCNW itself recognized that there might be practical challenges in turning people unaccustomed to tenancy into homeowners: "For many low-income families the concept of ever owning a home is remote, therefore, actually undertaking the responsibilities and privileges of homeownership is difficult."[59]

These various challenges were also reflected in the fact that the private housing industry overwhelmingly ignored the needs of poor people, assuming there was no market. Duke and her colleagues would somehow have to convince private builders and banks that there was a market in producing housing – for owner occupancy, no less – for poor people with unstable incomes, in large, often female-headed households. Such a feat was even more impressive given that several associations representing the private housing industry in the state were completely unaccustomed to cooperating with African American organizations, and had never offered their support for public housing agencies.[60]

---

[56] Office of Economic Opportunity, "Housing and the Poverty Program," March 30, 1967, in NCNW, Series 20, Box 3, Folder 28.

[57] NCNW, n.d. "How to Get Started with Housing," in NCNW Series 20, Box 21, Folder 7, 3.

[58] Henderson, *Housing and the Democratic Ideal*, 203.

[59] National Council of Negro Women, "Turnkey III Project Homes: Interim Report to the Ford Foundation," January 6, 1970, in NCNW Series 20, Box 4, Folder 95, 10.

[60] As Blackwell recalled, many of the local bankers, builders, and government officials she was supposed to negotiate with had "never dealt with a black person – a black woman at that – on this level." Duke helped prepare the "local white men" for this encounter by explaining "that I was a professional woman and they'd have to say 'Negro,' not 'nigger' or 'nigra,' or even 'colored.' (We hadn't yet become African Americans – or even black

And finally, there was the challenge of policy itself. Duke's discovery of the unbuilt but approved public housing stock was promising, but it was hardly a commitment to allow that stock to be used. It was far from clear that Duke's conjecture about using the committed but unbuilt housing stock to circumvent the 1962 laws had any legal basis. And even if this was the case, who would build the project, how would it get financed, and through what agency? NCNW saw an opportunity in Section 23 of the 1965 Housing and Community Development Act, which allowed organizations to rehabilitate housing for lease to local housing authorities, which would in turn rent the housing to low-income tenants. But when they first took their proposal to HUD, officials responded with skepticism before deeming it too "people oriented" to qualify for demonstration funding from an agency concerned with the "bricks and mortar" aspects of housing.[61]

FINDING KNOTHOLES IN THE FENCE

Despite these challenges, NCNW pushed forward by finding and exploiting, as it called them, the "knotholes in the fence."[62] The organization's vast knowledge of the federal government, nonprofit foundations, and their resources; its ability to tap into the government (it probably did not hurt that NCNW had long ties to Robert C. Weaver, HUD secretary at the time); and the local connections it had forged in its years working in Mississippi made a low-income homeownership program all the more plausible.

While HUD's initial lack of interest in the project may have been viewed as a setback, it did two things that ultimately helped advance NCNW's proposal. First, it referred Duke to the Office of Economic Opportunity's Housing Program, whose director received the proposal enthusiastically. By June of 1967, OEO had agreed to provide the first $45,000 in funds for a small-scale demonstration, and also helped NCNW set up meetings with business associations and state and local officials. Second, HUD Secretary Weaver assigned the agency's assistant

---

people.) And she practiced with them saying 'knee-grow' over and over, having them touch their knees on 'knee' and stretch their arms up high on 'grow.' She told them that I would have to sit in the front seat of the car and they would have to call me *Mrs.* Blackwell." In Blackwell, *Barefootin'*, 183–4.

[61] Harwell, *Wednesdays in Mississippi*, 176–8; Blackwell, *Barefootin'*, 180; Height, *Open Wide the Freedom Gates*, 195.

[62] Nancy Spraker, "Untitled," n.d., in NCNW Series 20, Box 16, Folder 23, 8.

general counsel, Joseph Burstein, to NCNW's project. The former was important in that it begat additional funding and support, including, eventually, $3 million from HUD to construct two hundred homes in North Gulfport, Mississippi, an additional $90,000 from OEO, and several grants from the Ford Foundation to try the initial pilot project in other locations, and allowed NCNW to put more resources into boosting community member participation in the program.[63]

Burstein's placement on the case was a significant, if serendipitous, boon to NCNW's original aim of creating homeownership opportunities. Like NCNW leaders, Burstein had a proclivity for creatively pushing the limits of existing government policies (Blackwell described him as "a brilliant thinker and a fantastic man").[64] Several years earlier, he had single-handedly reinterpreted the 1937 Housing Act to allow for greater private participation in the construction and management of public housing on Native American tribal lands for the Bureau of Indian Affairs. That work also opened the door to the eventual owner occupancy of public housing tenants on the lands. The projects had been named Turnkey I and Turnkey II.[65] Burstein's innovations had been confined initially to Native American tribal lands, but he immediately saw the potential in rural areas, which contained many of the same salient features as tribal lands.

Burstein also saw in this a financial rationale: "If the government subsidizes rental housing," he reasoned to Height, "why not subsidize homeownership for low-income families?"[66] Burstein persistently emphasized that it would cost the federal government less money to encourage homeownership than it would to maintain public housing. At worst, Burstein argued at an early planning meeting, the government had nothing to lose, since it would, in any case, be subsidizing poor citizens, whether as tenants or eventual homeowners. Some of the savings would

---

[63] Cathy Aldridge, "$3 Million Granted NCNW, Miss. Housing Planned," *New York Amsterdam News* (February 24, 1968); "OEO Extends Contract with National Council of Negro Women" OEO Press Release, February 7, 1968, in NCNW Series 20, Box 4, Folder 86.

[64] Blackwell, *Barefootin'*, 182.

[65] Mark K. Ulmer, "The Legal Origin and Nature of Indian Housing Authorities and the HUD Indian Housing Programs," *American Indian Law Review* 2, no. 2 (1987/88), 109–74; Outline of Remarks by Joseph Burstein, "The New Assistance Methods of the Housing Act of 1937," National Association of Housing and Redevelopment Officials Housing Policy Forum, February 13, 1967, in NCNW Series 20, Box 3, Folder 9.

[66] Height, *Open Wide the Freedom Gates*, 196.

accrue as the high costs of public housing management were replaced by self-managing homeowners associations. But some of the savings also had to do with downstream effects: people who owned their houses, it was believed, would be more eager to maintain their properties than those renting from a local housing authority.[67]

Burstein set to work on the administrative infrastructure for what would be the Turnkey III program, while at the same time working to persuade HUD to go along with the plan and state officials to accept the legal reasoning behind it. "It was a thrilling, exhilarating creative process," Blackwell recalled of their work together. "We were designing something that had never existed before to address the needs of poor people and, at the same time, working around the concerns of community power structures."[68] By May 1967, Burstein had succeeded in convincing the Mississippi attorney general to allow the plan of using untapped housing to be grandfathered from the 1962 legislation. That July, after Burstein attended several all-day meetings and spent a "great deal of time on the phone" with the executive director of the Region VIII Public Housing Authority, the thirteen-member commission also gave its unanimous approval for the program to proceed. This freed up at least fifteen hundred of the housing units Duke had discovered back in February, now available to be constructed without a referendum.[69]

Thus, by mid-1967 (only a few months after the Oxford, Mississippi, meeting that spurred the initiative), the project had morphed from a modest program aimed at rehabilitating existing housing that the local housing authority could lease to low-income tenants to a program for the private development of entirely new communities, consisting of single-family houses that would first be owned by the housing authority and then, eventually, by tenants. Rather than focusing exclusively on the "bricks and mortar" aspect of housing, the new project would include training and community resources intended to provide a more holistic support for homeownership.

[67] Burstein, in Spraker, "Untitled"; Meeting Notes, November 2, 1967, in NCNW Series 20, Box 13, Folder 15.

[68] Blackwell, *Barefootin'*, 182.

[69] For example, Spraker, "Untitled"; Nonprofit Housing Center, Urban America, Inc., "Turnkey III: A Case Study of the Pilot Program of Homeownership under Public Housing in North Gulfport Mississippi, 1970," in NCNW Series 20, Box 12, Folder 30, 14; Duke, "How It Began," 10–11.

FORGING RELATIONSHIPS WITH BUSINESS
AND COMMUNITY ACTORS

Beyond Burstein, HUD, OEO, and Ford, NCNW tapped into and cultivated a broad network of relationships with other key governmental, organizational, business, and community players. In The HUD Secretary's words, NCNW acted "as a liaison between builders, bankers, Federal and local officials, and prospective tenants"; in NCNW's words, they were "building bridges" between these groups.[70] These alliances helped secure policy victories (for example, getting the state attorney general to go along with the interpretation of the 1962 plan), but NCNW also realized that policy alone was insufficient to meaningfully improve the lives of the women who had shared their concerns at Wednesdays and Workshops in Mississippi. They would need more than on-paper policy successes: they would need to convince businesses that participation was in their interest, persuade local housing authorities and low-income residents to trust one another, and convince residents that the program was less of a threat than they otherwise believed. Height, Duke, and Blackwell accepted the challenge.

Duke and others operated under the principle that by informing business partners of the program's profit opportunities, they would be more inclined to lend support, which might explain the National Association of Home Builders' positive reception of the program. NAHB became an early and important partner. Meetings in March and April 1967 in DC between the NAHB leadership, Duke, and Burstein culminated in the organization's formal endorsement as well as the formation of a working group consisting of NCNW, homebuilders, and the Housing Assistance Administration (a federal agency responsible for the public housing program).[71] Far less involved in the planning, the National Association of Real Estate Boards also eventually endorsed the program, a first for an organization that had been "actively opposed to all public housing programs."[72]

---

[70] Robert C. Weaver, Address to the Annual Convention of NCNW, "Charting a Pathway to the Future," Washington, DC, November 9, 1967, in NCNW, Series 20, Box 5, Folder 1; Duke, "How It Began," 15.

[71] Richard Canavan (Staff VP, Builder Services Division of NAHB) to Dorothy Duke, April 16, 1967, in NCNW, Series 20, Box 3, Folder 9.

[72] John C. Williamson (NAREB) to Dorothy Duke, May 8, 1968, in NCNW, Series 20, Box 2, Folder 14; Duke, "How It Began," 3–4. See also, Height *Open Wide the Freedom Gates*, 195.

The Mississippi Home Builders (MHB) also proved a useful ally when, as with the NAHB, they were informed of the opportunities posed by such a project. The past president of MHB, Francis X. Collins, took a particular interest in Duke's proposal. Duke recalled a meeting in May 1967 when "Mr. Collins has proved to me without a shadow of a doubt that he is interested in more than just the economic gain that can be derived, even though I am sure this is part of his concern."[73] The two organized an all-day meeting at the Mississippi Research and Development Center in Jackson, with representatives of the Mississippi Home Builders, lumber and construction companies, the Ford Foundation, and the Job Training Corps. Duke later highlighted that the meeting was "a first in two areas." It was the first time the MHB "sat down to discuss housing problems with a high-ranking official of the PHA." It was also the first time the organization "sat down with a representative of a Negro organization to discuss housing for poor people." MHB registered its interest in pursuing the low-income programs proposed by NCNW, revising the program of its state homebuilders convention to include a presentation for the program, and also taking steps to change the Mississippi law that required a referendum for new public housing units. At this meeting, MHB agreed with NCNW that the program's success would require "maximum cooperation with the person to be housed," approving NCNW's community participation approach.[74]

Finally, the organization also worked locally to drum up interest in and support for local builders, developers, and lenders. NCNW reasoned that since private housing interests were unaccustomed to serving this sector of the market, they were likely unaware of opportunities that might be unleashed by the new Turnkey III program and skeptical about its political feasibility.[75] NCNW reached out to inform them on both points, because the local housing industries, as Duke put it, had "access to the power structure in their city that no one else has."[76]

By August 1967, NCNW had enlisted a number of builders, bankers, and supply dealers eager to participate in a Turnkey project. Collins offered to develop a demonstration Turnkey III project in the Gulfport area.[77] This would become the first of the Turnkey III

---

[73] Duke, "How It Began," 6.   [74] Ibid., 6–7.

[75] John Ogilvie, "Report and Projections on Project Turnkey Homes," December 4, 1967, in NCNW Series 20, Box 5, Folder 1, 3.

[76] Duke, "How It Began," 27.

[77] When Unita Blackwell first needed to meet with the housing authorities, officials, builders, and bankers in Gulfport – all white – Dorothy Duke suggested she take a plane

developments, and continued the productive relationship between Collins and NCNW. In addition to the planned Gulfport project, NCNW now had commitments to similar projects in towns across Mississippi, including Moss Point, Cleveland, and Greenville.[78] Duke described the "developing awareness of the banker and the builder that such programs make sound economic sense" as "remarkable."[79] As it turned out, once educated about the economic opportunities of the project, members of the housing industry became not only willing business partners, but also social partners and political advocates.[80] To quote Blackwell at length:

When Miss Height and I – two black women – sat down with these Mississippi people – most of them white men – I believe it was the first time white leaders had ever met with black people *as equals* to solve problems of poor black people in our state. And with us was a southern white woman, Dorothy Duke. I don't think they quite knew what to make of us. I'm certain they had never spoken with a black woman with the confident, businesslike manner of Miss Height. She spoke directly and didn't sidestep issues or beat around the bush, but she was always "ladylike" and usually wore a hat. Dorothy Duke was professional – polite but persistent. And then there was *me*, the civil rights worker who was supposed to be a raging militant. But of course I wasn't. I listened carefully to the tone of their voices and watched the looks on their faces to figure out what they were thinking. Then I'd speak up with realistic, practical suggestions and comments, which were all just the "mother wit" I'd been brought up with. We explained how the plan we were developing would benefit the Mississippi business community as well as the poor people who needed housing. It would bring millions of dollars into the state economy. We were successful in convincing the business leaders of the community of the value of our program, and they gave us their support. We were off and running.[81]

---

to Gulfport and pretend to be a DC consultant whose final approval "would be necessary for the project to go forward" (Blackwell was actually from Mississippi). Blackwell, *Barefootin'*, 183.

[78] The Greenville project was also significant because there was no housing authority in place to administer such a program, requiring the establishment of the first new housing authority in the state since the 1962 law requiring public referenda for public housing. A perhaps even bigger accomplishment was Duke's negotiation with the mayor of Greenville to include two black members (one a woman) on the five-member housing authority. Prior to this, no African Americans had ever been appointed to a housing authority in the state. All of this was accomplished with no publicity, in a deliberate effort by the mayor and Duke to not draw attention. Duke, "How It Began," 11–12.

[79] Ibid., 13.

[80] See, for example, Ogilvie, "Report and Projections on Project Turnkey Homes," December 4, 1967, 4.

[81] Blackwell, *Barefootin'*, 180–1.

Though they were off and running, there was still one hitch: the need for congressional appropriations in order to build the Gulfport project. One person they needed to win over, or at least neutralize, was James Eastland, the senator from Mississippi and a segregationist, who typically voted against antipoverty projects. Sensing the futility of approaching Eastland herself, Blackwell instead met with Eastland's chauffeur and asked him to bring up the program to the senator and explain its importance to people in Mississippi. The chauffeur reported back to Blackwell that "Senator Eastland had just nodded positively. He said that meant Eastland would not oppose but did not want to go on the record as supporting it. That's all we needed from him. Senator Eastland was a powerhouse and could have destroyed the project with one statement, but he didn't say a single word, for or against it. Appropriations for Turnkey III sailed through Congress."[82]

LOCAL POLITICS AND CHALLENGES

NCNW also worked to bridge the gap between the local housing authorities (LHAs) that would administer the programs and residents who would become the ultimate tenants and eventual owners of the houses. This would require a twofold effort: first, proving to the low-income community that Turnkey III could "be successfully administered by an agency that has historically ignored their needs" and, second, communicating "to the Housing Authority that meaningful community involvement and participation in planning and implementation is an integral component of the Turnkey III program which does not threaten the role of the Authority but enhances it in a new kind of relationship."[83]

To address the "credibility gap" between the promises of the program and the skepticism of its potential target population, NCNW decided that it was important that the target community be integral to the program's planning from the beginning. The organization held a series of small group meetings in Gulfport (and later in other communities) to explain the program to residents, plan how to advertise for and select tenants, and, more generally, build trust with residents. NCNW also employed community surveys as a means to cultivate local trust. In Gulfport, it sent out local community representatives (rather than professional data

---

[82] Ibid., 183.
[83] NCNW, "Turnkey III Project Homes: Interim Report to the Ford Foundation," January 6, 1970, 8.

collectors, who they worried would be too far removed from the population) to collect data about families' living conditions, income, and whether they might be suitable for homeownership under the Turnkey III program.[84] Gathering such statistics in a manner that was sensitive to local communities helped to win their support, and NCNW recommended the practice to all prospective Turnkey III planners. Data from surveys and other research they collected also helped NCNW build a bridge to the LHAs, helping to address some of their doubts.[85]

NCNW also bridged the divide between residents and the LHAs by introducing community participation committees (CPCs) in the planning and management phases of Turnkey III projects. A CPC would work with the local housing authority and a private management company to meet with and evaluate applicants, sending those whom they "recommended for homeownership" to the local housing authority. The inclusion of a CPC was "a new step in processing applications," unique to Turnkey III. While the housing authority would still have final say, the CPC would have formal recognition by the housing authority to carry out the homeownership plan.[86]

NCNW reached out to communities to try to sell them on the potential benefits of the Turnkey projects and quell residents' concerns about public housing projects. In April 1967, Duke met with an official from HUD's public affairs department and convinced him to draw up new materials on housing, aimed at both local decision-makers and "the poor person who to date has been completely left out."[87] They worked at the ground level to inform community leaders about the potential advantages to communities (as well as employers) of improving housing conditions and the stability of low-income residents.[88]

THE OPENING OF THE GULFPORT PROJECT

The first Turnkey III project opened in North Gulfport, Mississippi, in September 1968. Named Forest Heights, in a nod to NCNW President

---

[84] Nonprofit Housing Center, Urban America, Inc., "Turnkey III: A Case Study of the Pilot Program," 10.

[85] Ibid., 11.

[86] Dorothy Duke, "Application Processing for Home Ownership Plan in Gulfport, Mississippi, 1968," n.d., in NCNW Series 20, Box 12, Folder 28, 3.

[87] Duke, "How It Began," 5.

[88] Nonprofit Housing Center, Urban America, Inc. "Turnkey III: A Case Study of the Pilot Program," 11.

Dorothy Height, the project represented the cooperation of a handful of public advocacy, business, and government actors. First National Bank of Biloxi and Hancock Bank of Gulfport provided $1.2 million in financing for the construction. Collins Building Service, the company owned by the former Mississippi Home Builders president, handled the construction of the development. Management of Forest Heights was initially performed by a partnership between the Harrison County Civic Action Committee and the Thiokol Chemical Corporation (based in Utah, with experience managing housing on Native American reservations), which would review applications and make recommendations to the local housing authority. They would be responsible for training the residents they selected in the care and maintenance of the new housing, as well as in how to take over the eventual leadership of the homeowners association.[89]

Prior to the Forest Heights opening, public housing in Gulfport was in the form of two ten-year-old segregated projects, with mostly two- or three-bedroom units unsuitable for families with more than four children. The units themselves consisted of double houses, resembling "railroad cars, precisely uncoupled in compact freight yards."[90] In contrast, the new development included 150 three-bedroom houses, 25 four-bedroom houses, and 25 five-bedroom houses. Against the prevailing opinion of both builders and federal housing agencies that affordable housing required a significant reduction in building materials and quality, the houses were built with standard wood frames using normal construction procedures.[91] The community itself was a refutation of many clichés about public housing, with its gardens, greenbelts, a community center, and on-site day care. Two years later, Forest Heights became home to a demonstration Head Start program.[92] Beyond the planned facilities, residents themselves developed other community amenities, including a skills bank that allowed them to barter with each other for different services.[93] Finally, NCNW addressed concerns about the suitability of low-income residents for homeownership by creating a training program (to be administered by the Harrison County Community Action Committee

---

[89] NAHB, "Scope," 5:38 (September 22, 1967), in NCNW Series 20, Box 21, Folder 1.
[90] Spraker, "Untitled."
[91] Nonprofit Housing Center, Urban America, Inc., "Turnkey III: A Case Study of the Pilot Program," 23.
[92] Letter from Lee Ambrose to John Balch, July 31, 1969, in NCNW, Series 20, Box 12, Folder 23.
[93] Blackwell, *Barefootin'*, 184.

and Thiokol Chemical Corporation) to equip residents with information about how to be successful in homeownership, and to help provide a basis for cooperative living in the community.[94]

These changes were not simply programmatic and abstract, but were experienced every day in people's lives. The man from the Mississippi delta with ten children whom Blackwell had spoken to got his first house through the Turnkey III program. "Now he's got a home where he's staying in the Mississippi Delta because of Turnkey III," Blackwell shared with an audience in 1970. "He's proud of it. He has self-respect and he walks 'tall.' That's what I see in the communities in the field, the people that move into these homes. I see the look on the people's faces. I see the children running from room to room saying, 'this my room.' For the first time they have room to grow. You also see people suffering, I mean really suffering. We're suffering all over, but when you see people move into a decent home and they paying – some a few dollars less than they was in the little shack – some a few dollars more and the Federal government gonna help them own it. *Now that's something!* ... Why pay for something that ain't nothing, when you can *do* something about something that *is* something? I believe that."[95]

If the quality of the housing and surroundings challenged prevailing norms about low-income housing, NCNW's strategy in bringing the public on board early challenged the prevailing methods of LHAs in their communities. Before devising plans for Forest Heights, NCNW contracted with low-income members of the community to conduct surveys to help them determine their current living and housing situations, what sorts of houses and amenities the community demanded, and even their broader aspirations and frustrations.[96] (NCNW also believed that low-income community members "found less resistance to their inquiries than would have been experienced by middle income, professional employees."[97]) Many of the design decisions were based on such consultations with members of the community who would ultimately become residents.

Forest Heights had its first test of resilience a year later, when Hurricane Camille, a Category 5 hurricane with 200-miles-per-hour winds,

---

[94] See also National Council of Negro Women, "Turnkey III Project Homes: Interim Report to the Ford Foundation," January 6, 1970, 5.

[95] Blackwell, "Views from the Field," 7.

[96] John Ogilvie, "Report and Projections on Project Turnkey Homes," December 4, 1967, 5.

[97] Ibid., 5.

swept through the Gulf Coast. It devastated communities across the area with a 20-foot storm surge and left 140 dead.[98] Forest Heights was not among the affected areas, in large part because one resident, Ike Thomas, risked his life to go out into the storm and close the floodgates. On a tour of the affected areas after the storm, HUD Secretary George Romney asked Thomas why he did it. Thomas replied that "it was because for the first time in their lives, they had something of their own."[99]

THE DIFFUSION OF TURNKEY III AND POLICIES ON HOMEOWNERSHIP FOR THE POOR

In more ways than one, NCNW's efforts helped to transform national thinking on public housing. Within a year of opening its pilot project in Gulfport, NCNW had extended the reach of the program, with plans under way for Turnkey III projects in a dozen locations, ranging from other communities in rural Mississippi to St. Louis to Elizabeth, New Jersey – all told, almost four thousand homes were planned. The organization was also "inundated with requests" from other local housing agencies to help start their own turnkey-style programs, and it responded by creating and disseminating materials that they could customize to their own local housing demands.[100] For local housing authorities, community action program agencies, tenant associations, local sections of the NCNW, builders, architects, students, academics, trade associations, local government officials, churches, nonprofits, and homebuyers associations interested in setting up a program or learning more, NCNW had become the clearinghouse. Its materials included a manual, "How to Get Started With Housing," that outlined the economic, political, and community concerns that any successful program would need to overcome.[101] By 1970, there would be nearly forty thousand Turnkey III or Turnkey IV

[98] Harwell, *Wednesdays in Mississippi*, 177.

[99] Blackwell, *Barefootin'*, 185; Harwell, *Wednesdays in Mississippi*, 177–8; Height, *Open Wide the Freedom Gates*, 195.

[100] See NCNW, "Project Homes Interim Report to Ford Foundation," September 11, 1968, Appendix, in NCNW Series 20, Box 4, Folder 12; Staff Report of Dorothy Duke, May 18, 1968, in NCNW, Series 20, Box 5, Folder 1; and letters to Dorothy Duke and NCNW dated December 22, 1970, June 6, 1969, September 15, 1972, and June 19, 1974, all in NCNW Series 20, Box 2, Folder 14.

[101] NCNW, "Final Report of the NCNW on the Promotion and Development of New Programs to Provide Homeownership Opportunities Utilizing Public Housing Subsidies," November 17, 1972, in NCNW, Series 20, Box 4, Folder 91, 43; NCNW, n.d., "How to Get Started with Housing," in NCNW Series 20, Box 21, Folder 7.

(a similar program) units in the pipeline across eighty-five municipalities. In short, NCNW had demonstrated the viability of homeownership for the poor through public housing subsidies, challenging the prevailing logic among businesses and federal and local governments, and challenging the beliefs of poor residents themselves that such a program was impossible.

By this time, another federal program had emerged to fill the low-income homeownership space that Turnkey III's proponents had identified. The 1968 Housing Act introduced Section 235, an FHA program aimed at bringing homeownership to public housing–eligible households, particularly in urban areas that had experienced so much unrest in the 1960s. Section 235 operated on a fundamentally different basis, rejecting the sweat equity model that prevented people from accessing the title, sometimes for decades, as well as the community participation approach that empowered communities to select tenants and self-manage the communities, which NCNW sought to develop and proselytize. Section 235 was instead an extension of the FHA's standard operating procedures, which directly empowered mortgage brokers to sell to prospective homeowners, albeit at terms that public housing–eligible applicants could afford, including relaxed down payment requirements. The program was deemed a massive failure almost from the start, for reasons that are illuminating with regard to the general challenges of creating markets where none existed, yet are outside the scope of this book.[102]

Section 235 was top-down, developed by a committee led by the industrialist J. Edgar Kaiser, with little input from the people who ultimately would utilize the programs. Unlike NCNW's model, Section 235 had no mechanisms for counseling or training residents on the skills for successful self-management of the projects and eventual homeownership. In contrast, as NCNW worked to further improve Turnkey III, the organization focused on community participation and management, developing materials that local organizations could use to create and design a CPC, and also dealing with nuts-and-bolts issues, including templates, such as a sample letter to request recognition of the CPC by the local housing authority, meeting agendas, organizational flow charts, sample bylaws, and site-suitability criteria.[103] NCNW also developed

---

[102] See Hyman, *Debtor's Nation*, and von Hoffman, "Calling upon the Genius," for discussions of Section 235's failures.

[103] NCNW, "Project Homes Interim Report to Ford Foundation," September 11, 1968, Appendix.

mechanisms through which participants in Turnkey and other subsidized programs could have "effective means of communicating their experience and problems to HUD."[104] In short, NCNW viewed citizen involvement as crucial and CPCs as ambassadors for potential homebuyers, representing their interests in the planning and development of homes.[105]

Indeed, citizen participation was also built into NCNW's efforts at building a national coalition in support of homeownership through public housing. In May 1970, NCNW convened a meeting with over a half-dozen possible stakeholders, including the National Association of Home Builders, the National Association of Housing and Redevelopment Officials, the National Association of Real Estate Boards, the Rural Housing Alliance, the National Tenants Organization, the National Urban Coalition, and League of Women Voters. The aim was to combine their resources and experience in the low-income homeownership field and translate it into broader support for national housing goals that would include homeownership for public housing–eligible citizens. The meeting culminated in a letter sent to HUD Secretary Romney, in which they requested that he set up a task force to study the problem.[106]

Following up, they convened and invited Romney to attend a national conference on homeownership through public housing, the first of its kind. The conference provided a national forum on information about existing programs, obtained a commitment from the Nixon administration to Turnkey III, and also established a representative task force of organizations interested in homeownership through public housing, to be headed by Joseph Burstein.[107] During his keynote address, Romney spoke favorably of NCNW's leadership on the issue and seemed receptive to the idea of homeownership through public housing. He requested that NCNW create a task force to advise him on Turnkey III and IV. Following NCNW's lead, he stressed the need to involve consumers in shaping low-income housing policy, and suggested that the task force include representatives of low-income and Turnkey III and IV homebuyers.[108]

---

[104] NCNW, Ford Foundation Proposal Draft, June 20, 1972, in NCNW, Series 20, Box 2, Folder 23.

[105] Blackwell, "Views from the Field."

[106] Letter from Dorothy Height to George Romney, May 18, 1970, in NCNW, Series 20, Box 1, Folder 6.

[107] Letter to Elizabeth Farmer from Dorothy Duke, July 22, 1970, in NCNW Series 20, Box 1, Folder 1.

[108] NCNW, "Final Report of the NCNW," November 17, 1972, 10.

NCNW played an important role in the task force and also made sure to incorporate community participation, developing the CPC idea into a nationwide Citizens Task Force and giving it a seat at the table in HUD developments.[109] After the HUD task force released a draft of guidelines for homeownership through public housing in the summer of 1971, NCNW convened a meeting of 112 section volunteers and homebuyers in Mississippi to analyze and discuss the draft. Noting that the guidelines themselves had few provisions for community participation or legal protections for participants, they pushed for both to be included in the final regulations.[110]

This is not to suggest that everything that NCNW did with Turnkey III went smoothly. There were often political barriers to its acceptance. In some areas, NCNW had to navigate outcry from potential neighbors of Turnkey III projects who were concerned about the image of public housing, the potential impact on their own property values, and, sometimes, the unfairness of the relative ease (whether real or imagined) with which poor people could become homeowners through the program. A planned Turnkey III project in St. Louis, Missouri, was nearly abandoned when residents raised the specter of Priutt-Igoe, the city's notorious public housing project, in their backyard. After learning of the planned Turnkey III project in their neighborhood, black and white citizens banded together to form a protest organization called the Northside Citizens for a Better Community, which launched suits against the Housing Authority, held neighborhood rallies, marched on City Hall, and wrote newspaper articles railing against the plan.[111] Similarly, San Antonio's Housing Authority was forced to abandon the plan it worked out with NCNW after an announcement of the project's locations "created a furor of intensity previously unknown to the City of San Antonio. The 'silent majority' rose to public meetings, letter writing and domination of the conventional news media. The overall tone of their protests was that of 'it may be a good idea, but not next-door to me.'"[112]

Another political barrier was the strained relationship between local housing authorities that would need to administer the program and low-income residents who would be its target beneficiaries. Rather than accepting the program enthusiastically, potential residents often had good

---

[109] Ibid., 3.   [110] Ibid., 14.

[111] National Council of Negro Women, "Turnkey III Project Homes: Interim Report to the Ford Foundation," January 6, 1970, 11–12.

[112] Ibid., 36.

reason to be skeptical, based on past experience with their local housing agencies, as well as LHAs' general practice of excluding local residents from their decision-making process. On the other side, NCNW was concerned that LHAs might be unwilling to fully accept a program that challenged their conventional view of public housing tenants as incapable of homeownership and self-management.[113]

Because of restrictions built into the program, the rights of those who used Turnkey III were circumscribed. For example, civil rights and women's rights advocates fought for greater access to standard home-ownership opportunities, by which borrowers would receive the title to the property upon closing, even if they had a mortgage. Not so for Turnkey III residents. They would not receive title until after an estimated twenty-one to twenty-two years of payments. Similarly, whereas a home-owner under normal circumstances was free to move and resell the property, Turnkey III homeowners had to promise to stay at least ten years, which reduced their ability to move in response to, say, better job opportunities. Finally, unique disincentives were built in for Turnkey III owners, including stringent restrictions on how tenants could recapture property through sweat equity and a restriction designed to prevent "windfall profits" (whether for the homeowner or a speculator) by pro-hibiting homeowners from "making any profit whatever on the resale of the unit for 10 years thereafter."[114] In short, as ArDee Ames wrote in his critique of the program, Turnkey III provided "more of an illusion of homeownership than a reality."[115] (While one could make the same argument about any purchase involving a mortgage, Ames was correct that Turnkey III residents had limited rights of homeownership relative to those who were able to buy their houses through traditional lending channels.)

Perhaps the most formidable challenge for Turnkey III's expansion and longer-term viability was in identifying the elusive "homeownership suit-able" poor the program needed in order to function. A Government Accountability Office (GAO) report issued in March 1974 concluded that the program had failed to attract a "sufficient number of low-income families with genuine homeownership potential." This was a problem, because the success of the program depended on its ability to ensure as

---

[113] Ibid., 8.

[114] ArDee Ames, "A Critique of HUD's Homeownership Program for Low-Income Families (Turnkey III)," February 2, 1969, in NCNW Series 20, Box 21, Folder 5.

[115] Ibid.

few vacancies in the projects as possible, lest they become targets of vandalism or fall into disrepair. Income instability was one major issue. Studying 209 Turnkey III families in Raleigh, GAO found that nearly one-quarter of the households experienced an income decrease within their first three years of occupancy, and 72 percent had incomes so low that they were unable to meet the minimum monthly payment that would "cover their share of project operation and administrative expenses and reserves." Nine of these families actually paid nothing in monthly payments because their income was so low.[116] Unable to find "homeownership suitable" applicants on the basis of the initial public housing eligibility criteria, some localities began to relax the criteria and open the program to families above the income cutoffs, perhaps allowing the program to function, albeit technically violating HUD guidelines.[117]

TAKING STOCK OF NCNW'S STRATEGY

A month after the first Turnkey III development opened in Gulfport, HUD Secretary Weaver addressed the NCNW National Conference in DC to congratulate the organization for its "unprecedented involvement" in the project, which "marks you as prime innovators in this field."[118] Describing NCNW's impressive effort to convene federal, state, and local governments, the private building industry, lenders, and national foundations, Weaver noted that "the most important lesson to be learned is that the Gulfport project would never have started if it hadn't been for the interest, and the whole-hearted involvement of the National Council of Negro Women." He added, "This is doubly impressive when you consider that yours is not a technically-trained housing group."[119]

NCNW followed a process of detecting, researching, contesting, and then expanding the boundaries of access to homeownership that is familiar from earlier case studies in this book. But in this case, activists focused on barriers of income and poverty compounded by race and, to a lesser

---

[116] US Government Accountability Office, "Problems in the Homeownership Opportunities Program for Low-Income Families," Report to Congress B-171630, March 27, 1974, 15.

[117] Ibid., 10.

[118] Robert C. Weaver, Address to the National Convention of the NCNW, "Charting a Pathway to the Future," Sheraton Park Hotel, Washington, DC, November 9, 1967, in NCNW Series 20, Box 5, Folder 1, 12.

[119] Ibid., 13.

extent, gender. For the many similarities in these activities, key differences are evident between the development of Turnkey III and the movements for racial and gender equality described in earlier chapters. In the other two cases, advocates bracketed the income issue and focused on cases where middle- and upper-middle-class black and female applicants had attempted and failed to gain access to homeownership on the same terms as white men. By setting aside class issues, activists could challenge the underlying economic justification by which their constituents had been denied access (which is not to say that their argument that women and African Americans posed no inherent economic risk was readily accepted). And by casting doubt on the economic logic of exclusion, advocates were then able to contest this exclusion on *political* grounds, debunking the notion that private market forces were responsible for unequal housing outcomes.

These activists argued against the common wisdom that government policy merely reflected segregation; on the contrary, the federal government had used its policies to normalize and reinforce market segregation. To the extent that exclusion from homeownership was the product of the "mighty hand of the federal government," the government had not only the authority to intervene, but an obligation to do so. Moreover, that obligation arguably could extend to those businesses with which it partnered.

Likewise, feminist activists focused on middle-class constituents whose economic credentials seemed unassailable to make visible their categorical, noneconomic exclusion from access to housing credit. They argued further that sex alone was not a relevant predictor of default risk, drawing on work by economists such as Gary Becker, who argued that noneconomic discrimination actually harmed businesses that discriminated, by narrowing their markets. With this argument in hand, women's rights advocates fought to have government regulators adopt a more robust role in monitoring and sanctioning businesses within their purview that discriminated against women. Women's rights advocates also used their middle-class status to contrast their plight with that of the failed Section 235, which had also been targeted to low-income (generally African American) households. Finally, though focusing on middle-class women's issues may have given them firmer ground on which to contest exclusion, that created its own dilemmas and disagreements within the movement, as some wondered whether it was reasonable to focus on an issue that mostly affected middle- and upper-middle-class women at the expense of more cross-cutting issues, and others questioned whether married women who were not in the paid workforce ought to still have the right to share in the credit history of their husbands and have access to credit themselves.

Turnkey III's advocates did not approach the challenge by trying to chip away at the barriers to accessing mainstream mortgage credit channels. Early on, they ruled out going through FHA's rural counterpart, FaHA, largely accepting that their constituents' incomes were too low and unstable for them ever to qualify for a mortgage. Instead, they contested poor peoples' exclusion from homeownership from a different angle: NCNW challenged the prevailing opinion that poor households were uninterested in homeownership, or incapable of meeting the responsibilities it entailed. Many pointed to the poor state of public housing projects and the dilapidated conditions of the housing most poor people lived in as evidence. The structure of the Turnkey III program would essentially challenge this logic by requiring tenants to prove they were up to the task of basic maintenance and upkeep. And recognizing that the skills of homeownership and management were not innate but teachable, they designed a model of homeownership rooted in counseling and community participation. Beyond challenging the idea that the poor were undeserving or unwilling to meet the responsibilities of homeownership, NCNW questioned the basic economic logic that had long kept this area of the market underserved. NCNW consciously set out to "prove the market" for low-income ownership, by going door-to-door to survey local communities and meeting with local businesses to help kindle interest.

But the political task – and business support – lay in the organization's ability to convert one form of housing subsidy, namely public rental, into another form, homeownership. Subsidies for the poor were inevitable, Turntey III's advocates contended, and, given this fact, homeownership should be viewed as a viable subsidy that could even prove to be cheaper in the long run. Moreover, the organization contended, homeownership for the poor should be considered a legitimate and socially acceptable use of public power and funds. In designing Turnkey III, NCNW and its allies made the state's boundary-setting operations in the field of homeownership visible, and therefore contestable, and expanded the scope of government activity to include homeownership for the poor as a legitimate use of public power and purse.

7

Markets, Marginalized Groups, and American Political Development

The provision of social goods in the United States has been marked by exclusion and shaped by the contestation of the excluded. Even as beneficiaries of social policies had trouble recognizing their links to government, members of marginalized groups recognized those links and attempted to reforge them.

This observation challenges a prevalent view in the welfare state literature that the US government's tendency to distribute benefits to citizens indirectly helps to promulgate a quiet politics characterized by low citizen awareness of the government's role in their lives. It does not refute the abundant evidence suggesting that citizen beneficiaries often do not recognize the role of the government in their lives; there is little doubt that such citizens have the luxury of viewing the things they enjoy, such as homeownership, retirement security, or health care, as the result of "a freely functioning market system at work."[1] But it does suggest that, for others who are less fortunate, the activist state is clearly evident, and often not for the better. This book refocuses scholarly attention onto those groups that have been excluded from access and the insider-outsider dynamics created when the state attempts to channel social benefits to people indirectly, through the use of market incentives.

Across multiple cases, this book documents and describes how outsider groups have come to recognize the role of the government in promoting their constituents' exclusion from access to homeownership. Boundary groups have transformed what otherwise might have been viewed as

[1] Mettler, *Submerged State*, 5.

individual market problems into collective political ones, thereby open to collective political contestation. They have also mobilized to change the government's role, calling for new laws and specific revisions to existing regulations, as well as pressing the government to use its existing authority to impel private actors to change their behavior.

For a policy area in which institutions are supposed to depoliticize issues of access and distribution, the public–private welfare state has proved a surprisingly prolific source for the tools and materials, both institutional and ideational, by which groups have advanced their constituents' positions. In particular, as the boundary groups in this book show, public–private policies create both new financial opportunities and new risks for businesses that can be utilized politically. And they simultaneously place the government in the position of having to define the terms on which someone may access market goods, which can then invite charges of government complicity in discrimination and exclusion. In short, rather than *removing* politics from the question of who gets access to particular goods, delegating provision to third-party providers actually proliferates a different *kind* of politics. It redirects politics toward battles over the terms of access, often waged by those whose access is systematically constrained.

This book explores these claims as they pertain to the politics of homeownership and mortgage credit, policy areas that have remained surprisingly underexplored by scholars of the public–private welfare state. Yet the cases depicted in this book also raise some rather fundamental issues pertaining to democratic politics and the American state. The cases highlight the transformative role of marginalized groups in challenging the scope of the American state and redefining its authority and role in the housing market. In doing so, they bring to the fore a particular kind of politics whose core features can be seen in areas beyond homeownership: the politics of discovery.

The politics of discovery is centrally focused on rendering the role of the government visible and legible in order to contest it. Through certain forms of collective action, in particular information gathering and dissemination, marginalized groups have been important forces in revealing the state and challenging the boundaries of state power. Their success in challenging and altering the boundaries of state power, to be sure, has been mixed. But as scholars begin to come to grips with the vast but hidden scope of the American state, it is crucial that they grapple with the politics of discovery as constitutive of American political development.

AMERICAN POLITICAL DEVELOPMENT AND THE POLITICS OF DISCOVERY

Understanding politics as a process of discovery – in which marginalized groups engage in collective action to reveal and contest the scope of the state – helps to bring together two distinct research agendas in American political development. The first of these is detailed in the introduction to this book, and is centrally concerned with challenging an earlier literature that viewed the American state as minimalist, laissez-faire, or even nonexistent. It does so by shedding light on the state's complex entanglements with private associations and third-party providers and use of indirect tools such as tax expenditures, regulations, or loan insurance to achieve objectives that other governments might have attempted through more direct means.[2] By bringing to light the myriad ways the US government has wielded power since the nineteenth century, this agenda has significantly redefined how scholars think about the American state.[3] The American state is not necessarily less activist than the European states to which it has been compared, but is perhaps more complex and, as a result, often more opaque.

The second of these agendas has focused on understanding the contribution of marginalized groups to American political development. Like other transformative political actors – including parties, voters, business associations, policy entrepreneurs – marginalized groups have opened up new areas of state responsibility. Unlike other actors, marginalized groups are characterized by their relative lack of access to formal mechanisms of political power, whether the ballot box or political office. Despite this lack of access, they have managed in important ways to articulate new demands and forge new state authorities and capacities. Women's organizations have secured for their members the right to vote and deprived men (who *could* vote) of the right to drink, creating a maternalist welfare state along

---

[2] Sparrow, Novak, and Sawyer, *Boundaries of the State in US History*; Novak, *The People's Welfare*; Clemens, "Lineages of the Rube-Goldberg State"; Hacker, *The Divided Welfare State*; Mettler, *The Submerged State*; Morgan and Campbell, *The Delegated Welfare State*; Howard, *The Hidden Welfare State*; Howard, *The Welfare State Nobody Knows*; Klein, *For All These Rights*; Gottschalk, *The Shadow Welfare State*; Sheingate, "Why Americans Can't See the State;" Novkov and Nackenoff, *Statebuilding from the Margins*.

[3] Indeed, an even more important outcome of this renewed focus on the American state has been to challenge where we should even refer to the American state as singular, given all the different activities it engages in, different modes of power, and different means of accomplishment. See Kimberly Morgan and Ann Orloff, *The Many Hands of the State Theorizing Political Authority and Social Control* (New York: Cambridge University Press, 2017)

the way.[4] Radical farmers also worked from the margins to develop several key economic institutions of the twentieth-century regulatory state, including the Federal Trade Commission, the Federal Reserve, and federal farm lending institutions, which formed somewhat of a template for government involvement in homeownership in the 1930s.[5] A final example, as Megan Francis shows, is how the NAACP's movement against racial violence in the early twentieth century also reshaped American government and society. She writes of the transformation the civil rights organization helped bring about: "Democracy no longer meant unbridled violence toward one group of people. Of course, all did not immediately change, but it was a critical first step in showing that marginalized citizens could impact the sacred boundaries of state power."[6]

Bringing these two strands of research into conversation helps to draw attention to the stratifying effects of indirect or complex uses of state power.[7] To be sure, scholars have not fully neglected the question of who benefits from the government when it operates out of sight, pointing to private businesses and associations, higher-income citizens, third-party providers, and certain favored occupational categories. Scholars have done much less to reckon with the ways that indirect arrangements, like their more visible counterparts, can stratify citizens along other lines, including race, gender, age, and geography.[8] Governing arrangements

---

[4] Theda Skocpol, *Protecting Soldiers and Mothers: The Political Origins of Social Policy in the United States* (Cambridge MA: Harvard University Press, 1992), 317–18; Elisabeth Clemens, *The People's Lobby: Organizational Innovation and the Rise of Interest Group Politics in the United States, 1890–1925* (Chicago: University of Chicago Press, 1997), 5.

[5] Elizabeth Sanders, *Roots of Reform: Farmers, Workers, and the American State, 1877–1917* (Chicago: University of Chicago Press, 1999).

[6] Megan Ming Francis, *Civil Rights and the Making of the Modern American State* (New York: Cambridge University Press, 2014), 174–5.

[7] This is not to suggest that these agendas have never been brought together. The essays in Novkov and Nackenoff's *Statebuilding from the Margins* certainly take this relationship seriously, focusing on efforts of reformers and activists outside of the state to remake state activity and build new state capacities. The volume also takes seriously how reformers' efforts relate to the interpenetration of public and private in the US; sometimes reformers and activists are responsible for building hybrid forms of governing capacity, other times they are at the forefront of the reform.

[8] The literature on the public–private welfare state often notes income, class, and employment disparities in who has access to its benefits. (See Hacker, *Divided Welfare State*, Tables 1.2–1.4; Mettler, *Submerged State*; Howard, *Hidden Welfare State*, 8–9, 31–3, Table 1.3; Beth Stevens, "Blurring the Boundaries: How the Federal Government Has influenced Welfare Benefits in the Private Sector," in Margaret Weir, Ann Shola Orloff, and Theda Skocpol, (eds.), *The Politics of Social Policy in the United States* (Princeton, NY: Princeton University Press, 1988), chap. 3. 129, 147). It has paid much less attention to ways that these types of arrangements can stratify populations on the basis of race,

that rely on the interplay of public and private power can produce different experiences of and with the state, in ways that policy-makers might not have intended at the outset. Scholars need to understand the consequences of this form of state power for different social groups.

Moreover, the conversation between these two literatures touches on a key objection to the entire project of uncovering the hidden state. In an essay critiquing the hidden state genre, Damon Mayrl and Sarah Quinn raise the possibility that scholars, in designating complex governing arrangements as "hidden," "submerged," or "out of sight," have perhaps unfairly conflated the complexity of some governing arrangements with their invisibility. As they point out, there is nothing inherent in complex governing arrangements that conceals them from citizens. Just as citizens can fail to see or acknowledge the government's role when it fulfills some of its most obvious and visible functions (such as when Social Security recipients fail in surveys to classify themselves as beneficiaries of government social programs), citizens are also capable of seeing government power manifested in complex ways (for example, when they recognize the impact of employment regulations on their working conditions).[9] The designation of some activities as part of the state and others as not, then, is a political or cognitive exercise in classification.[10]

---

gender, or other ascriptive characteristics, though Hacker notes in passing that racial and gender inequalities in unionization and employment made employer-sponsored insurance mostly for the benefit of white men, and Mettler's study of the history of higher education finance briefly describes how policy-makers decided to channel the benefits directly to students, because it allowed them to "circumvent contentious issues of the era, most obviously surrounding race." (See Hacker, *Divided Welfare State*, 132, and Mettler, *Degrees of Inequality*, 60.) Literature on more "traditional" welfare state institutions has a longer history of treating stratification as a crucial dimension by which to understand and judge welfare state generosity. See, for example, Gøsta Esping-Andersen, *The Three Worlds of Welfare Capitalism* (Princeton, NJ: Princeton University Press); Julia Lynch, *Age in the Welfare State: The Origins of Social Spending on Pensioners, Workers, and Children* (New York: Cambridge University Press, 2006); Julia O'Connor, "Gender, Class and Citizenship in the Comparative Analysis of Welfare State Regimes: Theoretical and Methodological Issues," *British Journal of Sociology* 44, no. 3 (1993), 501–18; Gøsta Esping-Andersen, *Social Foundations of Postindustrial Economies* (Oxford: Oxford University Press, 1999); Kimberly Morgan, *Working Mothers and the Welfare State: Religion and the Politics of Work-Family Policies in Western Europe and the United States* (Palo Alto, CA: Stanford University Press, 2006); Margot Canaday, *The Straight State: Sexuality and Citizenship in Twentieth-Century America* (Princeton, NJ: Princeton University Press, 2011); and Lieberman, *Shifting the Color Line*.

[9] Mettler, *Submerged State*; Damon Mayrl and Sarah Quinn, "Beyond the Hidden American State: Classification Struggles and the Politics of Recognition," in Kimberly Morgan and Ann Shola Orloff (eds.), *The Many Hands of the State: Theorizing Political Authority and Social Control* (New York: Cambridge University Press, 2017), chap. 2.

[10] Mayrl and Quinn, "Beyond the Hidden American State," 65.

How do these two points relate to the politics of discovery? Well, if we consider the possibility that complex state arrangements can stratify the population into insiders and outsiders or affect citizens' lived experiences differently, *and* we take seriously the possibility raised by Mayrl and Quinn that the "hiddenness" of the state is contingent and contestable, then it follows that one mode of state building involves revealing the state – reclassifying economic or social activities and outcomes formerly viewed as private, natural, or wholly outside the scope of government – in order to contest its effects on society. Those who understand the coercive power of the state as being used against them may be the ones who are most likely to initiate such classification struggles. Organizations are central to this dynamic, given their advantages in helping people make meaning out of individual experiences and transform them into collective political grievances.

Boundary groups challenging the state to address their constituents' exclusion from homeownership often faced skepticism that the state had any role at all to play in their exclusion.[11] In an outcome many viewed as shaped by impersonal market forces, it could (and at times did) seem inappropriate to suggest that the state could play any role in remedying these groups' complaints without placing lenders at risk. Boundary groups engaged in the necessary task of proving the state's involvement. In bringing to light the role of the state, marginalized groups then challenged it, in effect altering its scope. If, as James C. Scott argues, states make society legible in order to govern it, so, too, might society make the state legible in order to contest and transform it.[12]

DETECT, REVEAL, AND ALTER: BEYOND HOMEOWNERSHIP AT MIDCENTURY

Viewed as a struggle to detect, reveal, and then alter the scope of the state, the possibilities for extending this book's core insights about the politics of discovery into other realms beyond homeownership and the public-private welfare state are clear. Conflicts over the appropriate scope of state authority are foundational to democratic politics and yet, as the

---

[11] Indeed, as David Freund points out, government homeownership policies helped to shape a new postwar racial politics, whereby white suburbanites could use economic arguments to justify racial exclusion in their neighborhoods, while also viewing blacks' lower attainment of homeownership as a sign of poor citizenship rather than government racial exclusion. Freund, *Colored Property*.

[12] James C. Scott, *Seeing Like a State: How Certain Schemes to Improve the Human Condition Have Failed* (New Haven: Yale University Press, 1998).

literature on the government out of sight well demonstrates, *that* the state even exercises authority in some areas is not always well known or understood. Revealing the state in order to contest it has been central to other conflicts in contemporary American politics, including in questions of whose medical needs get covered in the insurance market and whose are considered too risky to insure; whose labor actually counts as "employment" for the purposes of the Fair Labor Standards Act (FLSA) and whose work falls outside of the act's purview; and who gets protection through the criminal justice system and who needs protection *from* it. In each of these areas, citizens who have been differentially excluded from or mistreated by the application of state power have joined efforts to make the state's role in their grievances legible and thereby contestable.

In the health policy arena, advocacy groups have mobilized in multiple ways to draw attention to the state's influence over the parameters of the private insurance market, in order to encourage the government to use that influence to ensure better access to treatments have been unprovided or underprovided by insurers. Patient advocacy groups and minority rights organizations have pointed to the multiple sources of leverage that laws and regulations provide the government over private insurers.[13] This includes the favorable tax treatment of employer-provided insurance and the Food and Drug Administration's oversight over the prescription drug market, as well as privacy laws under the Health Insurance Portability and Accountability Act of 1996, whose nondiscrimination clause "paved the way for federal legislation mandating the inclusion of specific benefits in health insurance plans."[14] The use of state power to induce private insurers to cover oral contraceptives, mental health treatment, and gender

---

[13] Learning, for example, that only 15 percent of insurance companies offered comprehensive oral contraceptive coverage in their plans, women's health advocates launched a campaign in the mid-1990s at the state and federal levels to mandate coverage. Their strategy relied on challenging the prevailing economic explanations offered by members of the insurance industry, bringing to bear evidence suggesting that contraceptive coverage was omitted from health plans by historical oversight and stressing the arbitrary nature of categorically excluding oral contraceptives while allowing patients access to a range of other prescription drugs, not to mention options like sterilization (offered by 85 percent of plans at the time) and abortion (about two-thirds of plans). But they also used the federal and state governments' role in defining the parameters of who could access health care and on what terms as both a tool in pressing for their own demands and a rationale for why such issues could be resolved politically rather than through insurers or employers directly. Between 1998 and 2003, twenty states adopted laws to mandate contraceptive coverage for the insurers they regulated. Cynthia Dailard, "Contraceptive Coverage: A 10-Year Retrospective," *The Guttmacher Report on Public Policy* 7, no. 2. (2004), 6–9.

[14] Ibid.

reassignment therapy is in part a result of the efforts of advocates who identified the state's role in the insurance market in order to press it to do more for groups whose needs had long been neglected.[15]

Activists working to improve the wages and working conditions of home care workers have also at times invoked a politics of discovery, challenging the conventional wisdom that their work conditions were rooted in their market status as "unskilled" labor. Instead, home care workers and the labor organizers they allied with argued that care workers' position in the labor market was shaped by policy decisions beginning in the 1930s, in particular the decision to exempt domestic labor from the Fair Labor Standards Act, which rendered the workers ineligible for overtime pay and other protections. By the 2000s, home health workers had become the fastest growing segment of the American labor union movement, and used their increasing clout and numbers to challenge the government's designation of their work as outside of the FLSA framework.[16] Their success has been mixed. In a 2007 case demanding overtime compensation for extra work performed, the Supreme Court ruled that home health workers still "fell outside the Fair Labor Standards Act, even when employed by a for-profit agency."[17] In 2013, the Obama administration explicitly recognized home health workers as employees eligible for FLSA protection, but a Supreme Court ruling a year later saying that they were not technically public employees dealt a blow to home care workers' organizing efforts.[18]

A final area where the politics of discovery has figured prominently is the movement to challenge and reform the criminal justice system. The carceral state offers a slight twist to the politics of discovery, in that few would deny the government's hand in policing and enforcing the law and punishing offenders. These functions are widely understood as being within the state's

---

[15] Elaine M. Hernandez and Christopher Uggen, "Institutions, Politics, and Mental Health Parity," *Society and Mental Health* 2, no. 3 (2012)154–71; Liza Khan, "Transgender Health at the Crossroads: Legal Norms, Insurance Markets, and the Threat of Healthcare Reform," *Yale Journal of Health Policy, Law, and Ethics* 11, no. 4 (2013), 1–44; Jaime Grant et al., *Injustice at Every Turn: A Report of the National Transgender Discrimination Survey* (Washington, DC: National Center for Transgender Equality and National Gay and Lesbian Task Force, 2011), 73–4; Dailard, "Contraceptive Coverage."

[16] Vanessa May, *Unprotected Labor: Household Workers, Politics, and Middle-Class Reform in New York, 1870–1940* (Chapel Hill: University of North Carolina Press, 2011); Eileen Boris and Jennifer Klein, *Caring for America: Home Health Workers in the Shadow of the Welfare State* (New York: Oxford University Press, 2012); Tamara Draut, *Sleeping Giant: How the New Working Class Will Transform America* (New York: Doubleday, 2016); Premila Nadasen, *Household Workers Unite: The Untold Story of African American Women Who Built a Movement* (Boston: Beacon Press, 2015).

[17] Boris and Klein, *Caring for America*, 5.   [18] Ibid., 226–7.

purview and indeed constitute a core function of any state. Yet in recent years, scholars, journalists, and social movement activists have worked to reveal precisely how seemingly colorblind institutions of the carceral state can still produce systematic racial disparities in who comes into contact with it.[19] They have also revealed the cascading effects that systematic racial and class inequality in interactions with the carceral state have on neighborhoods, families, and democratic representation and legitimacy more broadly.[20] Movements to reform all areas of the carceral state, including policing, surveillance, and sentencing, have operated on the premise that the government's role needs to be made visible to the public in order to build support. Video and other forms of evidence have made it harder to contend that people's experience with the criminal justice system is shaped solely by whether they are law-abiding or not, showing how geography, class, gender, and, most of all, race condition one's experience with this aspect of state power and sense of systemic injustice.[21]

SUCCESS, FAILURE, AND THE LIMITS OF THE POLITICS OF DISCOVERY

Across multiple areas of American society and economy, groups who have felt the power of the state directed against their members have mobilized to alter the scope of state authority and responsibility, and have done so by first identifying and then rendering legible the role of the state in their grievances. This should be notable precisely because these are areas that do not have to be understood as definitively shaped by the state and may be given little or no thought by those whose experiences with these less visible or direct forms of state power are not marked by exclusion or coercion. Precisely because state power is so often

[19] Michelle Alexander, *The New Jim Crow: Mass Incarceration in the Age of Colorblindness* (New York: The New Press, 2010); Keeanga-Yamahtta Taylor, *From #Blacklivesmatter to Black Liberation* (Chicago: Haymarket Books, 2016).

[20] Traci Burch, *Trading Democracy for Justice: Criminal Convictions and the Decline or Neighborhood Political Participation* (Chicago: University of Chicago Press, 2013); Marie Gottschalk, *Caught: The Prison State and the Lockdown of American Politics* (Princeton, NJ: Princeton University Press, 2016); Amy Lerman and Vesla Weaver, *Arresting Citizenship: The Democratic Consequences of American Crime Control* (Chicago: University of Chicago Press, 2014).

[21] Hannah Walker, "Extending the Effects of the Carceral State: Proximal Contact, Political Participation, and Race" *Political Research Quarterly* 67, no. 4 (2014), 809–22; Hannah Walker, *Mobilized by Injustice: Criminal Justice Contact, Political Participation and Race*, PhD Diss., University of Washington, 2016.

operated through indirect and invisible mechanisms, it is critically important that we grapple with the politics of discovery that such groups with
grievances against the use of state power find themselves engaged in. This
book offers a first step in that agenda.

The second step should be to examine what limits the politics of
discovery. This book is largely an exercise in concept development and
theory building, examining the processes by which marginalized groups
come to understand their exclusion as generated not by the invisible hand
of the market, but by policy decisions, and then go on to contest their
exclusion on those grounds. The cases could be considered "successful"
to the extent that all four of the steps described in Chapter 1 (detection,
information, contestation, and expansion) ultimately materialized. But it
leaves open questions about latent grievances that never materialized into
movements, as well as movements that did materialize but failed to bring
about policy change. Moreover, and as the cases themselves illuminate,
the presence of this four-step process of detection, information, contestation, and expansion does not mean that all expansions are equally
successful. Policy changes can be cosmetic, yielding few meaningful
changes on the ground. Or they can reflect second-best options that fall
short of what boundary groups would prefer. They are also subject to
reversal, erosion, or lack of enforcement, though as Chapters 4 and 5
demonstrate, groups can also play a role in post-enactment politics,
helping to monitor and enforce policies once enacted.[22]

Engaging in a politics of discovery can carry its own political risks as
well. Boundary group mobilization can provoke public backlash, as
particularly visible demonstrations to render the state legible can also
spur resistance: consider how the Black Lives Matter movement helped
to generate a Blue Lives Matter countermovement that rejected the movement's central claims, or how the 1970s community reinvestment movement to address the lack of capital investment in minority neighborhoods
became implicated in the fight over the causes of the financial crisis.[23]

A final issue returns us to the narrower focus of this book on the politics
of contesting exclusion in the public–private welfare state. This book
identifies marginalized groups as potential change agents within a set of
policy arrangements thought to generate little involvement or attention
from citizens more broadly. At the least, marginalized groups have

---

[22] Patashnik, *Reforms at Risk*, Patashnik and Zelizer, "The Struggle to Remake Politics."
[23] See Desmond King and Rogers Smith, *Still a House Divided: Race and Politics in
Obama's America* (Princeton, NJ: Princeton University Press, 2011), 139–42.

identified and called attention to the role of the government in outcomes that many people assume to be attributable to the market. At their most successful, marginalized groups have helped to reform some of these institutions, thereby contributing to American political development.

But it is worth lingering a bit on whether there are costs to this strategy. Boundary groups focused on those who were arguably the best off among their constituents, presaging the representative inequalities that Dara Strolovitch finds characterize contemporary advocacy groups. (Recall that even in the low-income case, NCNW's emphasis was on its selection of "homeownership suitable" participants among its pool of low-income applicants.) And as much as boundary groups held to the idea that race, class, and gender were irrelevant to the narrow question of whether an individual applicant should be deemed less qualified, challenging such blanket exclusions on economic grounds allowed them to sidestep the structural inequalities faced by many of their constituents. Finally, these movements, while bringing benefits to a few, may have helped entrench a system of debt-financed homeownership that still produces inequalities on the same lines on which those earlier advocates contested it. Millions of Americans have been able to rely on homeownership as a form of asset building, yet for far too many Americans, homeownership has been used as a form of asset stripping, enriching some in the housing industry while leaving households vulnerable. It should not be forgotten that many of the victims of the 2007–8 foreclosure crisis belonged to groups that had historically been denied access to homeownership on the new terms brought about by the New Deal.

A FINAL NOTE

The US government conducts a vast amount of its policy provision discreetly, through indirect and market-based channels that few people associate with the visible hand of the state. Scholars and political commentators have raised questions as to whether this is actually a desirable way to distribute benefits. They point to concerns about the greater costs to taxpayers that can accrue in a "kludgey" policy system.[24] Even more than the financial costs, they point to concerns about democratic responsiveness and legitimacy in policies that are difficult to trace to the government and yet can deliver large and unaccountable profits to businesses.

---

[24] Steven M. Teles, "Kludgeocracy in America" *National Affairs* 17 (2013), 97–114.

Nonetheless, the government out of sight is not a fleeting trend: it is a longstanding mode of policy provision that produces its own distinctive political dynamics. Since at least as early as the 1950s, when the sociologist Richard Titmuss wrote of the "iceberg" quality of the American welfare state, scholars have recognized and grappled with this mode of policy provision and its implications both for democratic politics and for the longer-term developmental trajectories of specific policy areas themselves, such as health care, retirement, and housing.

Hence, the persistent contestation and renegotiation of boundaries over time that this book describes actually constitute one type of a larger form of American political development. Arguably, the advent of a "policy state," as Karen Orren and Stephen Skowronek characterize twentieth-century American political development, has enormously expanded opportunities to contest the boundaries of state activity. *But that contestation can only occur to the extent that the boundaries of the state are visible and the state's role in shaping some social outcome is legible.* From homeownership to health care to incarceration, many people are unaware of the coercive power of the state across the many realms of its activities. They can afford to be, because they exist well within the boundaries of the state and are largely immune from its coercive operations. *Marginalized groups, though, may be aware of the state precisely because its coercive powers are directed against them. To them, the state is clearly evident, and not necessarily an impartial observer.*

Boundary groups described in this book show how delegated authority not only pushed state functions onto private actors, but also pulled private functions into the realm and responsibility of state actors. In interrogating the sources of homeownership, civil society groups helped to make private exchange a matter of public policy, which then opened the way for political struggles over the meaning and effect of these market mechanisms. The activities of boundary groups reveal an entirely overlooked terrain of democratic politics that has not been given adequate attention by scholars of American political development. Much of the story of American political development has been about revealing the scope of the state in order to contest it, and to transform it.

Appendix: Archival Sources
and Congressional Hearings

ARCHIVAL SOURCES

Franklin D. Roosevelt Presidential Library, Hyde Park, NY

DNC	Democratic Party National Committee Papers
HH	Harry Hopkins Papers
HM	Henry Morgenthau Papers
JF	John Fahey Papers
FDR-OF	Presidential Papers, Official File
FDR-PM	Printed Materials

Library of Congress, Washington, DC

CNPR	Center for National Policy Review
CACSW	Citizens Advisory Committee on the Status of Women
NAACP	National Association for the Advancement of Colored People
NUL	National Urban League
RBG	Ruth Bader Ginsburg Papers

Lyndon B. Johnson Presidential Library, Austin, TX

LBJ-PP	Lyndon B. Johnson Presidential Papers
NACRP	National Advisory Commission on Rural Poverty
LBJ-WHCF	White House Central File
LBJ-WHCF2	White House Central File, Confidential File

National Archives II, College Park, MD

RG 31 Records of the Federal Housing Administration, 1930–1965

CCSF   Commissioner's Correspondence and Subject Files, 1938–1958

RS   Division of Research and Statistics, UD-UP 6

RG 220 Records of Temporary Commissions, Commissions, and Boards

NCCF   National Commission on Consumer Finance

National Archives for Black Women's History, Landover, MD

NCNW   National Council for Negro Women
      Series 19: Women in Mississippi
      Series 20: Project Housing
      Series 34: Housing

PC   Polly Cowan Papers

National Association of Realtors Library, Chicago, IL

SFAC   Subject Files, A-C

Special Collections, Northwestern University, Evanston, IL

KDC   Karen DeCrow Papers

Schlesinger Library, Harvard University, Cambridge, MA

CE   Catherine East Papers
CH   Cynthia Harris Papers
NOW   National Organization for Women
WEAL   Women's Equity Action League

CHRONOLOGICAL LIST OF HEARINGS

United States. Congress. Senate. Committee on Banking and Currency. *Creation of a System of Federal Home Loan Banks: Hearings before the Committee on Banking and Currency.* 72nd Cong., 1st sess., January 14, 16, 19, 20, and 21, 1932.

United States. Congress. House. Committee on Agriculture. *Farm Mortgage Relief: Hearings before the Committee on Agriculture.* 73rd Cong., 1st sess., April 5 and 6, 1933.

United States. Congress. Senate. Committee on Banking and Currency Subcommittee. *Home Owners' Loan Act: Hearings before Committee on Banking and Currency Subcommittee.* 73rd Cong., 1st sess., April 20 and 22, 1933.

United States. Congress. Senate. Committee on Banking and Currency. *National Housing Act: Hearings before the Committee on Banking and Currency.* 73rd Cong., 2nd sess., May 16–25, 28, 29, and 31 and June 1, 2, and 4, 1934.

United States. Congress. Senate. Committee on Finance Subcommittee. *Amendments to the Servicemen's Readjustment Act of 1944: Hearings before the Committee on Finance Subcommittee.* 79th Cong., 1st sess., October 8–12, 1945.

United States. Congress. Senate. Committee on Banking and Currency. *Study of Mortgage Credit: Hearings before the Subcommittee on Housing of the Committee on Banking and Currency.* 86th Cong., 1st sess., May 13–15, 19–21, 25, 26, and 28–29, 1959.

United States. House. Civil Rights Subcommittee of the Committee on the Judiciary. *Federal Government's Role in the Achievement of Equal Opportunity in Housing: Hearings before the Civil Rights Subcommittee of the Committee on the Judiciary.* 92nd Cong., 1st sess., October 27, November 3, 4, 10, and 11 and December 2, 8, and 9, 1971, and June 15, 1972.

National Commission on Consumer Finance. *Hearings on The Availability of Credit to Women before National Commission on Consumer Finance.* May 22 and 23, 1972.

United States. Congress. House. Subcommittee on Consumer Affairs of the Committee on Banking and Currency. *Credit Discrimination Part 1: Hearings before the Subcommittee on Consumer Affairs of the Committee on Banking and Currency.* 93rd Cong., 2nd sess., June 20 and 21, 1974.

United States. Congress. House. Subcommittee on Housing and Community Opportunity of the Committee on Financial Services. *Promoting the American Dream of Homeownership through Downpayment Assistance: Hearing before the Subcommittee on Housing and Community Opportunity of the Committee on Financial Services.* 108th Cong., 1st sess., April 8, 2003.

Bibliography

Aaron, Henry J. *Shelter and Subsidies: Who Benefits from Federal Housing Policies?* Washington, DC: Brookings Institution, 1972.

Abbott, Andrew. "Things of Boundaries." *Social Research* 62, no. 4 (1995): 857–82.

Abrams, Charles. "The New 'Gresham's Law of Neighborhoods' – Fact or Fiction?" *Appraisal Journal* 19, no. 3 (1951): 324–37.

Alexander, Michelle. *The New Jim Crow: Mass Incarceration in the Age of Colorblindness.* New York: The New Press, 2010.

Alston, Lee, Wayne Grove, and David Wheelock. "Why Do Banks Fail? Evidence from the 1920s." *Explorations in Economic History* 31, no. 4 (1994): 409–31.

American Institute of Banking. *Home Mortgage Lending, 1st Ed.* New York: American Institute of Banking, 1937.

American Savings and Loan Institute. *Lending Principles and Practices, 1st Ed.* Chicago: American Savings and Loan Institute Press, 1971.

Anderson, Carol. *White Rage: The Unspoken Truth of Our Racial Divide.* New York: Bloomsbury, 2016.

Arnold, R. Douglas. *The Logic of Congressional Action.* New Haven: Yale University Press, 1990.

Babcock, Frederick M. *The Appraisal of Real Estate.* New York: Macmillan Company, 1924.

Baldwin, Peter. "Beyond Weak and Strong: Rethinking the State in Comparative Policy History." *Journal of Policy History* 17, no. 1 (2005): 12–33.

Balogh, Brian. *A Government Out of Sight: The Mystery of National Authority in Nineteenth-Century America.* New York: Cambridge University Press, 2009.

Baumgartner, Frank, Jeffrey Berry, Marie Hojnacki, David Kimball, and Beth Leech. *Lobbying and Policy Change: Who Wins, Who Loses, and Why.* Chicago: University of Chicago Press, 2009.

Becker, Gary. *The Economics of Discrimination.* Chicago: University of Chicago Press, 1957.

Bensel, Richard. *The Political Economy of American Industrialization, 1877–1900.* Cambridge: Cambridge University Press, 2000.

Berk, Gerald. *Louis D. Brandeis and the Making of Regulated Competition, 1900–1932.* Cambridge: Cambridge University Press, 2009.

Bingham, Robert and Stanley McMichael. *City Growth and Values.* Cleveland: McMichael Publishing Company, 1913.

Blackwell, Unita. *Barefootin': Life Lessons from the Road to Freedom.* New York: Crown, 2006.

Boleat, Mark. *National Housing Finance Systems.* London: Croom Helm, 1985.

Boris, Eileen and Jennifer Klein. *Caring for America: Home Health Workers in the Shadow of the Welfare State.* New York: Oxford University Press, 2012.

"Organizing Home Care: Low-Waged Workers in the Welfare State." *Politics & Society* 34, no. 1 (2006): 81–108.

Botein, Hilary. "Labor Unions and Affordable Housing." *Urban Affairs Review* 42, no. 6 (2007): 799–822.

Bowdish, Lawrence. *Invidious Distinctions: Credit Discrimination against Women, 1960s–Present.* PhD Diss. The Ohio State University, 2010.

Boyle, Kevin. *Arc of Justice: A Saga of Race, Civil Rights, and Murder in the Jazz Age.* New York: Henry Holt and Company, 2004.

Break, George. *The Economic Impact of Federal Loan Insurance.* Washington, DC: National Planning Association, 1961.

Buckley, Jack and Mark Schneider. "Are Charter School Parents More Satisfied with Schools? Evidence from Washington, D.C." *Peabody Journal of Education* 81, no. 1 (2006): 57–78.

Burch, Traci. *Trading Democracy for Justice: Criminal Convictions and the Decline of Neighborhood Political Participation.* Chicago: University of Chicago Press, 2013.

Burk, Robert. *The Eisenhower Administration and Black Civil Rights.* Knoxville: University of Tennessee Press, 1984.

Calder, Lendol. *Financing the American Dream: A Cultural History of Consumer Credit.* Princeton, NJ: Princeton University Press, 2001.

Campbell, Andrea. "Policy Makes Mass Politics." *Annual Review of Political Science* 15 (2012): 333–51.

Canaday, Margot. *The Straight State: Sexuality and Citizenship in Twentieth-Century America.* Princeton, NJ: Princeton University Press, 2011.

Card, Emily. *Staying Solvent: A Comprehensive Guide to Equal Credit for Women.* New York: Holt, Rinehart and Winston, 1985.

Women and Mortgage Credit: An Annotated Bibliography. Report for the United States Department of Housing and Urban Development, Office of Policy Development and Research. March 1979.

Carpenter, Daniel. *The Forging of Bureaucratic Autonomy: Reputations, Networks, and Policy Innovation in Executive Agencies, 1862–1928.* Princeton, NJ: Princeton University Press, 2001.

Reputation and Power: Organizational Image and Pharmaceutical Regulation at the FDA. Princeton, NJ: Princeton University Press, 2010.

Castles, Francis. "The Really Big Trade-Off: Home Ownership and the Welfare State in the New World and the Old." *Acta Politica* 33, no. 1 (1998): 5–19.

Chambers, Matthew, Carlos Garriga, and Don E. Schlagenhauf. "Did Housing Policies Cause the Postwar Boom in Home Ownership?" In Eugene N. White, Kenneth Snowden, and Price Fishback, eds. *Housing and Mortgage Markets in Historical Perspective*, chap. 11. Chicago: University of Chicago Press, 2014.

Chapman, Jane Roberts. "Policy Centers: An Essential Resource." In Irene Tinker, ed. *Women in Washington: Advocates for Public Policy*. Beverly Hills, CA: Sage Publications, 1983.

Chappell, L. C. "Judging a Mortgage's Soundness." *Insured Mortgage Portfolio* 1, no. 1 (1936): 12.

Clemens, Elisabeth. "Lineages of the Rube Goldberg State: Building and Blurring Public Programs, 1900–1940." In Ian Shapiro, Stephen Skowronek, and Daniel Galvin, eds. *Rethinking Political Institutions: The Art of the State* New York: New York University Press, 2006.

The People's Lobby: Organizational Innovation and the Rise of Interest Group Politics in the United States, 1890–1925. Chicago: University of Chicago Press, 1997.

Cohen, Lizabeth. *A Consumer's Republic: The Politics of Mass Consumption in Postwar America*. New York: Vintage Books, 2003. [Kindle Edition]

Colean, Miles. *The Impact of Government on Real Estate Finance in the United States*. Cambridge, MA: National Bureau of Economic Research, 1950.

Collins, William J. and Robert A. Margo. "Race and Home Ownership from the End of the Civil War to the Present." *The American Economic Review: Papers and Proceedings* 101, no. 3 (2011): 355–9.

Congressional Quarterly. *Congress and the Nation, 1945–1964*, Volume 1. Washington, DC: Congressional Quarterly Press, 1965.

Cramer Walsh, Katherine. "Putting Inequality in Its Place: Rural Consciousness and the Power of Perspective." *American Political Science Review* 106, no. 3 (2012): 517–32.

Culpepper, Pepper. *Quiet Politics and Business Power: Corporate Control in Europe and Japan*. Cambridge, MA: Cambridge University Press, 2010.

Dailard, Cynthia. "Contraceptive Coverage: A 10-Year Retrospective." *The Guttmacher Report on Public Policy* 7, no. 2 (2004): 6–9.

Davies, Pearl Janet. *Real Estate in American History*. Washington, DC: Public Affairs Press, 1958.

Davies, Richard. *Housing Reform in the Truman Administration*. Columbia: University of Missouri Press, 1966.

Davis, Flora. *Moving the Mountain: The Women's Movement in America since 1960*. New York: Simon & Schuster, 1991.

de Tocqueville, Alexis. *Democracy in America*. New York: McGraw-Hill, 1981 [1835].

Diamond, Douglas and Michael Lea. "The Decline of Special Circuits in Developed Country Housing Finance." *Housing Policy Debate* 3, no. 3 (1992): 747–77.

Doling, John and Nick Horsewood. "Home Ownership and Pensions: Causality and the Really Big Trade-Off." *Housing, Theory and Society* 28, no. 2 (2011): 166–82.

Draut, Tamara. *Sleeping Giant: How the New Working Class Will Transform America*. New York: Doubleday, 2016.

Durand, David. *Risk Elements in Consumer Installment Financing*. Cambridge, MA: National Bureau of Economic Research, 1941.

Eaton, Charlie and Margaret Weir. "The Power of Coalitions: Advancing the Public in California's Public–Private Welfare State." *Politics & Society* 43, no. 1 (2015): 3–42.

Epp, Charles. *Making Rights Real: Activists, Bureaucrats, and the Creation of the Legalistic State*. Chicago: University of Chicago Press, 2010.

Esping-Andersen, Gøsta. *Social Foundations of Postindustrial Economies*. Oxford: Oxford University Press, 1999.

  The Three Worlds of Welfare Capitalism. Princeton, NJ: Princeton University Press, 1990.

Ewalt, Josephine. *A Business Reborn: The Savings and Loan Story, 1930–1960*. Chicago: American Savings and Loan Institute Press, 1962.

Farhang, Sean. *The Litigation State: Public Regulation and Private Lawsuits in the US*. Princeton, NJ: Princeton University Press, 2010.

Federal Housing Administration. *Underwriting Manual*. Washington, DC: Government Printing Office, 1936.

  Underwriting Manual. Washington, DC: Government Printing Office, 1938.

  Underwriting Manual. Washington, DC: Government Printing Office, 1955.

Federal National Mortgage Association. *Circular No. 1: Information Regarding the Activities of the Association*. Washington, DC: Government Printing Office, 1938.

Fetter, Daniel K. "How Do Mortgage Subsidies Affect Home Ownership? Evidence from the Mid-Century GI Bills." *American Economic Review: Economic Policy* 5, no. 2 (2013): 111–47.

  "The Twentieth-Century Increase in US Home Ownership: Facts and Hypotheses." In Eugene N. White, Kenneth Snowden, and Price Fishback, eds. *Housing and Mortgage Markets in Historical Perspective*. Chicago: University of Chicago Press, 2014.

Fishback, Price, Jonathan Rose, and Kenneth Snowden. *Well Worth Saving: How the New Deal Safeguarded Homeownership*. Chicago: University of Chicago Press, 2013.

Fleming, David, William Mitchell, and Michael McNally. "Can Markets Make Citizens? School Vouchers, Political Tolerance, and Civic Engagement." *Journal of School Choice* 8, no. 2 (2014): 213–36.

Fligstein, Neil. "Markets as Politics: A Political-Cultural Approach to Market Institutions." *American Sociological Review* 61, no. 4 (1996): 656–73.

Francis, Megan Ming. *Civil Rights and the Making of the Modern American State*. New York: Cambridge University Press, 2014.

Fraser, Arvonne S. "Insiders and Outsiders: Women in the Political Arena." In Irene Tinker, ed. *Women in Washington: Advocates for Public Policy*. Beverly Hills, CA: Sage Publications, 1983.

Freeman, Richard B. "It's Financialization!" *International Labour Review* 149, no. 2 (2010): 163–83.

Freund, David. *Colored Property: State Policy and White Racial Politics in Suburban America*. Chicago: University of Chicago Press, 2010.

Frydl, Kathleen. *The GI Bill*. New York: Cambridge University Press, 2009.

Galvin, Daniel. "Qualitative Methods and American Political Development." In Richard Valelly, Suzanne Mettler, and Robert Lieberman, eds. *The Oxford Handbook of American Political Development*. New York: Oxford University Press, 2016.

Gates, Margaret. "Credit Discrimination against Women: Causes and Solutions." *Vanderbilt Law Review* 27, no. 3 (1974): 409–42.

Gelb, Joyce and Marian Lief Palley. *Women and Public Policies: Revised and Expanded Edition*. Princeton, NJ: Princeton University Press, 1987.

Gotham, Kevin Fox. "Racialization and the State: The Housing Act of 1934 and the Creation of the Federal Housing Administration." *Sociological Perspectives* 43, no. 2 (2000): 291–317.

Gottschalk, Marie. *Caught: The Prison State and the Lockdown of American Politics*. Princeton, NJ: Princeton University Press, 2016.

The Shadow Welfare State: Labor, Business, and the Politics of Health Care in the United States. Ithaca, NY: Cornell University Press, 2000.

Grant, Jaime M., Lisa A. Mottet, Justin Tanis, Jack Harrison, Jody L. Herman, and Mara Kiesling. *Injustice at Every Turn: A Report of the National Transgender Discrimination Survey*. Washington, DC: National Center for Transgender Equality and National Gay and Lesbian Task Force, 2011.

Green, Richard and Susan Wachter. "The American Mortgage in Historical and International Context." *Journal of Economic Perspectives* 19, no. 4 (2005): 93–114.

Greer, James. "The Better Homes Movement and the Origins of Mortgage Redlining in the United States." In Julie Novkov and Carol Nackenoff, eds. *Statebuilding from the Margins: Between Reconstruction and the New Deal*. Philadelphia: University of Pennsylvania Press, 2014.

Haar, Charles M. *Federal Credit and Private Housing: The Mass Financing Dilemma*. New York: McGraw Hill, 1960.

Hacker, Jacob. *The Divided Welfare State: The Battle over Public and Private Social Benefits in the United States*. New York: Cambridge University Press, 2002.

Hacker, Jacob and Paul Pierson. "After the 'Master Theory': Downs, Schattschneider, and the Rebirth of Policy-Focused Analysis." *Perspectives on Politics* 12, no. 3 (2014): 634–62.

Harrington, Michael. *The Other America: Poverty in the United States*. New York: Macmillan Publishing Co., 1962.

Hartz, Louis. *The Liberal Tradition in America: An Interpretation of American Political Thought*. San Diego: Harcourt Brace & Company, 1955.

Harwell, Debbie. *Wednesdays in Mississippi: Proper Ladies Working for Radical Change, Freedom Summer 1964*. Oxford: University Press of Mississippi, 2014.

Height, Dorothy. *Open Wide the Freedom Gates: A Memoir*. New York: Public Affairs, 2005.

Henderson, A. Scott. *Housing & the Democratic Ideal: The Life and Thought of Charles Abrams*. New York: Columbia University Press, 2000.

Henderson, James D. *Real Estate Appraising: A Practical Work on Appraising and Appraisal Methods.* Cambridge, MA: Banker & Tradesman, 1931.

Hernandez, Elaine M. and Christopher Uggen. "Institutions, Politics, and Mental Health Parity." *Society and Mental Health* 2, no. 3 (2012): 154–71.

Hillier, Amy. "Redlining and the Home Owners' Loan Corporation." *Journal of Urban History* 29, no. 4 (2003): 392–420.

Hirsch, Arnold. "'The Last and Most Difficult Barrier': Segregation and Federal Housing Policy in the Eisenhower Administration, 1953–1960." Report Submitted to the Poverty & Race Research Action Council, March 2005.

Hoffman, Susan. *Politics and Banking: Ideas, Public Policy, and the Creation of Financial Institutions.* Baltimore: Johns Hopkins University Press, 2001.

Hornstein, Jeffrey. *A Nation of Realtors: A Cultural History of the Twentieth Century.* Durham, NC: Duke University Press, 2005.

Howard, Christopher. *The Hidden Welfare State.* Princeton, NJ: Princeton University Press, 1997.

The Welfare State Nobody Knows. Princeton, NJ: Princeton University Press, 2007.

Hoyt, Homer. *One Hundred Years of Land Values in Chicago.* Chicago: University of Chicago Press, 1933.

Hunt, J. Bradford. "Was the U.S. Housing Act a Pyrrhic Victory?" *Journal of Planning History* 4, no. 3 (2005): 195–221.

Hyman, Louis. *Debtor's Nation: The History of America in Red Ink.* Princeton, NJ: Princeton University Press, 2011.

"Ending Discrimination, Legitimating Debt: The Political Economy of Race, Gender, and Credit Access in the 1960s and 1970s." *Enterprise & Society* 12, no. 1 (2011): 200–32.

Immergluck, Daniel. *Foreclosed: High Risk Lending, Deregulation, and the Undermining of America's Mortgage Market.* Ithaca, NY: Cornell University Press, 2009.

International Monetary Fund. *World Economic Outlook.* Washington, DC: International Monetary Fund, 2003.

Jackson, Kenneth. *Crabgrass Frontier: The Suburbanization of the United States.* Oxford: Oxford University Press, 1987.

Jacobs, Alan and Steven Teles. "The Perils of Market Making: The Case of British Pension Reform." In Marc Landy, Martin Levin, and Martin Shapiro, eds. *Creating Competitive Markets: The Politics of Regulatory Reform.* Washington, DC: Brookings Institution Press, 2007.

John, Richard. "Governmental Institutions as Agents of Change: Rethinking American Political Development in the Early Republic, 1787–1835." *Studies in American Political Development* 11, no. 2 (1997): 347–80.

Spreading the News: The American Postal System from Franklin to Morse. Cambridge, MA: Harvard University Press, 1995.

Katznelson, Ira. *When Affirmative Action Was White: An Untold Story of Racial Inequality in Twentieth Century America.* New York: W. W. Norton Press, 2006.

Kemeny, Jim. "'The Really Big Trade-Off' between Home Ownership and Welfare: Castles' Evaluation of the 1980 Thesis, and a Reformulation 25 Years On." *Housing, Theory and Society* 22, no. 2 (2005): 59–75.

Khan, Liza. "Transgender Health at the Crossroads: Legal Norms, Insurance Markets, and the Threat of Healthcare Reform." *Yale Journal of Health Policy, Law, and Ethics* 11, no. 4 (2013): 1–44.

King, Brayden and Sarah Soule. "The Stages of the Policy Process and the Equal Rights Amendment, 1972–1982." *American Journal of Sociology* 111, no. 6 (2006): 1871–1909.

King, Desmond. *Separate and Unequal: African Americans and the U.S. Federal Government.* New York: Oxford University Press, 2007.

King, Desmond and Mark Stears. "How the U.S. State Works: A Theory of Standardization." *Perspectives on Politics* 9, no. 3 (2011): 505–18.

King, Desmond and Robert C. Lieberman. "Ironies of State Building: A Comparative Perspective on the Weak American State." *World Politics* 61, no. 3 (2009): 547–88.

King, Desmond and Rogers Smith. *Still a House Divided: Race and Politics in Obama's America.* Princeton, NJ: Princeton University Press, 2011.

Klein, Jennifer. *For All These Rights: Business, Labor and the Shaping of America's Public–Private Welfare State.* Princeton, NJ: Princeton University Press, 2003.

Kniskern, Philip Wheeler. *Real Estate Appraisal and Valuation.* New York: The Ronald Press Co., 1933.

Krippner, Greta. *Capitalizing on Crisis: The Political Origins of the Rise of Finance.* Cambridge, MA: Harvard University Press, 2011.

Lamb, Charles. *Housing Segregation in Suburban America since 1960: Presidential and Judicial Politics.* Cambridge: Cambridge University Press, 2005.

Lamont, Michele and Virag Molnar. "The Study of Boundaries in the Social Sciences." *Annual Review of Sociology* 28 (2002): 167–95.

Larson, John Lauritz. *Internal Improvement: National Public Works and the Promise of Popular Government in the Early United States.* Chapel Hill: University of North Carolina Press, 2000.

Laurenti, Luigi M. "Effects of Nonwhite Purchases on Market Prices of Residences." *Appraisal Journal* 20, no. 3 (1952): 314–29.

Lavelle, Kathryn. *Money and Banks in the American Political System.* Cambridge: Cambridge University Press, 2013.

Lerman, Amy and Vesla Weaver. *Arresting Citizenship: The Democratic Consequences of American Crime Control.* Chicago: University of Chicago Press, 2014.

Levitsky, Sandra. *Caring for Our Own: Why There Is No Political Demand for New American Social Welfare Rights.* New York: Oxford University Press, 2014.

Lieberman, Robert. *Shifting the Color Line: Race and the American Welfare State.* Cambridge, MA: Harvard University Press, 1998.

Light, Jennifer. "Discriminating Appraisals: Cartography, Computation, and Mortgage Insurance in the 1930s." *Technology and Culture* 52, no. 3 (2011): 485–522.

Lipset, Seymour Martin. *American Exceptionalism: A Double-Edged Sword.* New York: W. W. Norton, 1997.

Lipset, Seymour Martin and Gary Marks. *It Didn't Happen Here: Why Socialism Failed in the United States.* New York: W. W. Norton, 2013.

Lodge, Edgar A. *A Mortgage Analysis: A Twenty-Eight Year Record of the Mortgages of Home Title Insurance Company, 1906–1934.* Brooklyn, NY: Home Title Guaranty Company, 1935.

Lovell, George I. *This Is Not Civil Rights: Discovering Rights Talk in 1939 America.* Chicago: University of Chicago Press, 2012.

Lowi, Theodore and Norman K. Nicholson. *Arenas of Power: Reflections on Politics and Policy.* New York: Routledge, 2009.

Lynch, Julia. *Age in the Welfare State: The Origins of Social Spending on Pensioners, Workers, and Children.* New York: Cambridge University Press, 2006.

Mason, David. *From Buildings and Loans to Bail-Outs: A History of the American Savings and Loan Industry, 1831–1995.* New York: Cambridge University Press, 2004.

Massey, Douglas and Nancy Denton. *American Apartheid: Segregation and the Making of the Underclass.* Cambridge, MA: Harvard University Press, 1993.

May, Arthur. *The Valuation of Residential Real Estate.* New York: Prentice-Hall, 1942.

May, Vanessa. *Unprotected Labor: Household Workers, Politics, and Middle-Class Reform in New York, 1870–1940.* Chapel Hill: University of North Carolina Press, 2011.

Mayrl, Damon and Sarah Quinn. "Beyond the Hidden American State: Classification Struggles and the Politics of Recognition." In Kimberly Morgan and Ann Shola Orloff, eds. *The Many Hands of the State: Theorizing Political Authority and Social Control.* New York: Cambridge University Press, 2017.
  "Defining the State from Within: Boundaries, Schemas, and Associational Policymaking." *Sociological Theory* 34, no. 1 (2016): 1–26.

McCabe, Brian. *No Place Like Home: Wealth, Community, and the Politics of Homeownership.* New York: Oxford University Press, 2016.

McCann, Michael. "Causal versus Constitutive Explanations (or, On the Difficulty of Being so Positive …)" *Law and Social Inquiry* 21, no. 2 (1996): 457–82.

McCarthy, John and Mayer Zald. "Resource Mobilization and Social Movements: A Partial Theory." *American Journal of Sociology* 82, no. 6 (1977): 1212–48.

Mettler, Suzanne. *Degrees of Inequality: How the Politics of Higher Education Sabotaged the American Dream.* New York: Basic Books, 2013.
  The Submerged State: How Invisible Government Policies Undermine American Democracy. Chicago: University of Chicago Press, 2011.

Morgan, Belden. "Values in Transition Areas: Some New Concepts." *The Review of the Society of Residential Appraisers* (March 1952): 5–10.

Morgan, Kimberly. *Working Mothers and the Welfare State: Religion and the Politics of Work-Family Policies in Western Europe and the United States.* Palo Alto, CA: Stanford University Press, 2006.

Morgan, Kimberly and Andrea Campbell. *The Delegated Welfare State: Medicare, Markets, and the Governance of Social Policy*. Oxford: Oxford University Press, 2011.

Morone, James. "American Ways of Welfare." *Perspectives on Politics* 1, no. 1 (2003): 137–46.

Nadasen, Premila. *Household Workers Unite: The Untold Story of African American Women Who Built a Movement*. Boston: Beacon Press, 2015.

National Advisory Commission on Civil Disorders. *Report of the National Advisory Commission on Civil Disorders*. Washington, DC: Government Printing Office, 1968.

National Association of Real Estate Boards, Department of Education and Research. *Session by Session Outline of a Course in Real Estate Appraisals*. Chicago: National Association of Real Estate Boards, 1926.

National Commission on Consumer Finance. *Consumer Credit in the United States*. Washington, DC: Government Printing Office, 1972.

Novak, William. "The Myth of the 'Weak' American State." *American Historical Review* 113, no. 3 (2008): 752–72.

The People's Welfare: Law and Regulation in Nineteenth-Century America. Chapel Hill: University of North Carolina Press, 1996.

Novkov, Julie and Carol Nackenoff, eds. *Statebuilding from the Margins: Between Reconstruction and the New Deal*. Philadelphia: University of Pennsylvania Press, 2014.

Oliver, Melvin and Thomas Shapiro. *Black Wealth, White Wealth: A New Perspective on Racial Inequality*. New York: Routledge, 2006.

Orren, Karen. *Corporate Power and Social Change: The Politics of the Life Insurance Industry*. Baltimore: Johns Hopkins University Press, 1974.

O'Connor, Julia. "Gender, Class and Citizenship in the Comparative Analysis of Welfare State Regimes: Theoretical and Methodological Issues." *British Journal of Sociology* 44, no. 3 (1993): 501–18.

Patashnik, Eric M. *Reforms at Risk: What Happens After Major Policy Changes Are Enacted*. Princeton, NJ: Princeton University Press, 2008.

Patashnik, Eric M. and Julian E. Zelizer. "The Struggle to Remake Politics: Liberal Reform and the Limits of Policy Feedback in the Contemporary American State." *Perspectives on Politics* 11, no. 4 (2013): 1071–87.

Pew Research Center. "Home Sweet Home. Still." April 12, 2011. www.pewsocialtrends.org/2011/04/12/home-sweet-home-still/.

Phelps, Edmund. "The Statistical Theory of Racism and Sexism." *American Economic Review* 62, no. 4 (1972): 659–61.

Pierson, Paul. "The New Politics of the Welfare State." *World Politics* 48, no. 2 (1996): 143–79.

Politics in Time: History, Institutions, and Social Analysis. Princeton, NJ: Princeton University Press, 2004.

Polanyi, Karl. *The Great Transformation: The Political and Economic Origins of Our Time*. Boston: Beacon Press, 1944.

Radford, Gail. *Modern Housing for America: Policy Struggles in the New Deal Era*. Chicago: University of Chicago Press, 1996.

Roosevelt, Franklin D. "Executive Order 9070 of February 24, 1942, Establishing the National Housing Agency." In Gerhard Peters and John T. Woolley, eds. The American Presidency Project. www.presidency.ucsb.edu/ws/?pid=16625.

Rothstein, Richard. *The Color of Law: A Forgotten History of How Our Government Segregated America*. New York: Liverlight, 2017.

Ruggles, Steven, J. Trent Alexander, Katie Genadek, Ronald Goeken, Matthew B. Schroeder, and Matthew Sobek. *Integrated Public Use Microdata Series: Version 5.0*. Minneapolis: University of Minnesota, 2010.

Ruschemeyer, Dietrich. "Can One or a Few Cases Yield Theoretical Gains?" In James Mahoney and Dietrich Ruschemeyer, eds. *Comparative Historical Analysis in the Social Sciences*. Cambridge: Cambridge University Press, 2003.

Russell, Horace. *Savings & Loan Associations*. Albany, NY: Matthew Bander & Company, 1956.

Sanders, Elizabeth. *Roots of Reform: Farmers, Workers, and the American State, 1877–1917*. Chicago: University of Chicago Press, 1999.

Schattschneider, E. E. *Politics, Pressure, and the Tariff: A Study of Free Private Enterprise in Pressure Politics, as Shown in the 1929–1930 Revision of the Tariff*. New York: Prentice Hall, 1935.

Schlesinger, Arthur. *Paths to the Present*. New York: Macmillan, 1949.

Scott, James C. *Seeing Like a State: How Certain Schemes to Improve the Human Condition Have Failed*. New Haven: Yale University Press, 1998.

Sheingate, Adam. "Why Can't Americans See the State?" *The Forum* 7, no. 4 (2009): Article 1.

Skocpol, Theda. *Protecting Soldiers and Mothers: The Political Origins of Social Policy in the United States*. Cambridge, MA: Harvard University Press, 1992.

Skowronek, Stephen. *Building a New American State: The Expansion of National Administrative Capacities, 1877–1920*. Cambridge: Cambridge University Press, 1982.

Skrentny, John D. *The Minority Rights Revolution*. Cambridge, MA: Harvard University Press, 2004.

Smith, Paul. "Measuring Risk on Consumer Installment Credit." *Management Science* 11, no. 2 (1964): 327–40.

Snowden, Kenneth A. "The Anatomy of a Residential Mortgage Crisis: A Look Back to the 1930s." In Lawrence E. Mitchell and Arthur E. Wilmarth Jr., eds. *The Panic of 2008: Causes, Consequences and Implications for Reform*. Cheltenham, UK: Edward Elgar Publishing Limited, 2010.

"Debt on Nonfarm Structures, by Type of Debt, Property, and Holder: 1896–1952." In Susan B. Carter, Scott Sigmund Gartner, Michael R. Haines, Alan L. Olmstead, Richard Sutch, and Gavin Wright, eds. *Historical Statistics of the United States, Earliest Times to the Present: Millennial Edition*. New York: Cambridge University Press, 2006.

"Mortgage Banking in the United States, 1870–1940." Research Institute for Housing America Special Report. Paper 13129. October 2013.

"Mortgage Foreclosures and Delinquencies: 1926–1979." In Susan B. Carter, Scott Sigmund Gartner, Michael R. Haines, Alan L. Olmstead, Richard Sutch, and Gavin Wright, eds. *Historical Statistics of the United States,*

Earliest Times to the Present: Millennial Edition. New York: Cambridge University Press, 2006.

"Terms on Nonfarm Home Mortgages, by Type of Mortgage and Holder: 1920–1967." In Susan B. Carter, Scott Sigmund Gartner, Michael R. Haines, Alan L. Olmstead, Richard Sutch, and Gavin Wright, eds. *Historical Statistics of the United States, Earliest Times to the Present: Millennial Edition.* New York: Cambridge University Press, 2006.

Soss, Joe and Sanford Schramm. "A Public Transformed? Welfare Reform as Policy Feedback." *American Political Science Review* 101, no. 1 (2007): 111–27.

Sparrow, James, William Novak, and Stephen Sawyer, eds. *Boundaries of the State in US History.* Chicago: University of Chicago Press, 2015.

Stevens, Beth. "Blurring the Boundaries: How the Federal Government Has Influenced Welfare Benefits in the Private Sector." In Margaret Weir, Ann Shola Orloff, and Theda Skocpol, eds. *The Politics of Social Policy in the United States.* Princeton, NJ: Princeton University Press, 1988.

Stone, Gregory Martin. *Ethnicity, Class and Politics among Czechs in Cleveland, 1870–1940.* PhD Diss. Rutgers University. 1993.

Strolovitch, Dara. *Affirmative Advocacy: Race, Class, and Gender in Interest Group Politics.* Chicago: University of Chicago Press, 2007.

Stuart, Guy. *Discriminating Risk: The U.S. Mortgage Lending Industry in the Twentieth Century.* Ithaca, NY: Cornell University Press, 2003.

Sugrue, Thomas. *The Origins of the Urban Crisis: Race and Inequality in Postwar Detroit.* Princeton, NJ: Princeton University Press, 1997.

Taylor, Keeanga-Yamahtta. *From #Blacklivesmatter to Black Liberation.* Chicago: Haymarket Books, 2016.

Teles, Steven M. "Kludgeocracy in America." *National Affairs* 17 (2013): 97–114.

Thurston, Chloe. "Policy Feedback in the Public–Private Welfare State: Advocacy Groups and Access to Government Homeownership Programs, 1934–1954." *Studies in American Political Development* 29, no. 2 (2015): 250–67.

Truman, Harry S. "Statement by the President upon Approving the Housing Act, August 10, 1948." In Gerhard Peters and John T. Woolley, eds. The American Presidency Project. http://presidency.ucsb.edu/ws/?pid=12975.

"Statement by the President upon Signing the Housing Act of 1949, July 15, 1949." In Gerhard Peters and John T. Woolley, eds. The American Presidency Project. www.presidency.ucsb.edu/ws/?pid=13246.

Trumbull, Gunnar. *Consumer Lending in France and America: Credit and Welfare.* New York: Cambridge University Press, 2014.

Strength in Numbers: The Political Power of Weak Interests. Cambridge, MA: Harvard University Press, 2012.

Ulmer, Mark K. "The Legal Origin and Nature of Indian Housing Authorities and the HUD Indian Housing Programs." *American Indian Law Review* 2, no. 2 (1987/88): 109–74.

United States Commission on Civil Rights. "Mortgage Money: Who Gets It? A Case Study of Mortgage Lending Discrimination in Hartford, Connecticut." Washington, DC: Government Printing Office, 1974.

United States Department of Housing and Urban Development. "Equal Access to Housing in HUD Programs Regardless of Sexual Orientation or Gender Identity." *Federal Register* 77, no. 23 (2012): 5662–76.

Fair Housing Laws and Presidential Executive Orders. www.hud.gov/program_offices/fair_housing_equal_opp/FHLaws.

"HUD-FHA Underwriting Analysis: October 1972." Washington, DC: Department of Housing and Urban Development, 1972.

United States Government Accountability Office. "Problems in the Homeownership Opportunities Program for Low-Income Families: Report to the Congress." Washington, DC: US General Accounting Office, 1974.

Vandell, Kerry. "FHA Restructuring Proposals: Alternatives and Implications." *Housing Policy Debate* 6, no. 2 (1995): 299–393.

Ventry, Dennis. "The Accidental Deduction: A History and Critique of the Tax Subsidy for Mortgage Interest." *Law and Contemporary Problems* 73, no. 1 (2009): 233–84.

von Hoffman, Alexander. "A Study in Contradictions: The Origins and Legacy of the Housing Act of 1949." *Housing Policy Debate* 11, no. 2 (2000): 299–326.

"Calling upon the Genius of Private Enterprise: The Housing and Urban Development Act of 1968 and the Liberal Turn to Public–Private Partnerships." *Studies in American Political Development* 27, no. 2 (2013): 165–94.

Vose, Clement E. *Caucasians Only: The Supreme Court, the NAACP, and the Restrictive Covenant Cases.* Berkeley: University of California Press, 1959.

Walker, Hannah. "Extending the Effects of the Carceral State: Proximal Contact, Political Participation, and Race." *Political Research Quarterly* 67, no. 4 (2014): 809–22.

Mobilized by Injustice: Criminal Justice Contact, Political Participation and Race. PhD Diss. University of Washington, 2016.

Ware, Leland. "Invisible Walls: An Examination of the Legal Strategy of the Restrictive Covenant Cases." *Washington University Law Quarterly* 67, no. 3 (1989): 737–72.

Wheelock, David. "The Federal Response to Home Mortgage Distress: Lessons from the Great Depression." *Federal Reserve Bank of St. Louis Review* 90, no. 3 (2008): 133–48.

Witko, Christopher. "The Politics of Financialization in the United States, 1949–2005." *British Journal of Political Science* 46, no. 2 (2016): 349–70.

Index